IMAGES
of America

PERQUIMANS COUNTY
NORTH CAROLINA

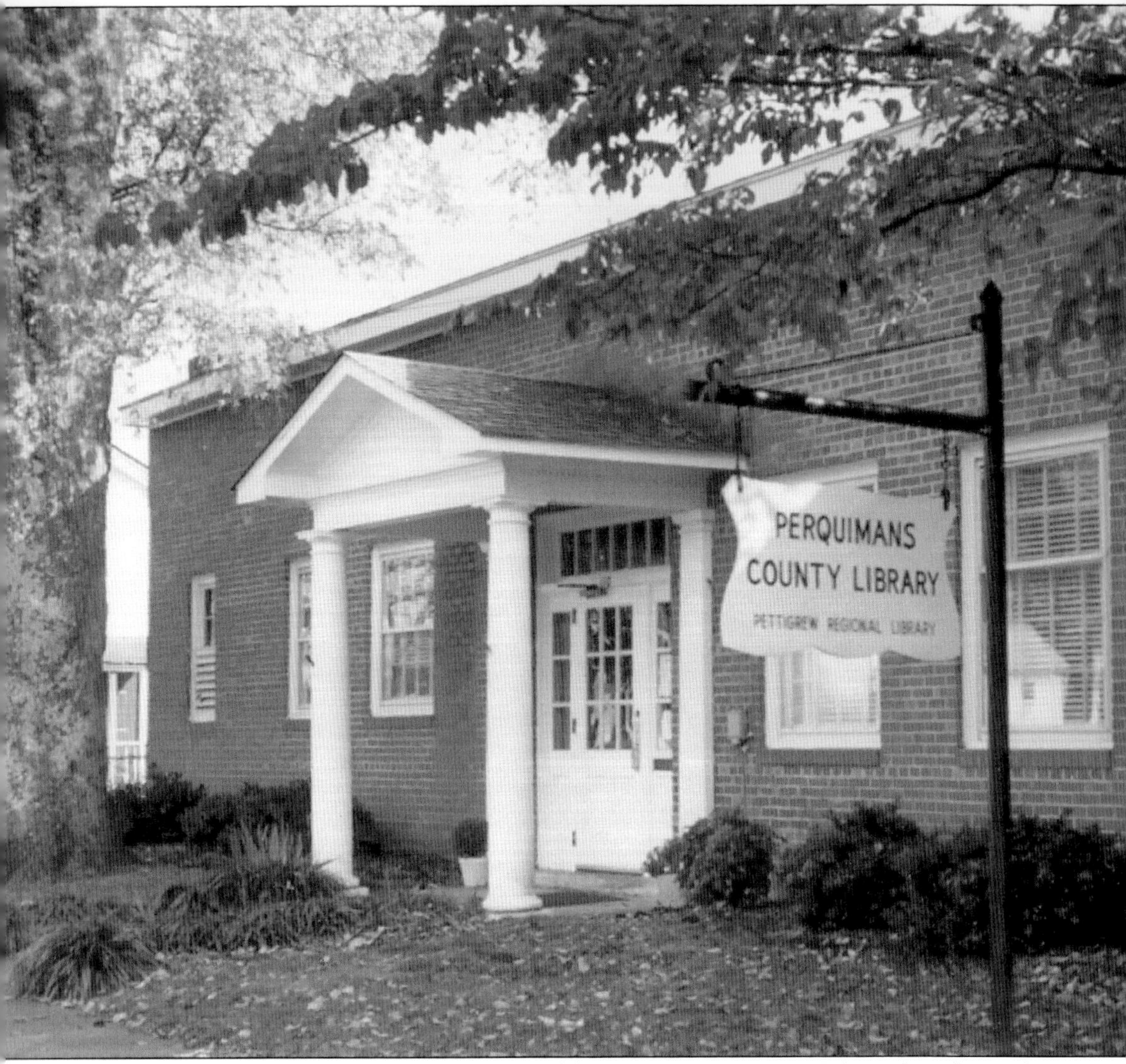

The front entrance of the building occupied by Perquimans County Library has changed very little since it served as a lunchroom for an elementary school in the 1950s. Handicapped access has been added since this photo was taken in 1994. (Courtesy of J.K. Oltman.)

(On the cover) Perquimans River offers many scenic spots for boating and picnicking. This outing probably occurred at Nixon's Point north of Hertford in the 1920s. (Courtesy of Mary Barbee Corprew.)

IMAGES
of America

PERQUIMANS COUNTY NORTH CAROLINA

Perquimans County Library and
Perquimans County Restoration Association

ARCADIA
PUBLISHING

ISBN 978-0-7385-1579-3

Published by Arcadia Publishing
Charleston, South Carolina

Printed in the United States of America

Library of Congress Catalog Card Number: 2003110229

For all general information contact Arcadia Publishing at:
Telephone 843-853-2070
Fax 843-853-0044
E-mail sales@arcadiapublishing.com
For customer service and orders:
Toll-Free 1-888-313-2665

Visit us on the Internet at www.arcadiapublishing.com

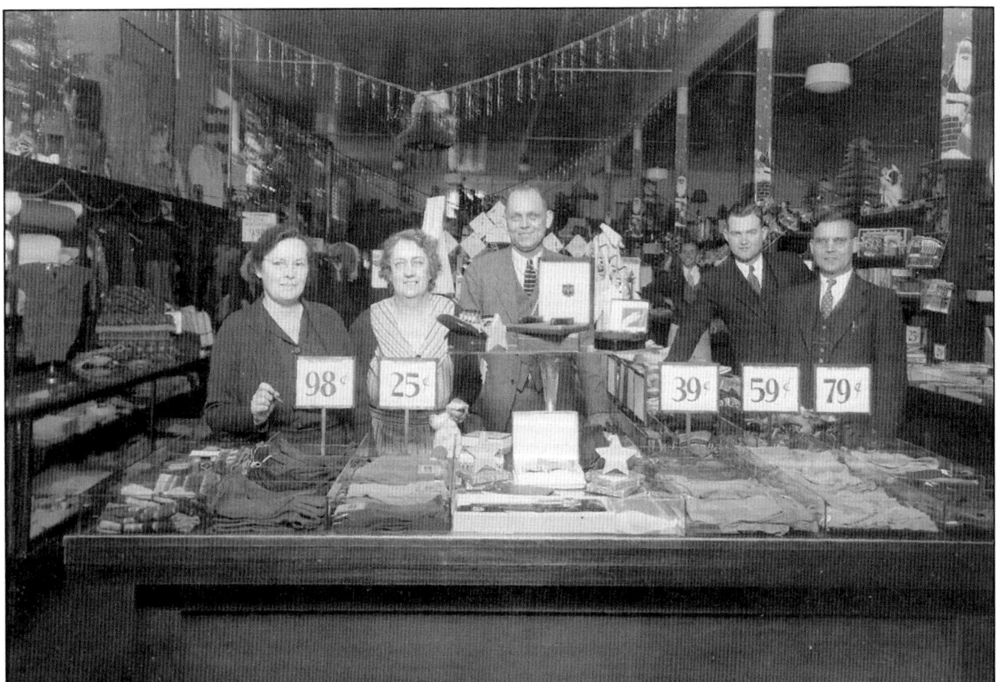

Lessie Gregory (left), who later died in a fire at J.C. Blanchard & Company, is shown in the mid-1930s with fellow employees, from left to right, Mattie Anse White, Linwood Skinner, Marshall Owens (in the background), Marion Riddick, and Mr. Hurt at Blanchard's store in downtown Hertford. (Courtesy of Joyce Riddick.)

Contents

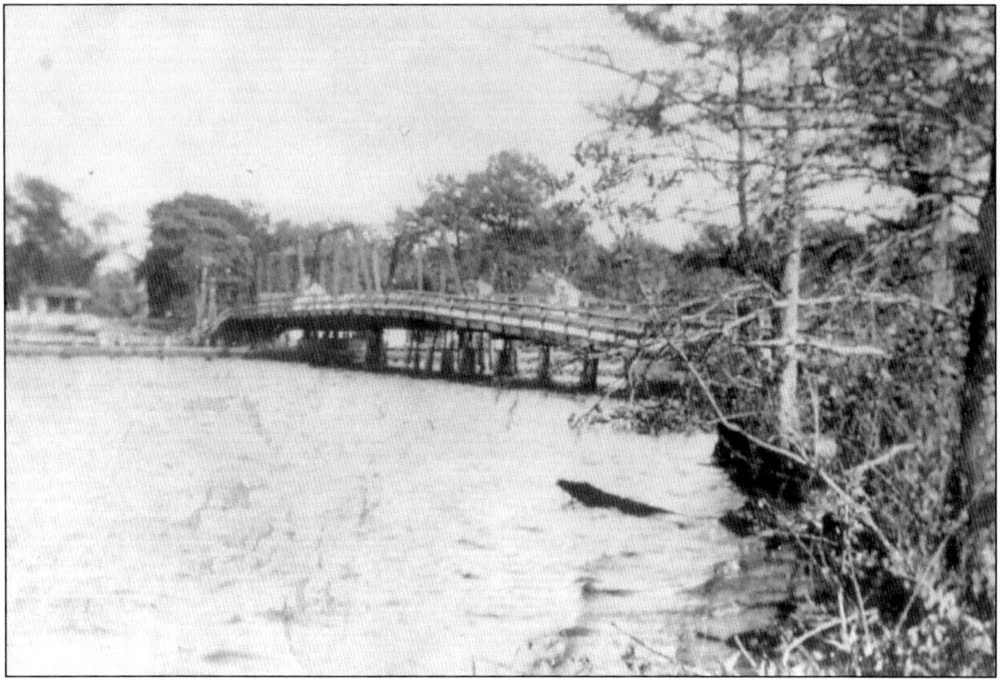

This steel and wood bridge spanned Perquimans River at Hertford from 1897 to 1928. Visible near center foreground in the partially submerged timber upon which generations of turtles have sunned themselves. Local people fervently believe the view from this river crossing inspired the well-known song "Carolina Moon." (Courtesy of Mary Barbee Corpew.)

ACKNOWLEDGMENTS

This pictorial history of Perquimans County, North Carolina, is the result of a generous outpouring of community support. Perquimans County Library and Perquimans County Restoration Association thank all those who so graciously shared their treasured photographs to be part of this book and the library's archives.

Both organizations are indebted to Raymond A. Winslow Jr. for his excellent research and writing and offer an additional thank-you to Debra Robinson, Margaret Brewin, Charles T. Skinner Jr., and Mary Corprew for their special contributions.

Mary K. Vidaurri, Ann Carol White, Wonder Lewis, and Jeri Oltman at Perquimans County Library, and LuAnne Pendergraft, representing the Perquimans County Restoration Association, devoted countless hours to the production of this book. They appreciate the support of their respective boards in this endeavor.

INTRODUCTION

It is the waters of Perquimans that draw people in and entice them to stay—from the early Yeopim Indians to the English settlers of the 17th century to the newcomers attracted to the county today. The most casual visitor immediately encounters the abundance of waterways in this northeastern corner of North Carolina, but a longer acquaintance reveals another characteristic of the place.

There is continuity with the past that invigorates the present. Much survives from the past—structures, records, artifacts, and attitudes toward life. Families present when the county was established in 1668 still have descendants in Perquimans, a Quaker Meeting formed in the 17th century still worships, buildings erected in the 18th century still stand, and a culture drawing upon generations of shared experience still prevails. Perquimans claims North Carolina's oldest public records, oldest religious congregation, and oldest house open to the public. It is a place where farmers till land their ancestors planted 14 generations ago and where citizens have done public business in the same courthouse for 175 years.

Perquimans County is a unique place where a walk along Hertford streets laid out in 1758 offers pleasing views of buildings dating from 1775 and may lead to a chat with a descendant of a colonial governor or a pioneer settler. It is a place where people appreciate a tranquil life and a slow pace in familiar surroundings enriched by memories of long ago.

The quiet character of Perquimans today masks the county's rich and noteworthy history. The county's historical significance is reflected by the wealth of public records that date to 1659, the earliest days of European settlement. Sir Walter Raleigh's explorers visited the waters of Perquimans as early as 1586. Perquimans, the de facto capital of the state until 1716, was a political center in colonial North Carolina.

John Harvey, a vanguard of the revolutionary movement, called Perquimans home, and Ann Durant, wife of the 17th-century settler George Durant, is considered to be the first woman in North Carolina to serve as an attorney. In 1792, Sarah Moore Delano DeCrow was appointed postmaster of Hertford, the first woman in the United States to hold that post. Perquimans saw the beginning of organized religion in North Carolina when, in 1672, George Fox, the founder of the Society of Friends (Quakers), held religious services here. The Society of Friends has continued to hold meetings in the county ever since.

This visual history, while containing historical images, relates intimate and personal stories from family photo albums, shoeboxes found in closets, and the archives of local historians. Other than six paintings of wealthy planters and their wives, these images are photographs, snapshots taken by ordinary citizens and studio poses for special occasions. There are images of departed individuals, vanished buildings, and altered landscapes. There are pictures of families at home and large groups in church and school. There are the faces of Confederate soldiers, a Union soldier, and a woman born a slave. There are planters and farmers, business tycoons and country storekeepers, preachers and teachers, barbers and freight haulers. The continuity of Perquimans life is illustrated with images of persons descended from the earliest settlers, of buildings that have survived centuries, and of the ever-present waters that impact daily life.

Over the years, many photographs have lost their context. No one remembers exactly when and where they were taken. Some depicted individuals remain unidentified. Yet, it is not necessary to know such details to appreciate a photograph. An image tells its own story or allows the viewer to imagine one. A poignant look can provoke a sigh, antique fashions a chuckle, and bygone scenes a reminiscence of youth. The images in this collection reflect life in Perquimans of yore, while providing instruction and entertainment for today.

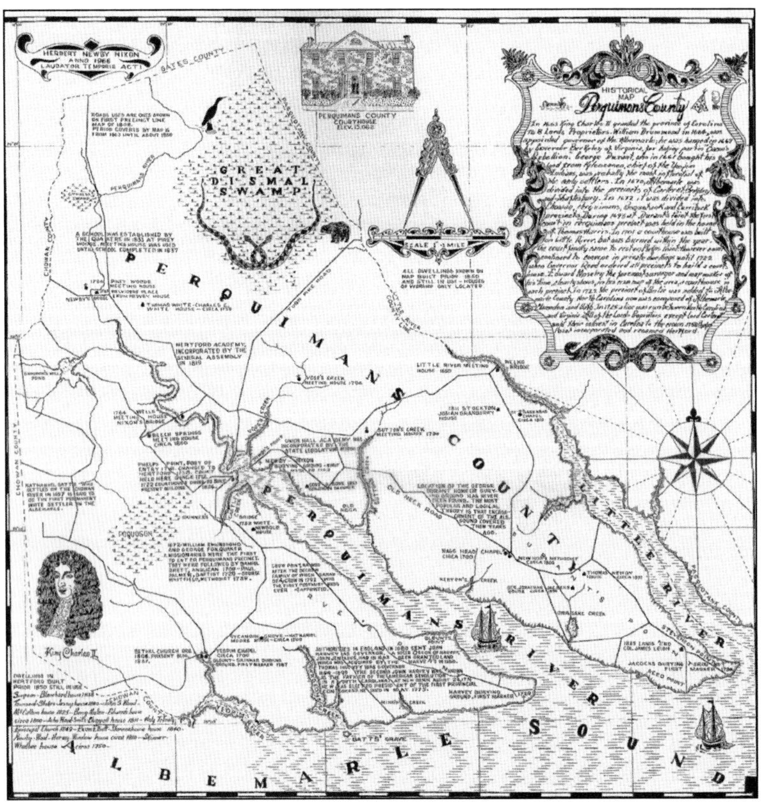

A hand-drawn map shows Perquimans County in 1966 with many embellishments furnished by the artist Herbert Newby Nixon.

One

At Home

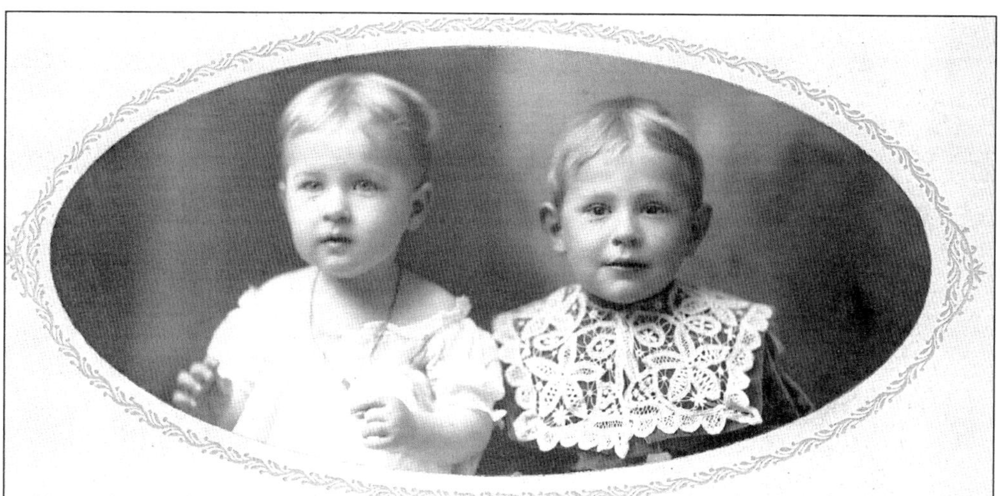

With his intricate collar, Philip S. McMullan (right) is more elaborately clothed than his younger sister Camilla, *c.* 1902. Their parents were mill bookkeeper Sidney M. McMullan and his wife Penelope. They lived on Church Street near Penelope's mother, Mary Frances Whedbee. (Courtesy of Anne McMullan and Philip McMullan.)

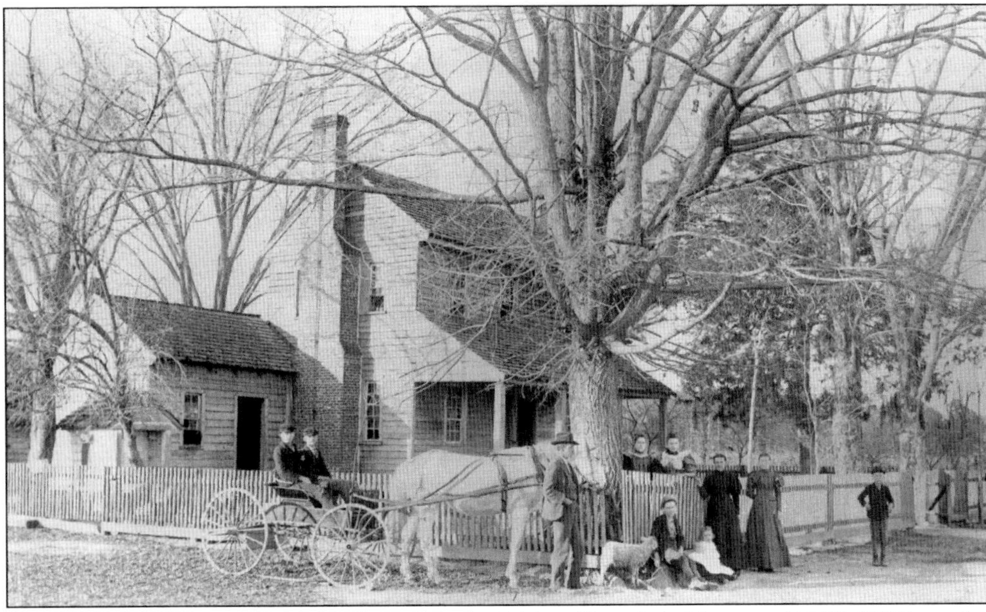

Thomas C. Morgan (1847–1915) and wife Addie (Speight) Morgan (1847–1919) gather their family at their homestead in Parkville Township, c. 1897. The home lot is well fenced to prevent cow, hog, or horse from chewing, digging, or dunging the yard. (Courtesy of *The Perquimans Weekly*.)

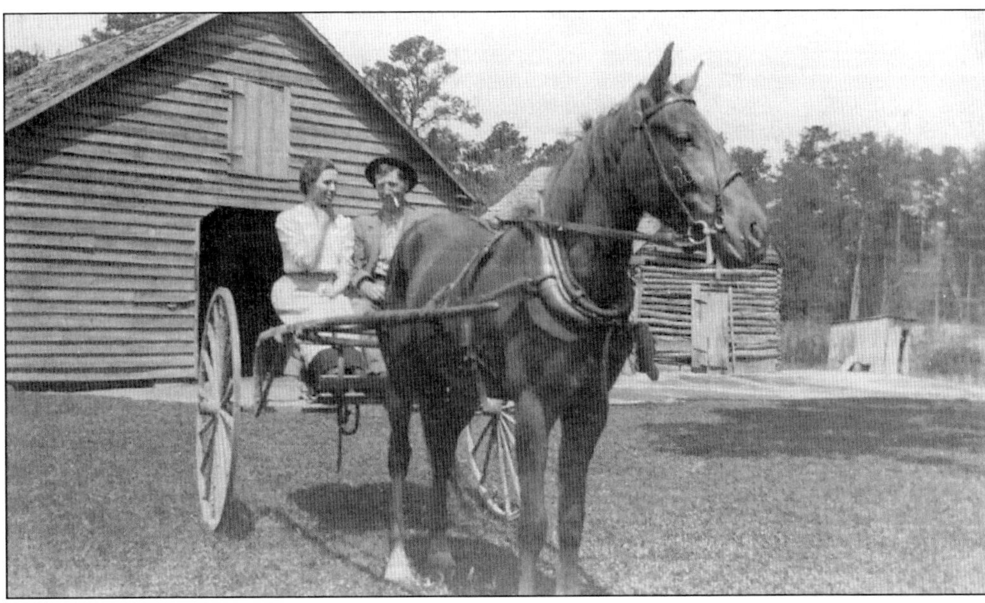

John Jordan Chappell Jr. (1891–1926) of Belvidere and wife Maude (Jessup) Chappell prepare for a buggy ride, c. 1915. Behind the horse's head is a log structure. (Courtesy of Thelma Chappell Riddick.)

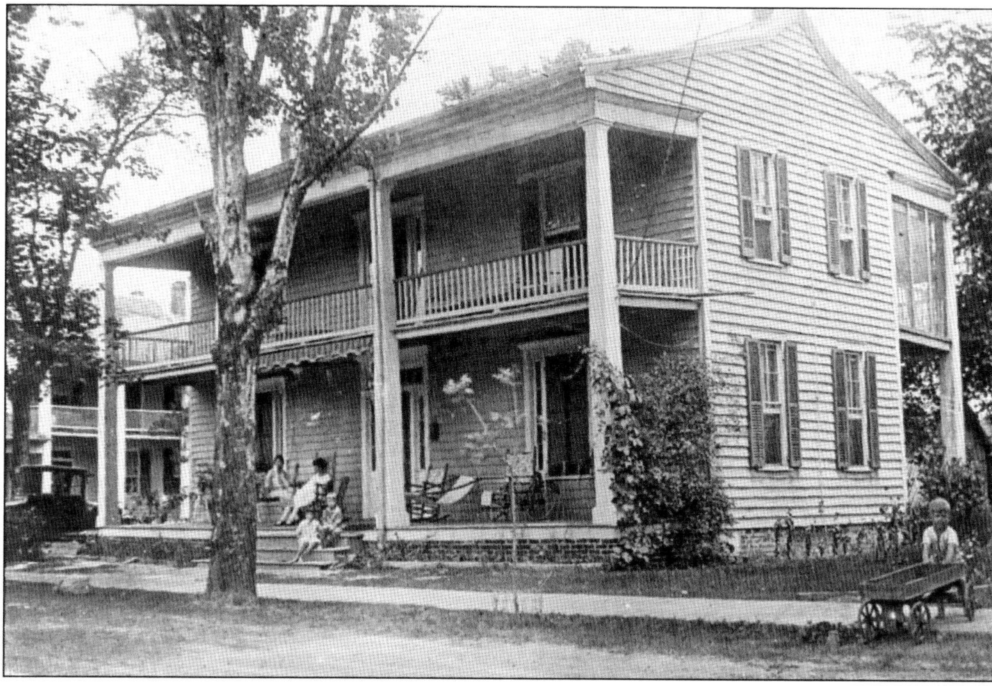

In this 1920s photograph, the Henry Stokes house on Front Street shows the classic lines of a building form typical of Perquimans. The double-tiered porches front and back offer shade, protection from rain, and restful places to pass the time with family and friends. The house still stands, much altered. (Courtesy of Bettie Gaither Stokes.)

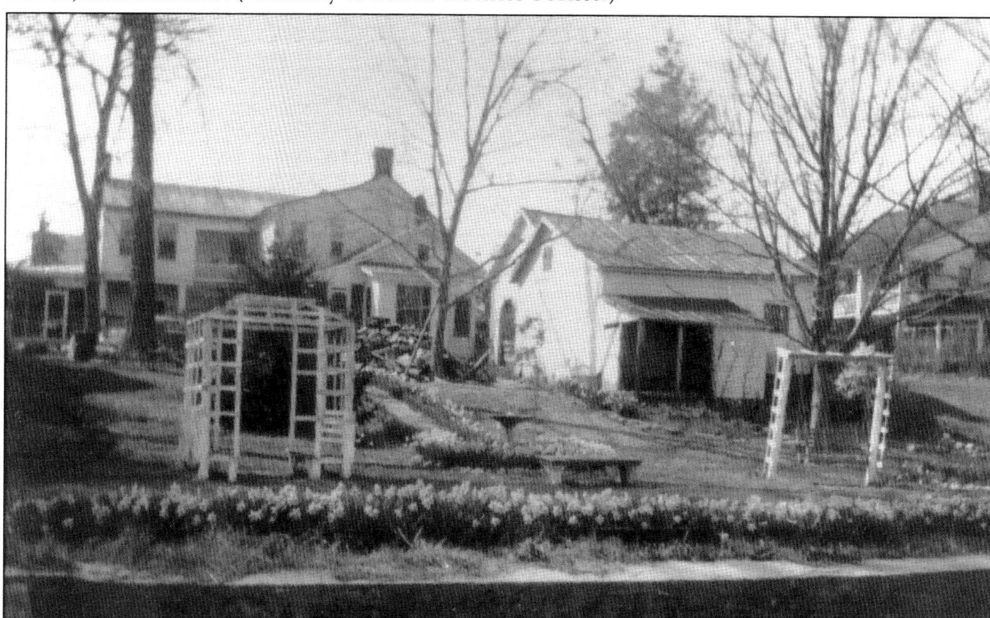

Viewed from the river, the backyard of the Henry Stokes house shows the additions and outbuildings that form a domestic complex like many others in Perquimans. A garage, a shed, and a garden—and in former times a kitchen, a dairy, a well, an outhouse, and a barn—each serve a useful purpose. (Courtesy of Bettie Gaither Stokes.)

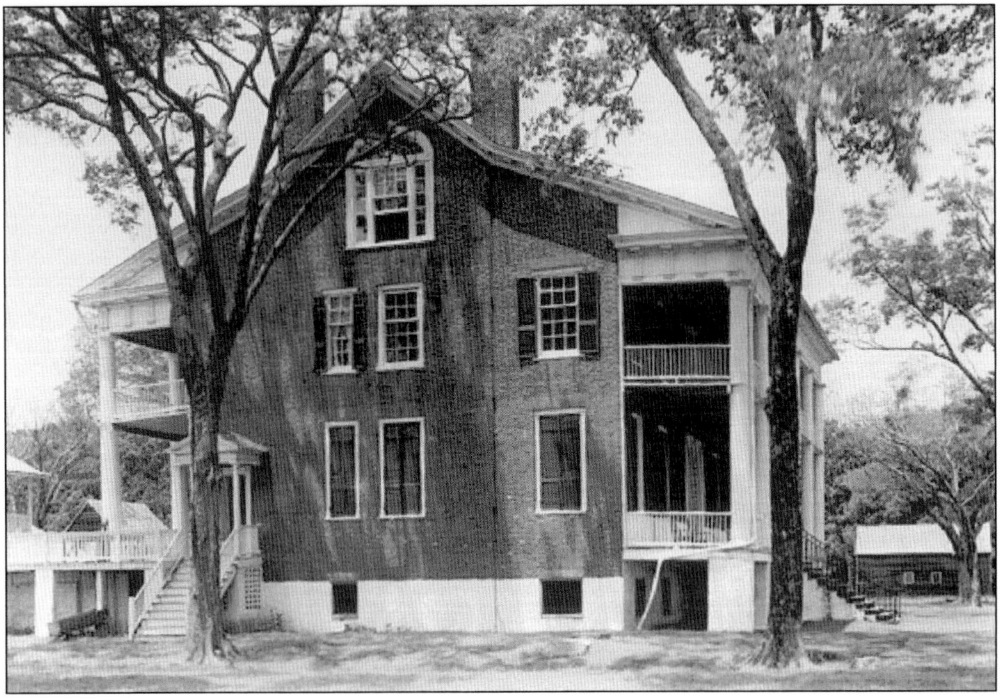

This 1940 photograph by Thomas Waterman, an architectural historian with the Historic American Buildings Survey, emphasizes the monumental scale of Land's End and its relation to outbuildings. The house was already a century old. (Courtesy of Library of Congress, Prints & Photographs Division, HABS, HABS, NC, 72-HERF.V, 1-1.)

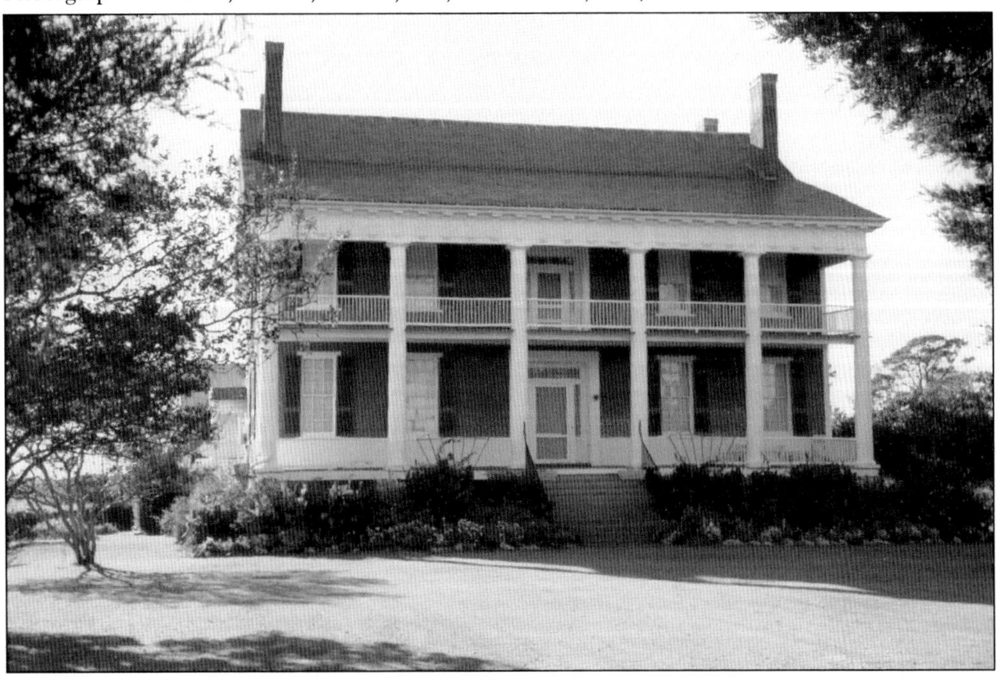

Built by Col. James Leigh in the 1830s, Land's End is the largest of the antebellum plantation houses in Perquimans County. (Courtesy of Bettie Gaither Stokes.)

Susan (Banks) Leigh (*c.* 1807–1837) was the second wife of Col. James Leigh. She did not long enjoy the great mansion her husband built. (Courtesy of Bettie Gaither Stokes.)

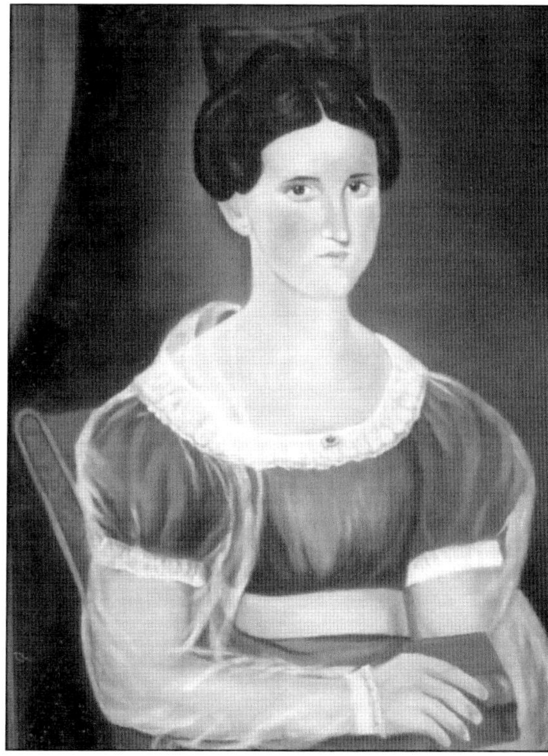

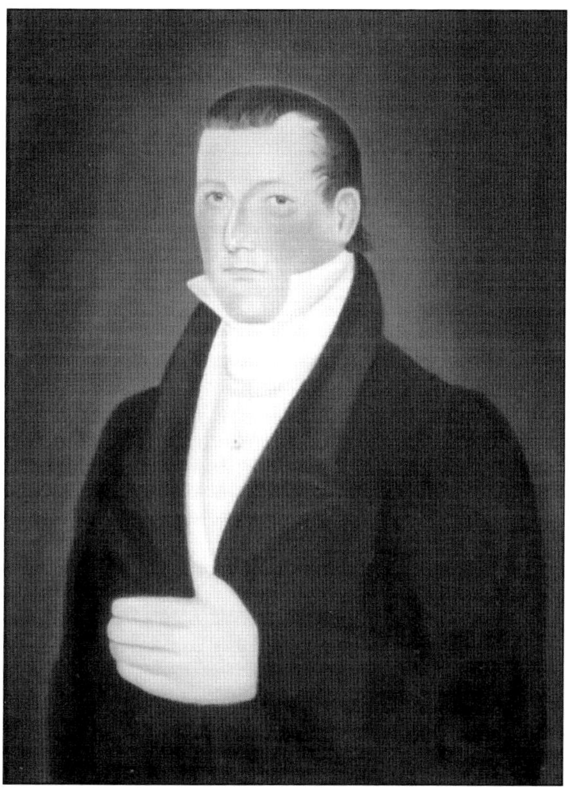

Col. James Leigh (1781–1854) was one of the wealthiest and most active citizens of Perquimans in antebellum days. From modest beginnings as a carpenter, he amassed a great fortune, including thousands of acres, a hotel, wharves, and schooners. (Courtesy of Bettie Gaither Stokes.)

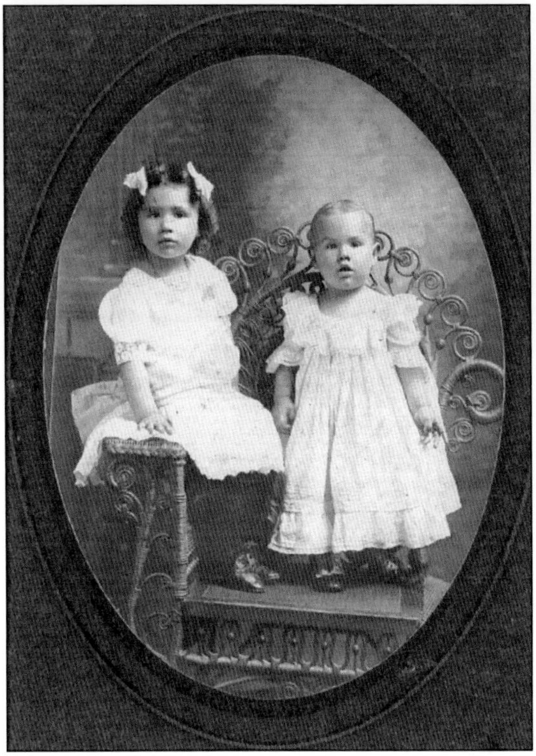

The Chappell sisters, Erma Marie (left) and Grace, are entranced by the photographer, *c.* 1905. (Courtesy of Mary Chappell White.)

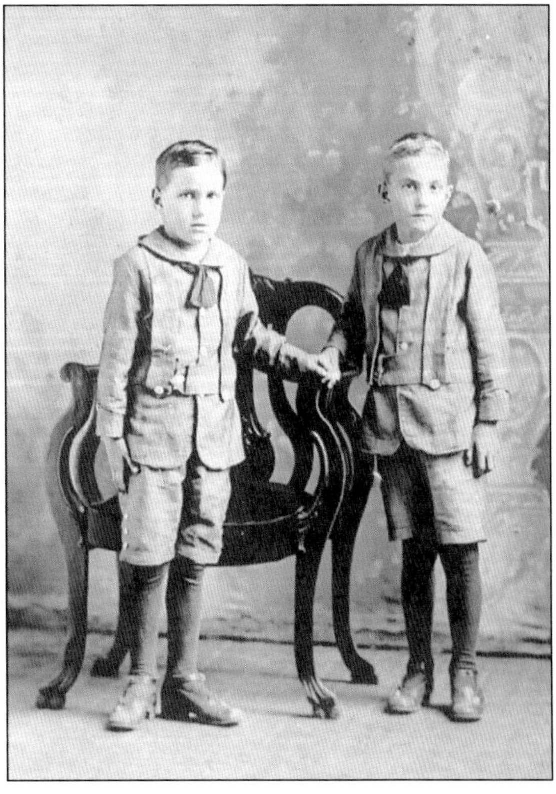

Twins Randolph Pinkney Winslow and Raymond Alexis Winslow pose in a studio, c. 1922. Knee pants were standard for boys in that era. Even close family members cannot identify which twin is which in this photo. (Courtesy of Raymond A. Winslow Jr.)

Ida Cornelia Goodwin (center) rests a protective hand on the shoulders of her father William Albert Goodwin (1846–1926) and mother Emma Jane (Goodwin) Goodwin (1855–1929) in the Bear Swamp vicinity, c. 1910. (Courtesy of Lynwood C. Winslow III.)

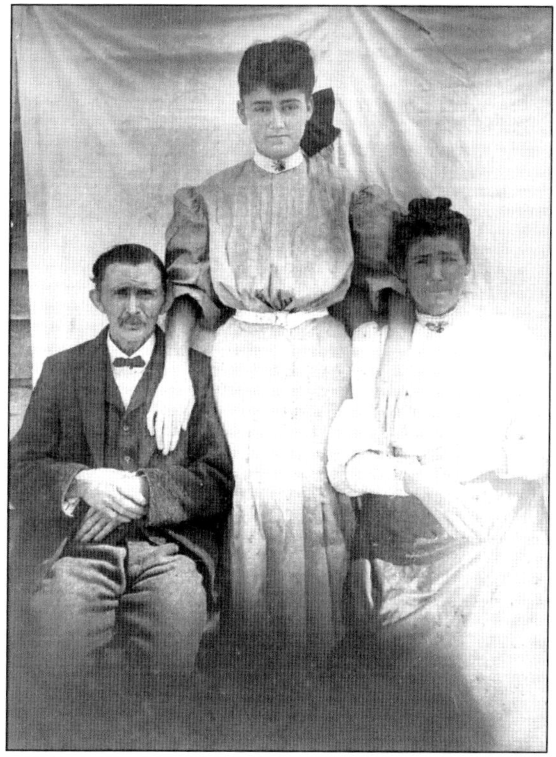

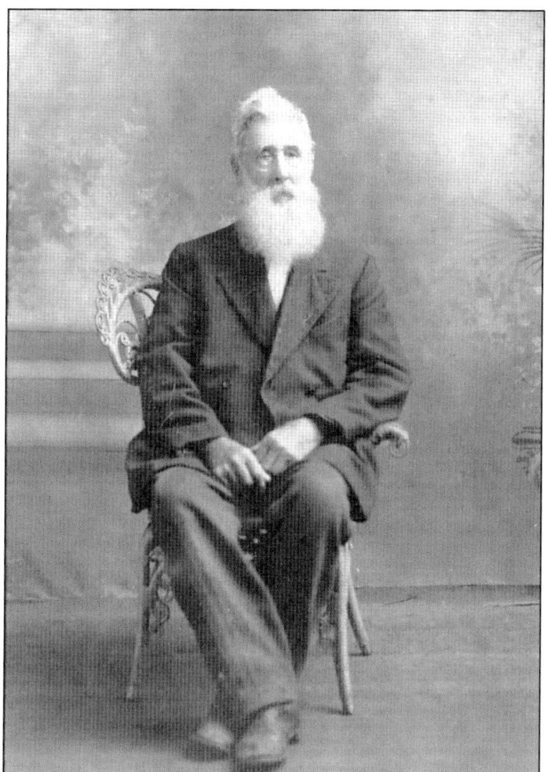

Thomas A. Morgan (1825–1916) was a farmer and brick mason in the New Hope vicinity. (Courtesy of Alice Jeanne Ward.)

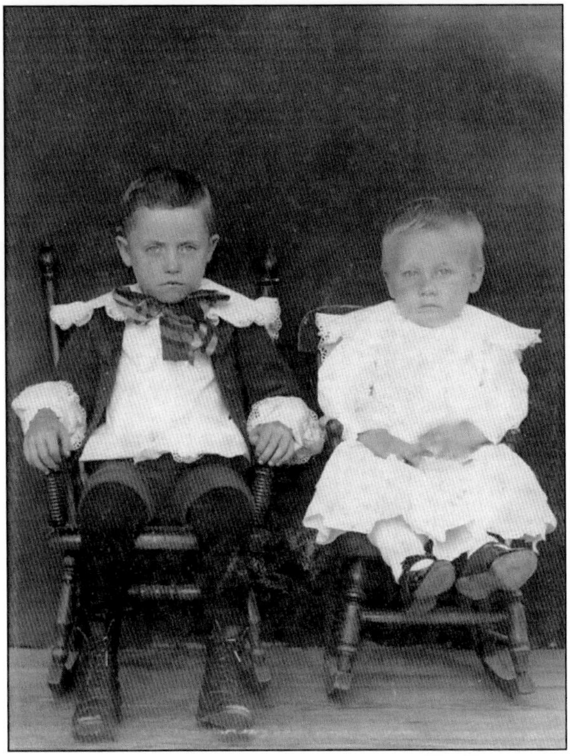

Raymond Skinner (left) and half-brother Lloyd Elliott do not seem happy wearing lace collars and having to sit still, *c.* 1902. Rocking chairs are for rocking, after all. (Courtesy of Sybil Skinner.)

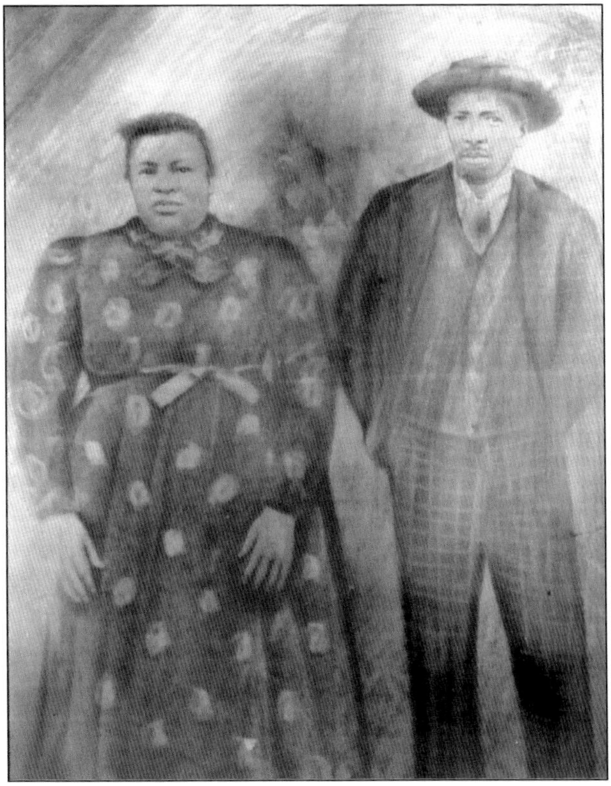

When deacon Alexander Ellis moved to Winfall in 1895, he found no Baptist church there. He organized one, which was named Ellis Temple in his honor. Deacon Ellis is shown here with his wife Deborah, *c.* 1895. (Courtesy of Margaret Jordan.)

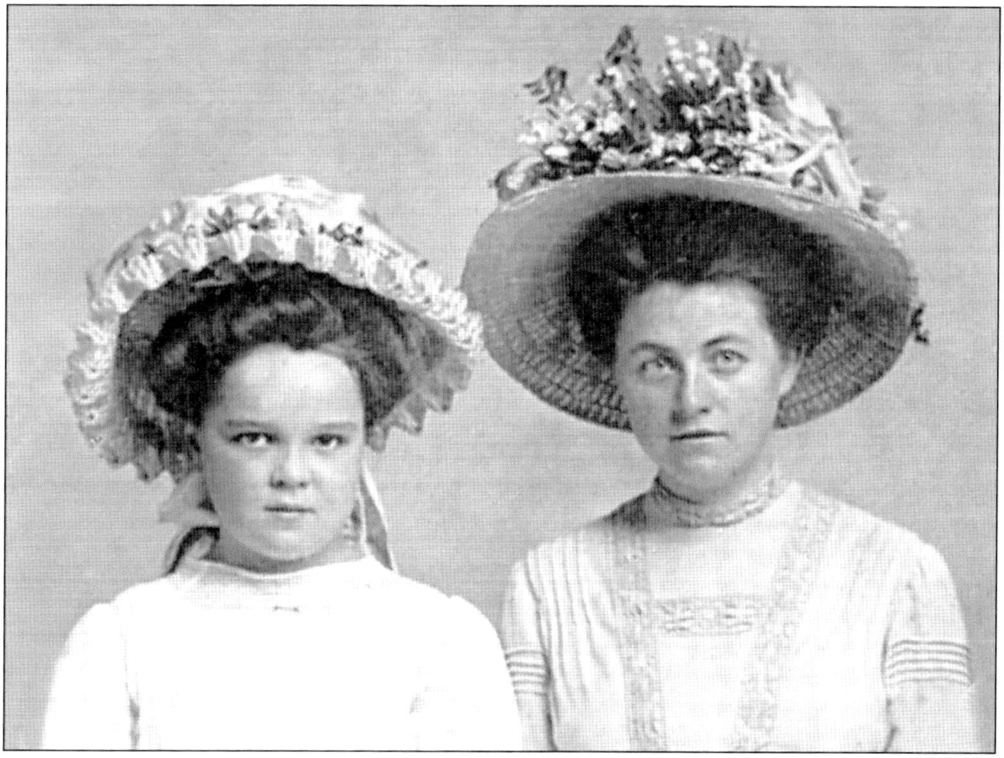

Eucel Hurdle (left) and Mary Elizabeth Jessup model two extravagant hats, which were the rage in 1909. (Courtesy of Thelma Chappell Riddick.)

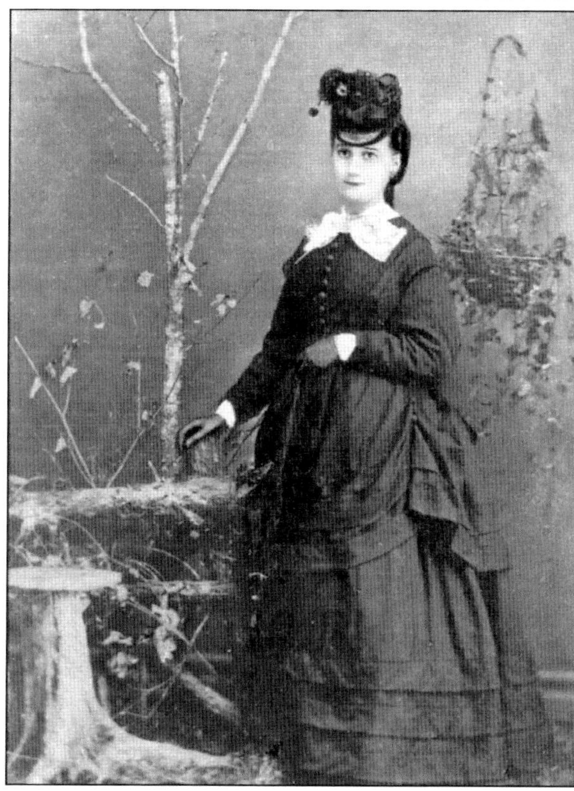

This very stylish Victorian lady is Mary Frances (Skinner) Whedbee (1844–1934). In addition to bearing six children, tending a household, and operating a hotel, she was postmaster of Hertford from 1897 to 1901. Her husband James Monroe Whedbee was active in Perquimans politics; her brothers Thomas and Henry Skinner were United States congressmen. (Courtesy of Anne McMullan and Philip McMullan.)

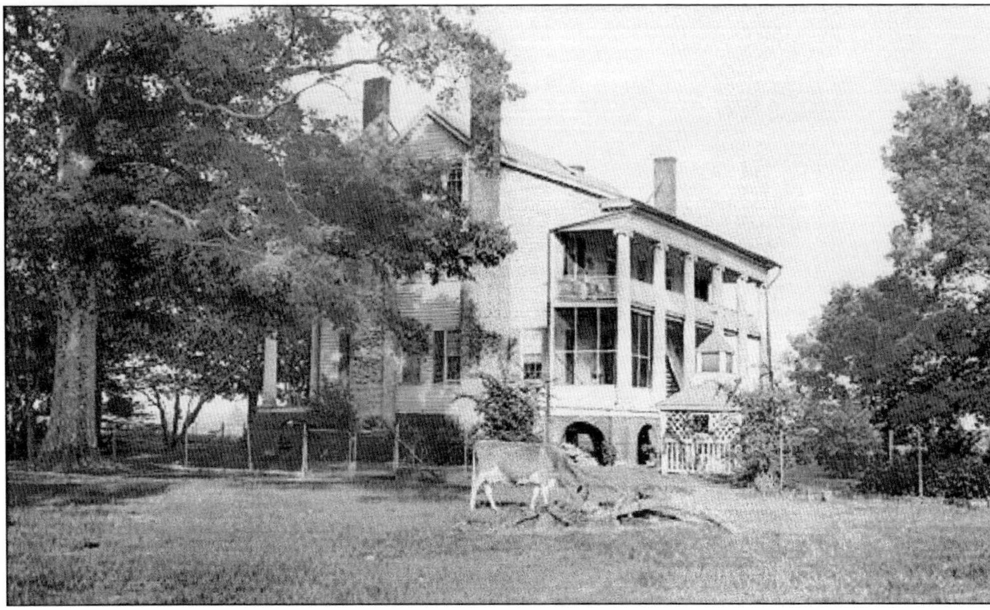

A cow grazes in the side yard behind 1830s mansion Cove Grove in a 1940 Thomas Waterman photograph. The low outbuilding is a gazebo protecting the well; in its cupola is the bell that calls workers in to meals from outlying fields. (Courtesy of Library of Congress, Prints & Photographs Division, HABS, HABS, NC, 72-HERF.V, 2-2.)

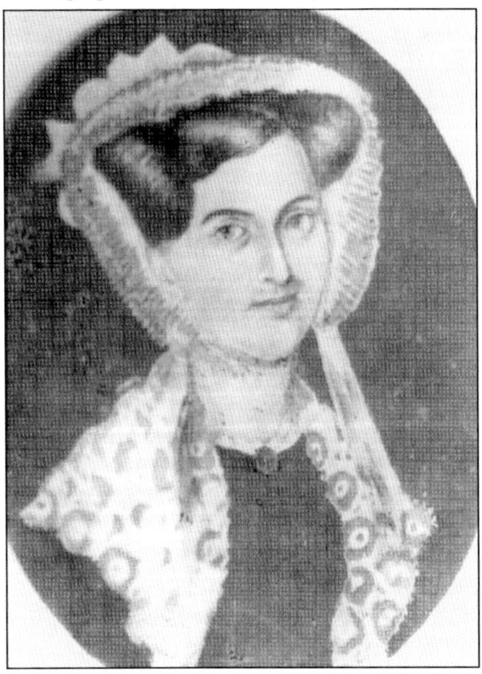

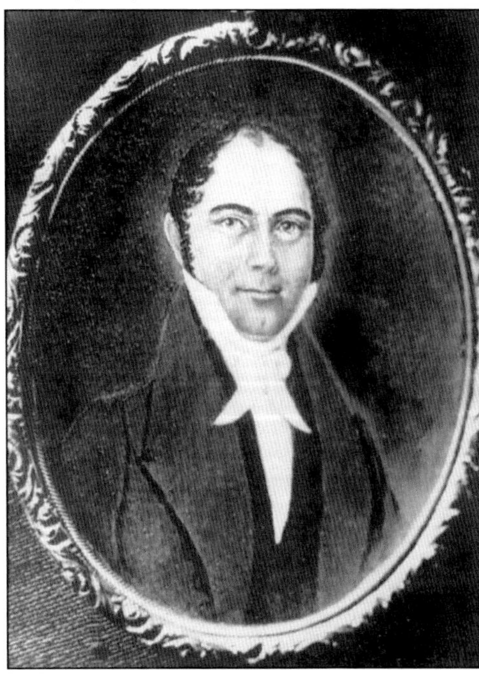

Benjamin Smith Skinner (1795–1861), shown here on the right, became one of the wealthiest men in the county, built one of the finest houses (Cove Grove), sent a son to Harvard, saw his daughters married well, and virtually founded the Episcopal church in Hertford. He married Elizabeth Leigh (1807–1874), pictured at left, a daughter of Col. James Leigh. (Courtesy of Bettie Gaither Stokes.)

Benjamin S. Skinner Jr. (1839–1864) graduated from Harvard in 1860 and inherited Cove Grove plantation in 1861, just days before joining the Confederate Army. While captain of the Perquimans Beauregards, he was killed in battle at Reams Station. By will, he freed his slaves and left funds to care for the needy men in his command. (Courtesy of Raymond A. Winslow Jr.)

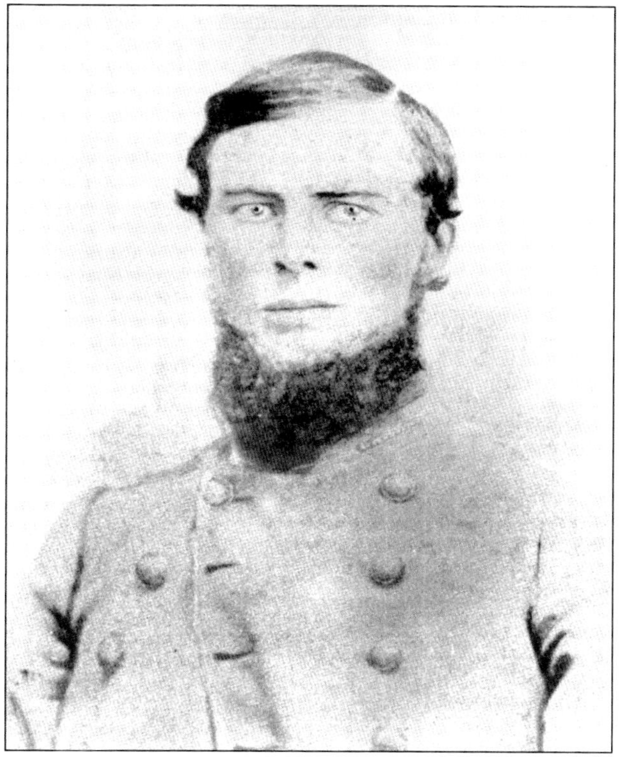

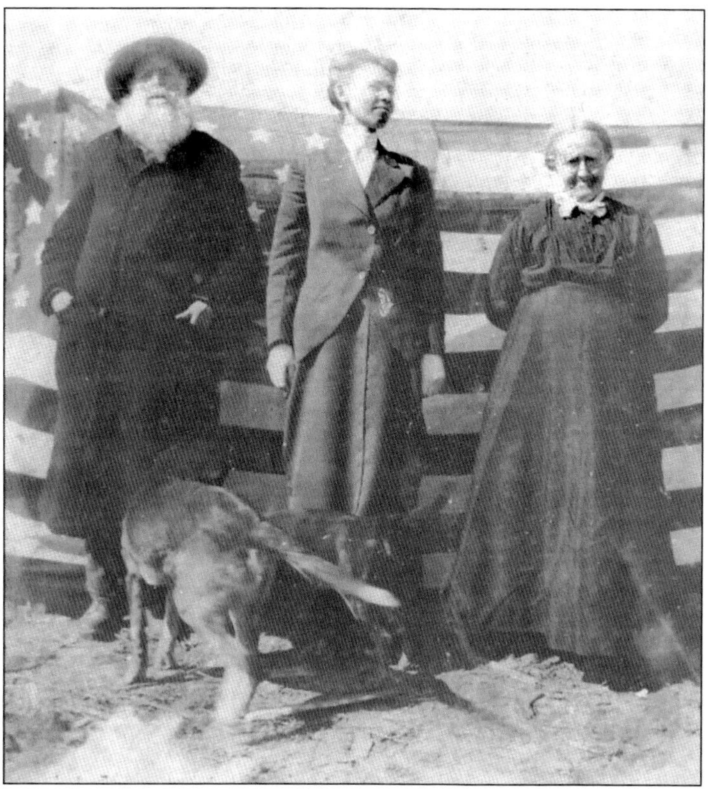

Amos Smith (1843–1918), at left, stands before the flag for which he fought as one of the numerous Perquimans men in the Union Army; he was a corporal in Company E, First North Carolina Union Volunteers. With him are his wife Sarah Ann (Winslow) Smith (1840–1919), shown at right, and their daughter Mamie. (Courtesy of Peggy Lane.)

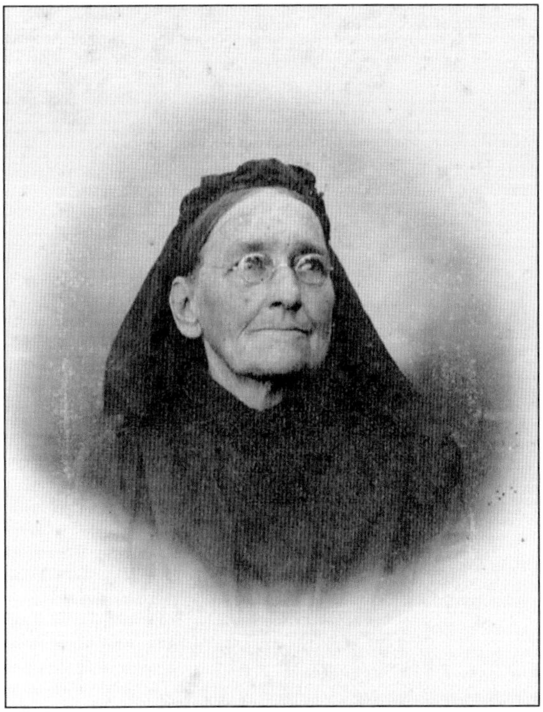

Mary Eliza (White) Jolliff (1839–1906) was educated at Belvidere Academy and New Garden Boarding School in Greensboro, North Carolina. She outlived her husband John Richard Jolliff, siblings, and seven of her twelve children. She donated land for Bethany Methodist Church; the circuit-riding preachers could expect Sunday dinner at her home. (Courtesy of Raymond A. Winslow Jr.)

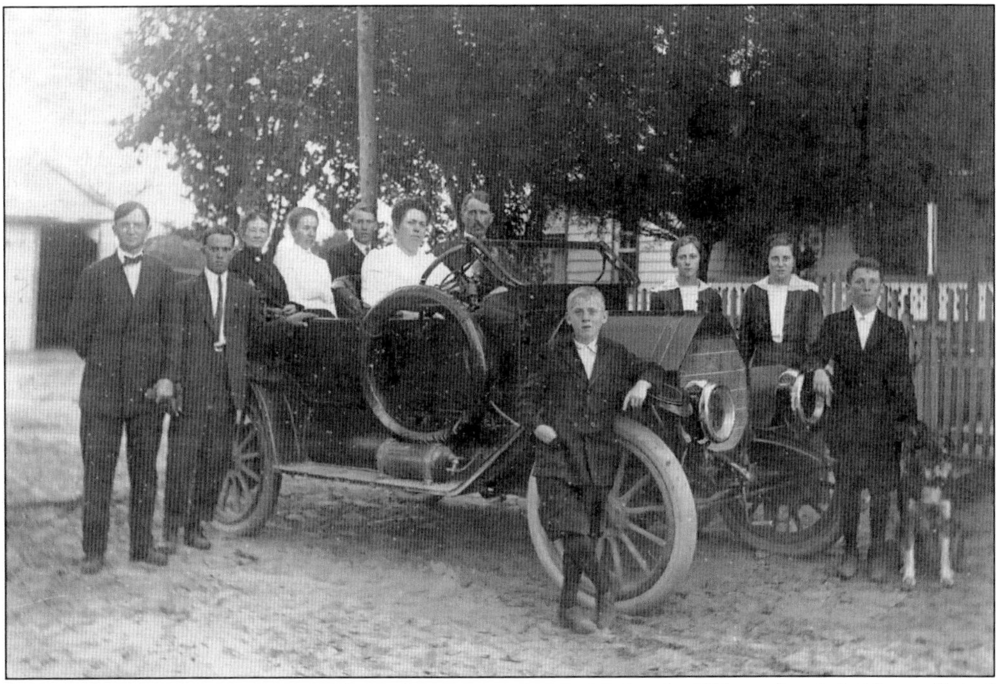

Like a cross between a convertible and a sport utility vehicle, the White family's Maxwell had ample room. Seen at Whiteston c. 1920, from left to right, are Leslie Pearson, John Lassiter, Dora Knight, Mattie Saunders, Murray White, Anna (Saunders) White, Fernando C. White, Edwin White, Sylvia White, Myrta White, Vivian White, and Fido. Mrs. Knight and Miss Saunders were teachers at Whiteston School. (Courtesy of Mary Chappell White.)

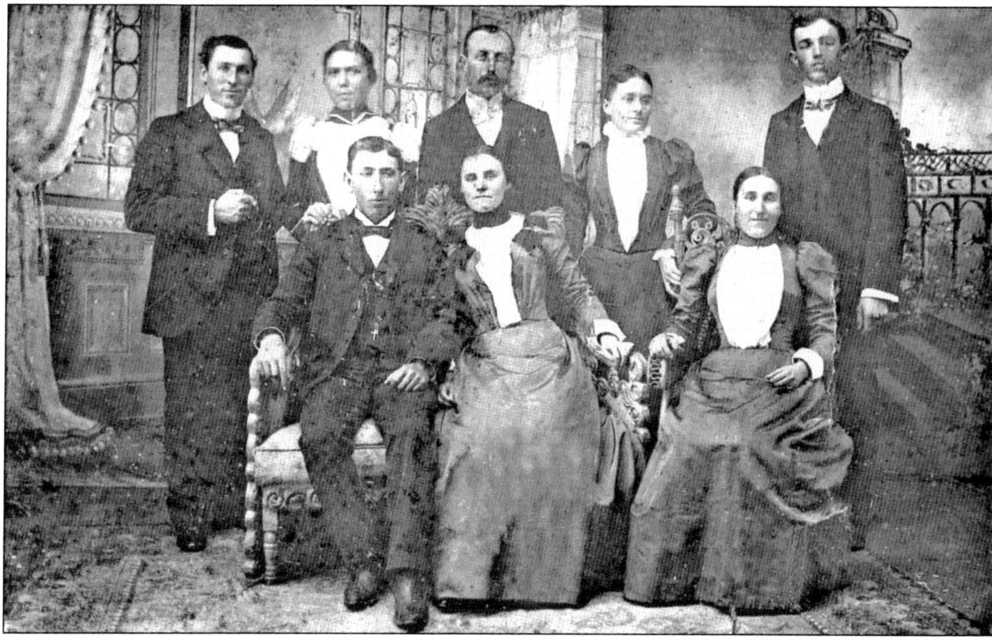

Charles R. Lane married Julianna E. Chappell in October 1898 at Piney Woods Meeting House. Their wedding picture highlights the groom (left) and bride (center) sitting in front. The Lane-Chappell connection would be enhanced in 1901 when the bride's brother Edward Chappell (back, left) married the groom's sister Mary Ann Lane (back, second from left). (Courtesy of Mary Chappell White.)

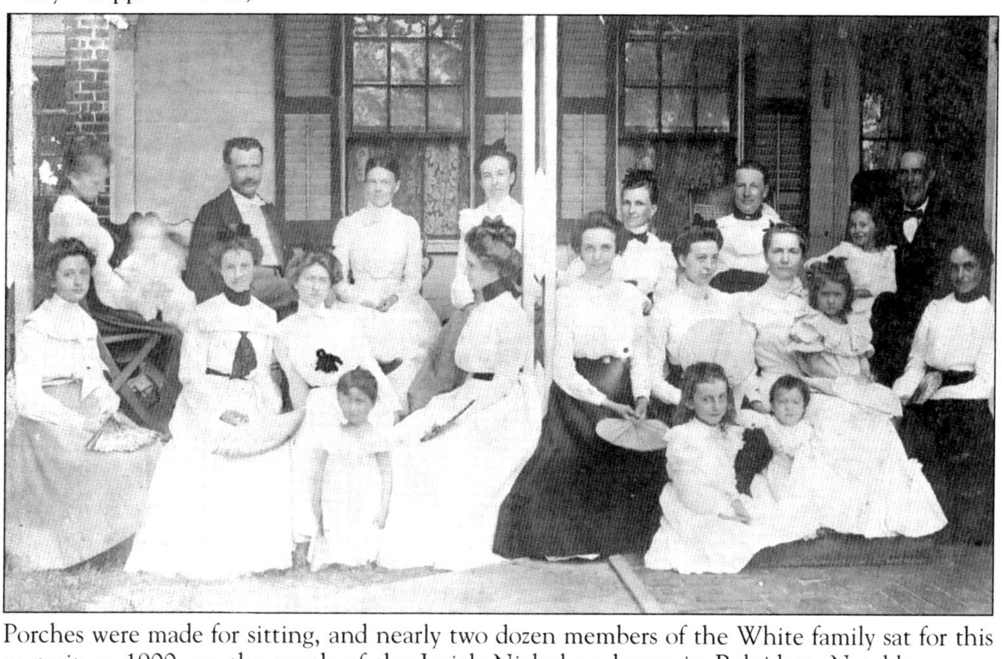

Porches were made for sitting, and nearly two dozen members of the White family sat for this portrait, *c.* 1900, on the porch of the Josiah Nicholson house in Belvidere. Notable among them is principal of Belvidere Academy Mary Jordan White (1859–1909), shown here in the back, framed by the window and to the right of the first gentleman. (Courtesy of Lynwood C. Winslow III.)

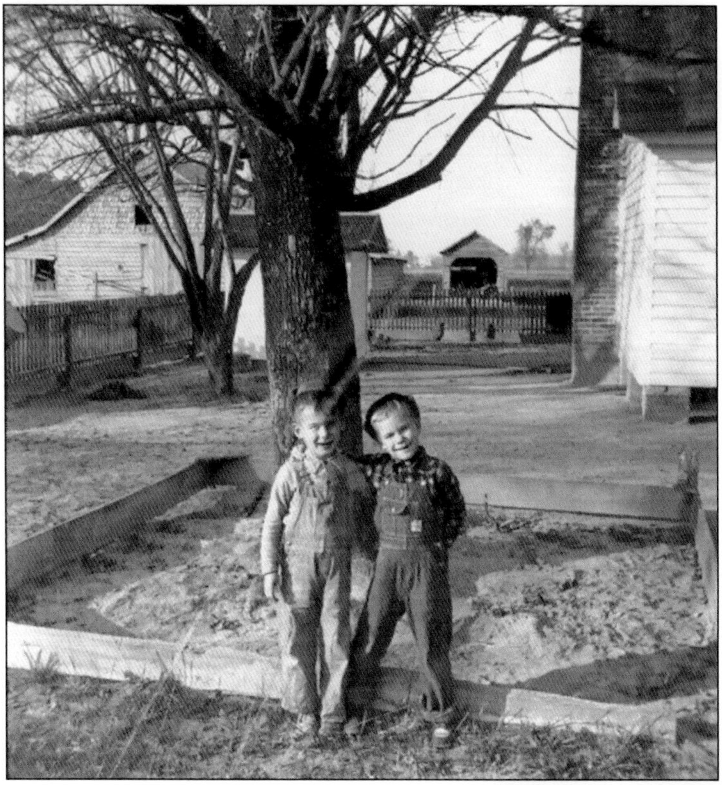

Much family activity occurs in the backyard. The Hobbs boys, John and Ben, have a sandbox for playtime in 1953, and work buildings appear in the background, including the barn (left) and dairy (behind the tree). (Courtesy of Joyce Hobbs.)

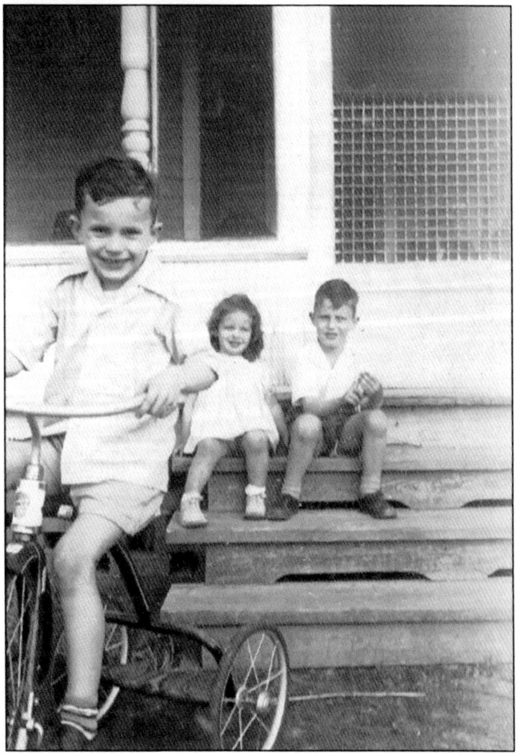

Cousins, from left to right, Raymond Alexis Winslow Jr., Susan Frances Riddick, and Thomas Lindsey Riddick are seen in front of their grandfather's house on Easter Sunday, 1947. The old homestead's porch has been screened in, a quiet but significant improvement to health by keeping flies and mosquitoes out of the house. (Courtesy of Raymond A. Winslow Jr.)

It takes a moment to realize that the middle child is a boy, Edward Chappell, flanked by his sisters Grace (left) and Mary, shown in Belvidere *c.* 1913. (Courtesy of Mary Chappell White.)

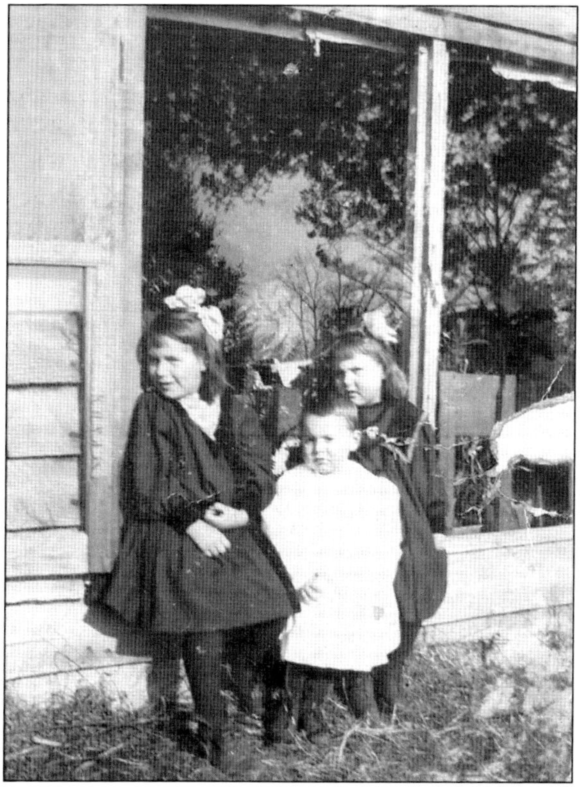

Cousins Laura Everett (left) and Helen Thompson are arm-in-arm, *c.* 1941. Having more in common than friendship alone, cousins saw a lot of each other at home, in school, and in church. (Courtesy of Helen Thompson Shaw.)

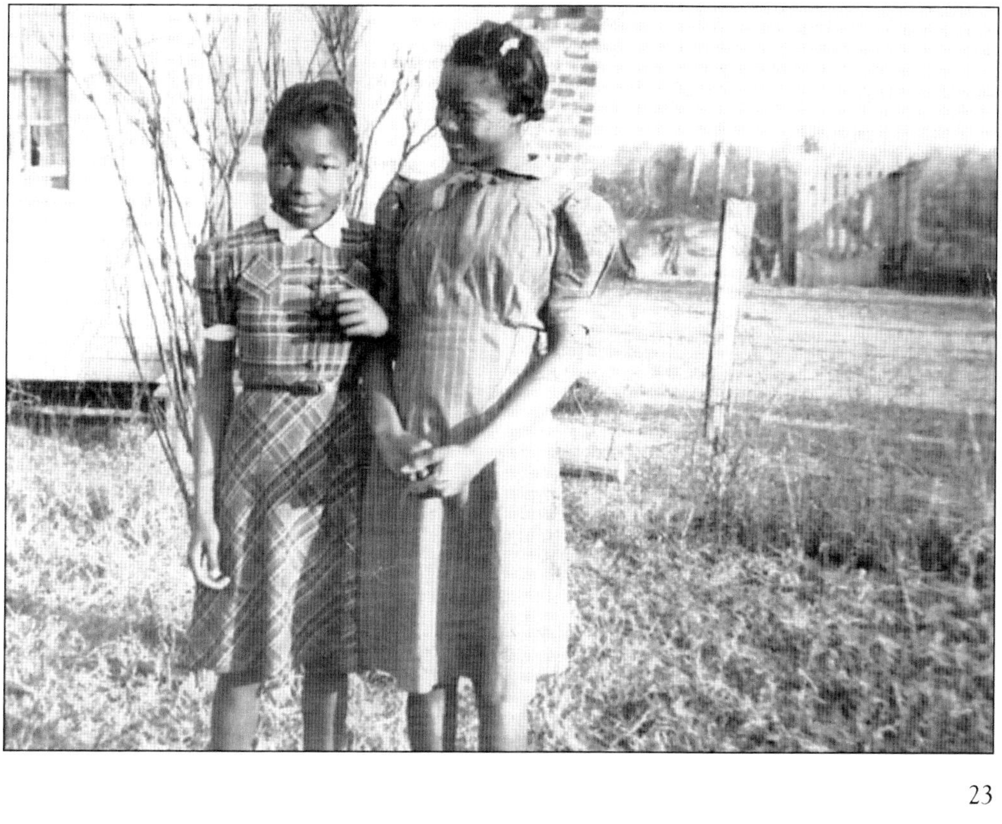

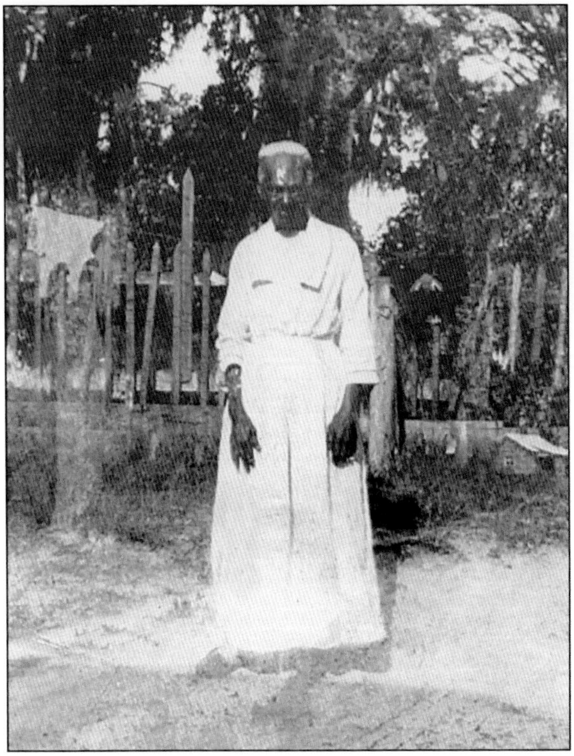

Rhoda Perry was already an adult when slaves were emancipated, but she was able to live in freedom for more than seven decades. Never married, she died at a nephew's home on Goodwins Mill Road in 1935, aged 98 years or more. Her neighbors called her "Aunt" Rhoda, a term which was then used to indicate respect. (Courtesy of Mary Chappell White.)

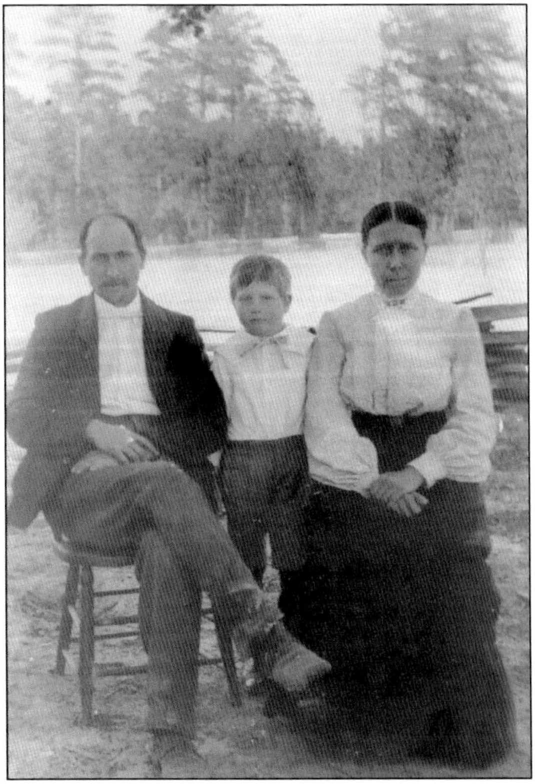

Sitting before their rail fence c. 1905 are (from left to right) John Jordan Chappell (1863–1934), son Julian (1898–1970), and wife Julia Anna (Ward) Chappell (1860–1945). (Courtesy of Thelma Chappell Riddick.)

Mark (left) and Margaret Gregory pose in a studio in 1895. Both wear dresses, but the sister has shoes as well. (Courtesy of Margaret Ainsley Brewin.)

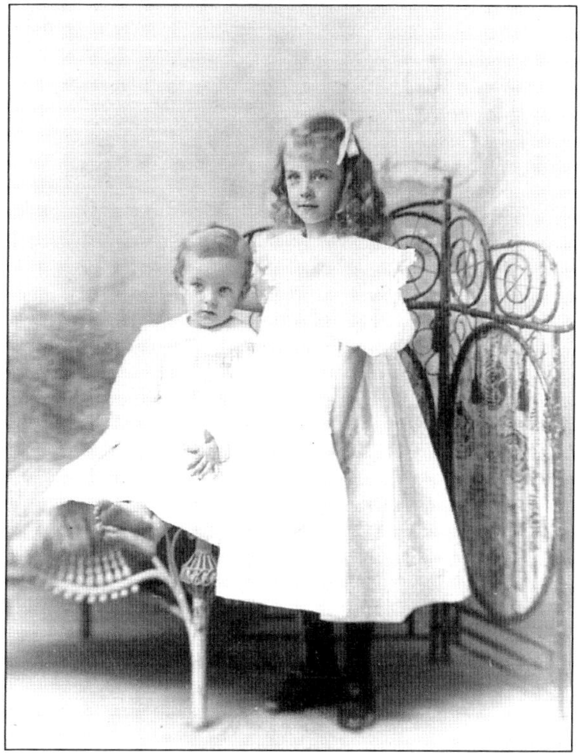

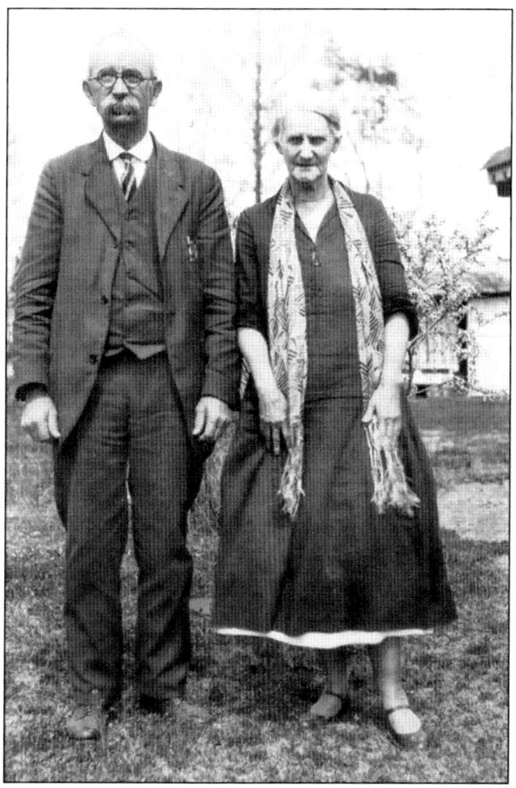

Jacob William Darden (1855–1937) and Martha Estelle (Stokes) Darden (1868–1947), who married in 1886, are shown at their 50th wedding anniversary celebration in 1936. (Courtesy of Florence Darden Christensen.)

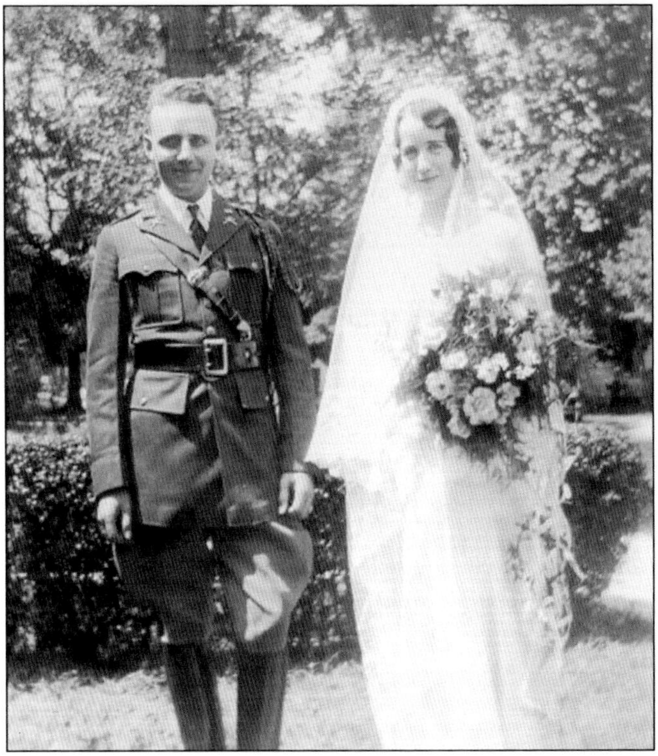

Nell Zora Spivey of Perquimans married James Elmer Totten of New York in August 1931; both were aged 27. James rose to the rank of colonel in the Air Force. A graduate of Duke University, Nell was a registered nurse. She is buried in Arlington National Cemetery. (Courtesy of Kay Matthews Whedbee.)

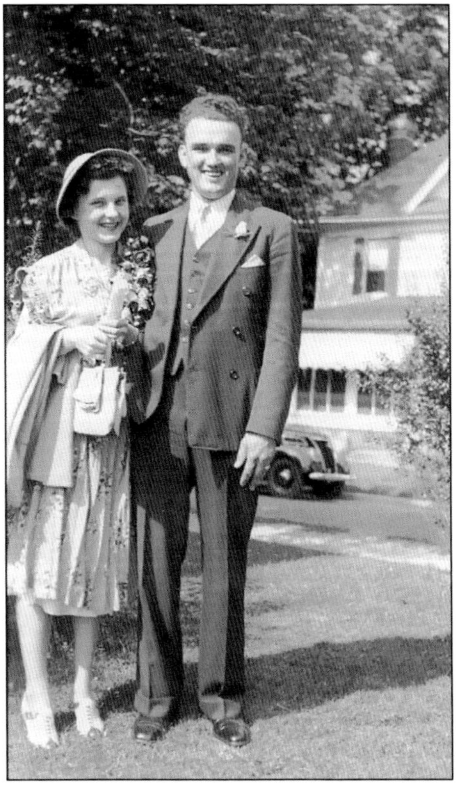

Eighteen-year-old June bride Doris (Gregory) Ainsley stands at their home on Covent Garden Street with new husband William F. Ainsley on their wedding day in 1937. (Courtesy of Margaret Ainsley Brewin.)

Wallace Hobbs is framed by the family home at Bethel in 1941. Heavily ornamented with scroll work, the porch has a swing ready for a leisurely afternoon. At right can be seen the well sweep, a vertical post supporting a pivoted horizontal pole from which a smaller pole or a rope could lower a bucket into the well. (Courtesy of Joyce Hobbs.)

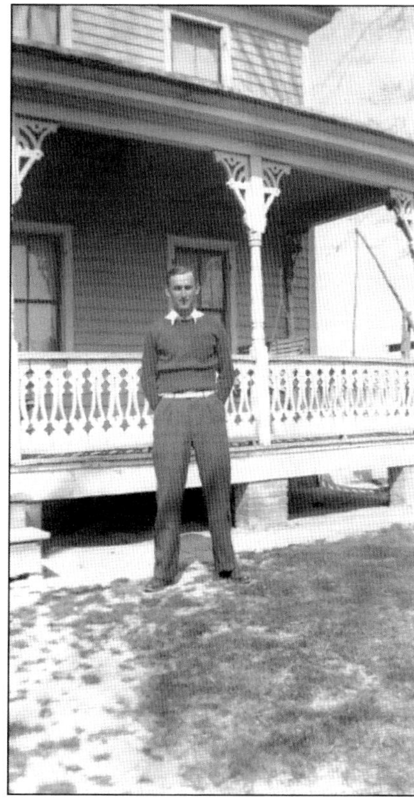

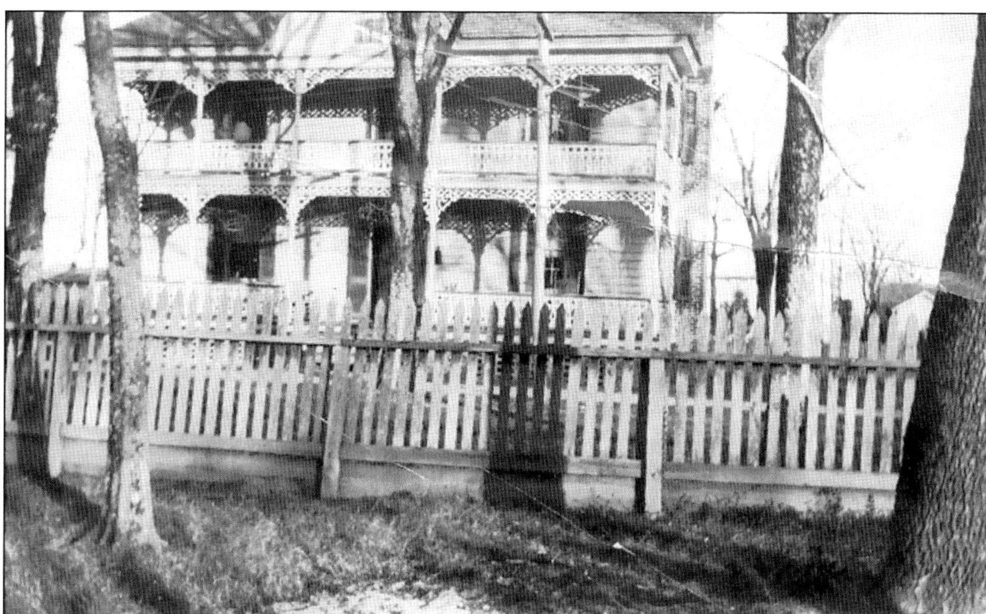

Scroll work (gingerbread) on the eaves casts interesting shadows across Rosser Brinn's house on Front Street, *c.* 1913. In the foreground is the fence around the Harvey sisters' backyard, one of the wide variety of barriers then needed to keep out livestock, which often roamed the streets freely. (Courtesy of Claudia Brinn Bunch.)

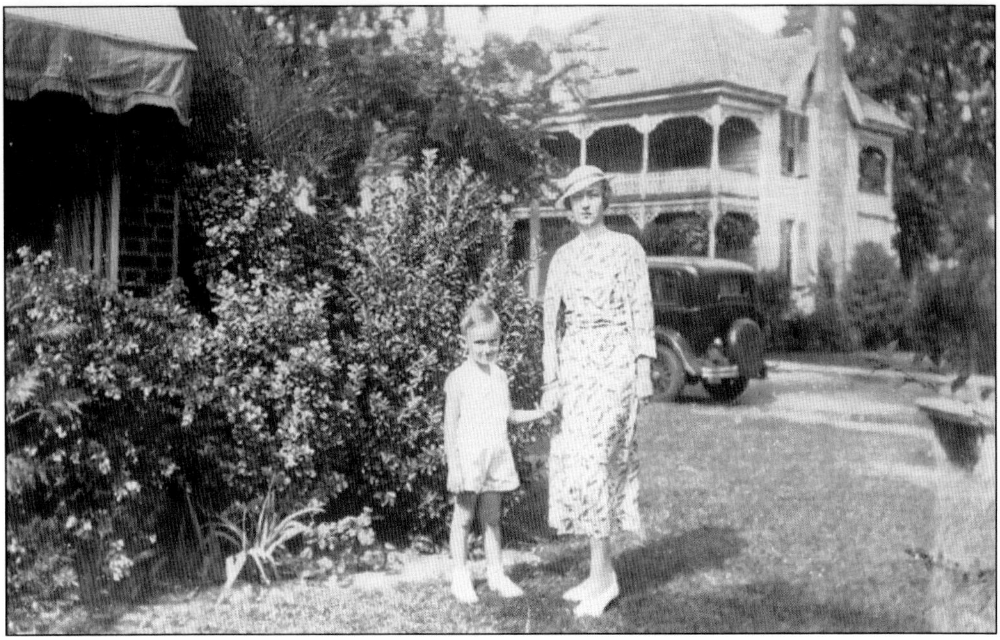

Marie (Schroeder) Davenport holds son Carlton's hand beside the luxuriant growth in their yard. Across Front Street is the Brinn house, which has been much altered since this picture was taken in 1934. (Courtesy of Carlton A. Davenport Jr.)

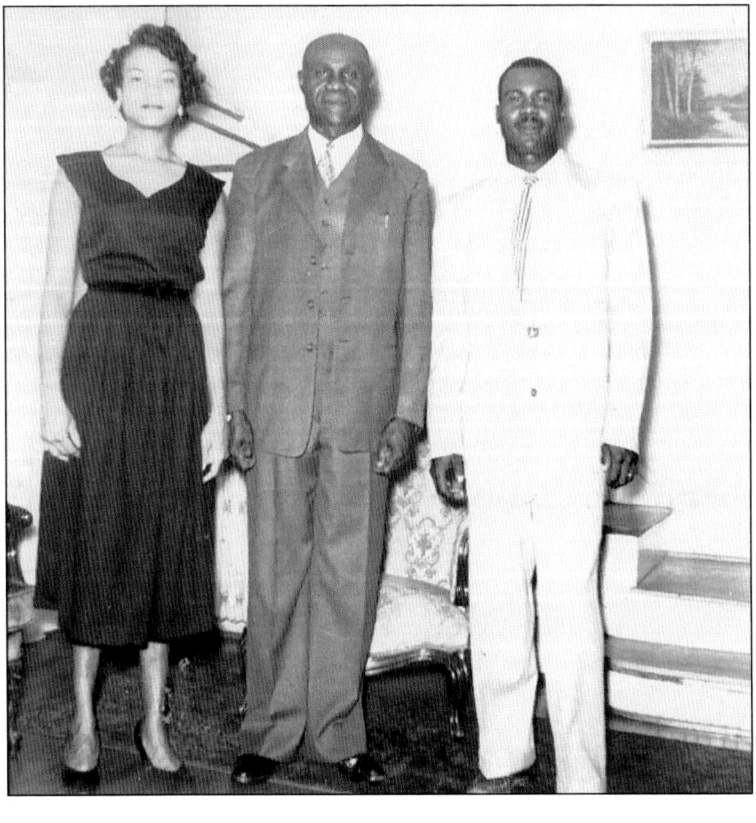

Helen Thompson is shown with her father Walter Thompson, who was principal at Hertford High School from 1930 to 1947, and her brother Walter Thompson Jr. in the early 1950s. Helen later served on the Perquimans County Board of Education for several years. (Courtesy of Helen Thompson Shaw.)

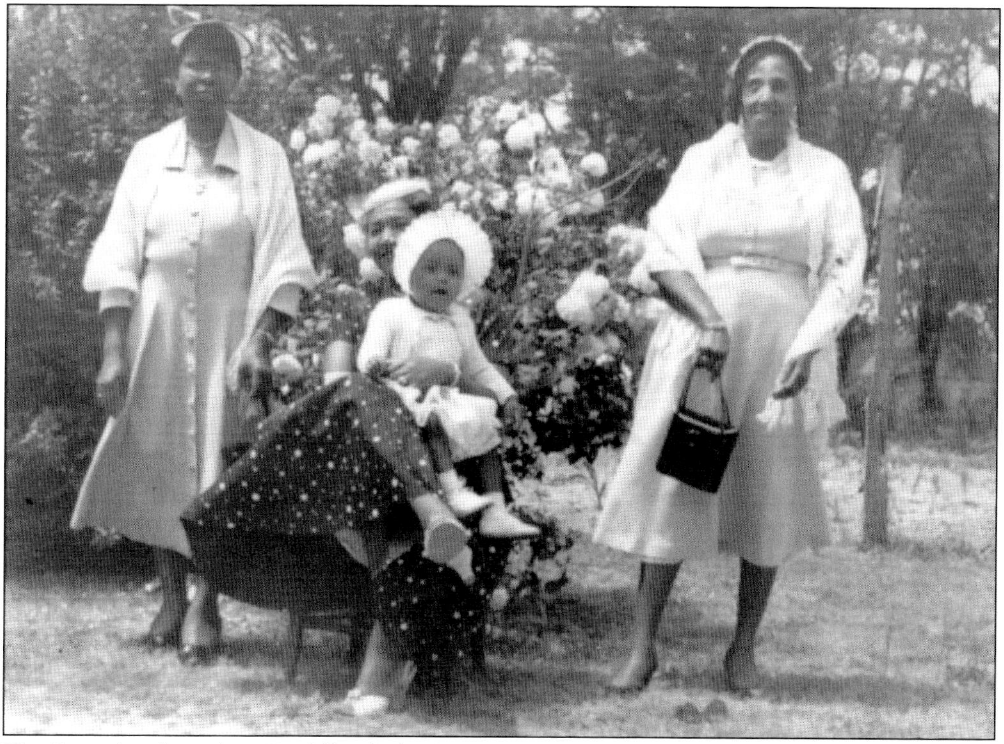

The Bowe family yard in Winfall is the background for, from left to right, Mary Lee Wiggins, Ruth Brookins holding daughter Debra, and Estella Bowe, *c.* 1955. (Courtesy of Ruth Brookins.)

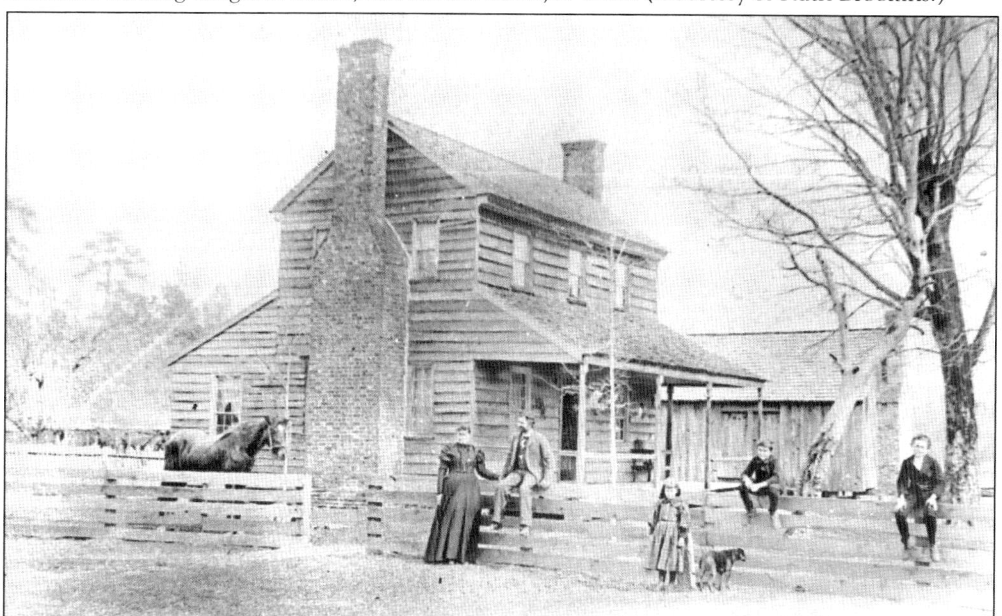

Edward Proctor's house in Bethel was typical of early 19th-century Perquimans architecture, being a two-story structure with end chimneys and a front porch balanced by a rear shed. In the background at right is an outbuilding with twin doors and board-and-batten walls. Seen here *c.* 1900, the house burned down half a century later. (Courtesy of Joyce Hobbs.)

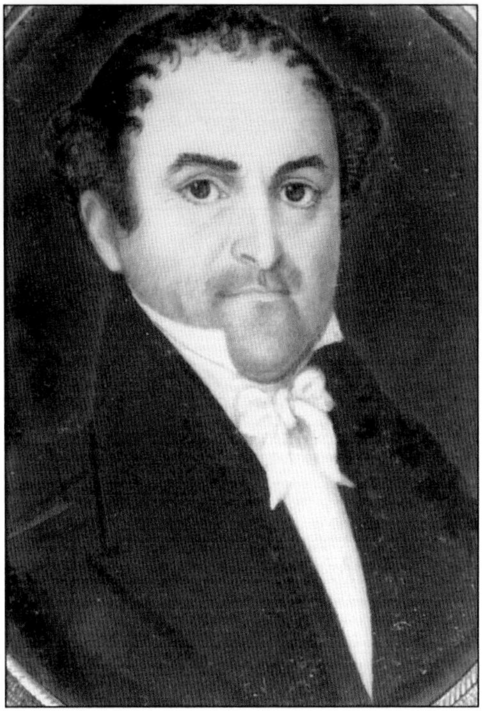

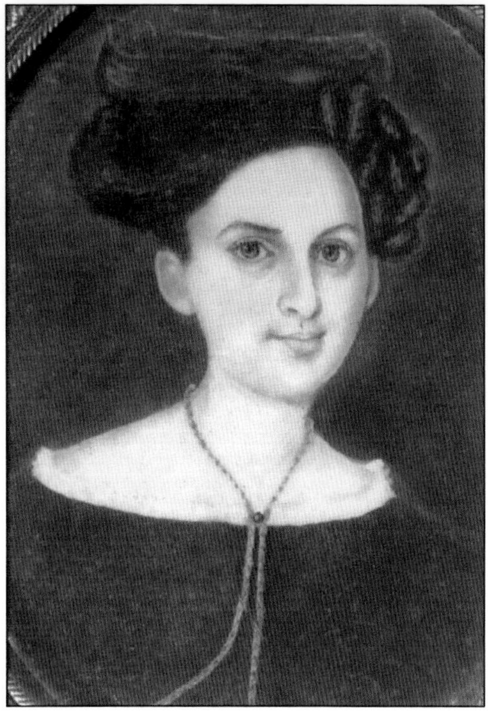

Jonathan Hill Jacocks (1792–1847), at left, was brigadier general of the militia, state legislator, and one of the wealthiest planters in the area. His second wife Grizzelle Pointer (Copeland) Fletcher Jacocks Jenkins (1811–1873), at right, married three times, but had children only by Jacocks. (Courtesy of Raymond A. Winslow Jr.)

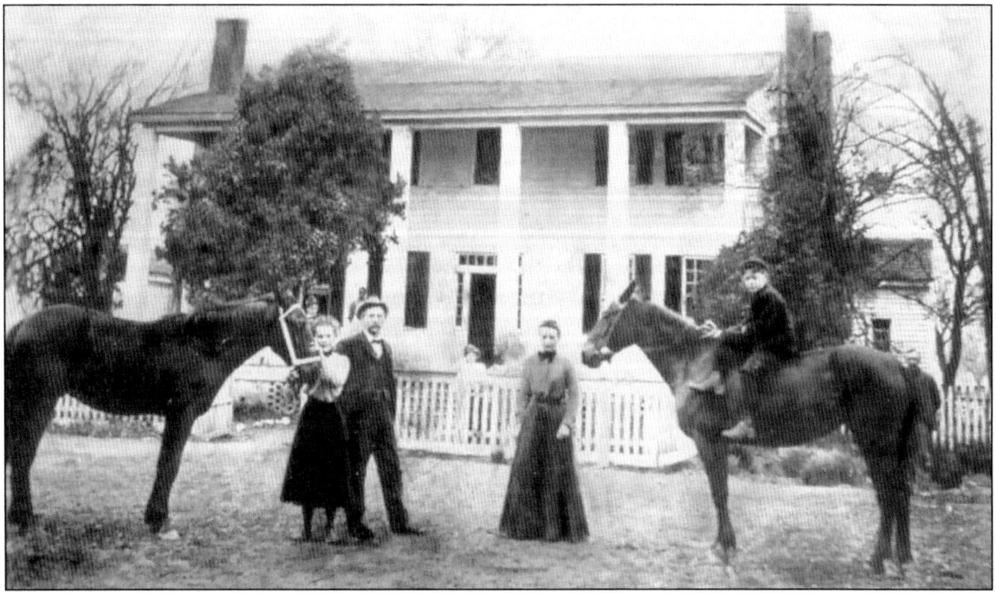

Gen. Jonathan Jacocks was enlarging his house in Durants Neck when he died in 1847. It is seen here *c.* 1895 when the family of Leonidas C. Relfe (1856–1919) occupied it. Relfe was postmaster for Jacocks Post Office from 1894 to 1911. Like many middle-class families of the day, the Relfes had a few live-in servants. (Courtesy of Elizabeth Relfe Hobbs Edwards.)

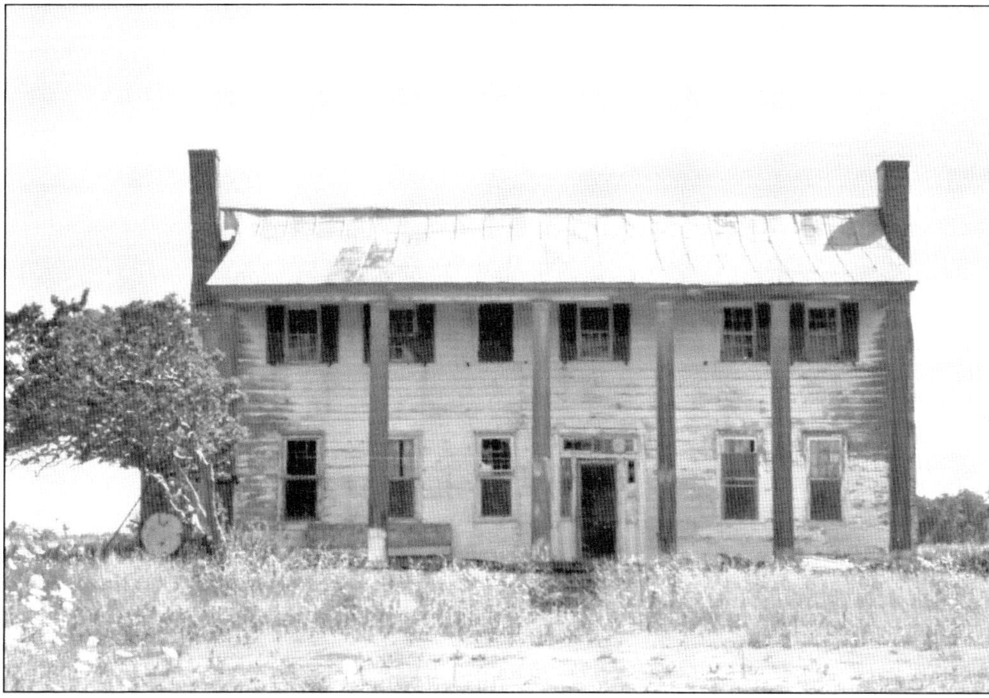

The Jacocks house was vacant and neglected for a long time in the late 20th century. (Courtesy of Beth Skinner Taylor.)

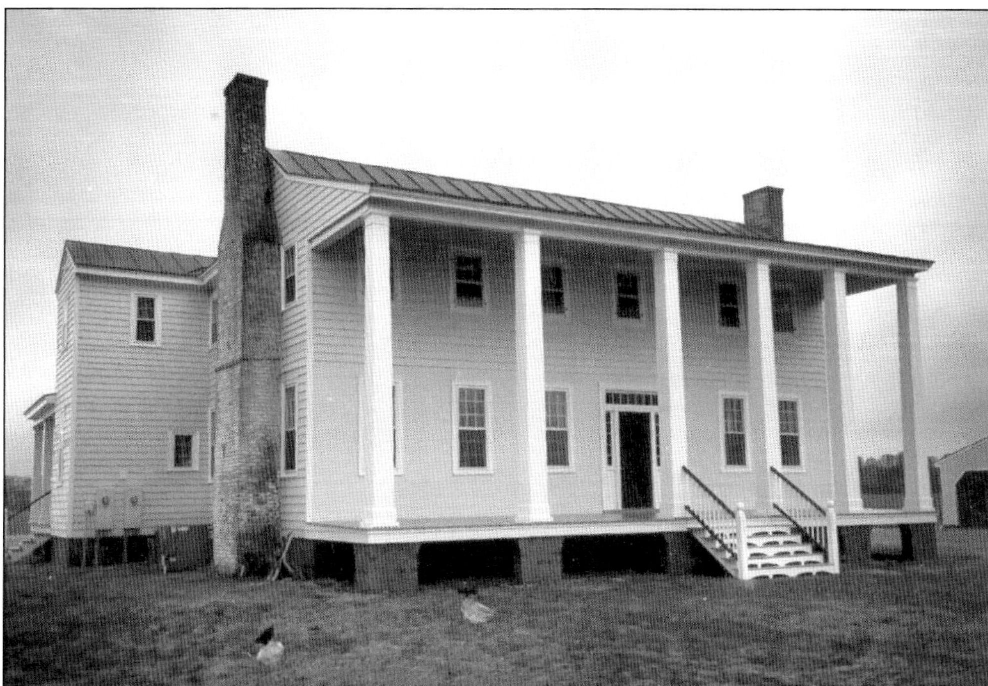

The Jacocks house was restored at the beginning of the 21st century by Paul and Jean Carr. Jean is a descendant of the Relfe family. (Courtesy of Beth Skinner Taylor.)

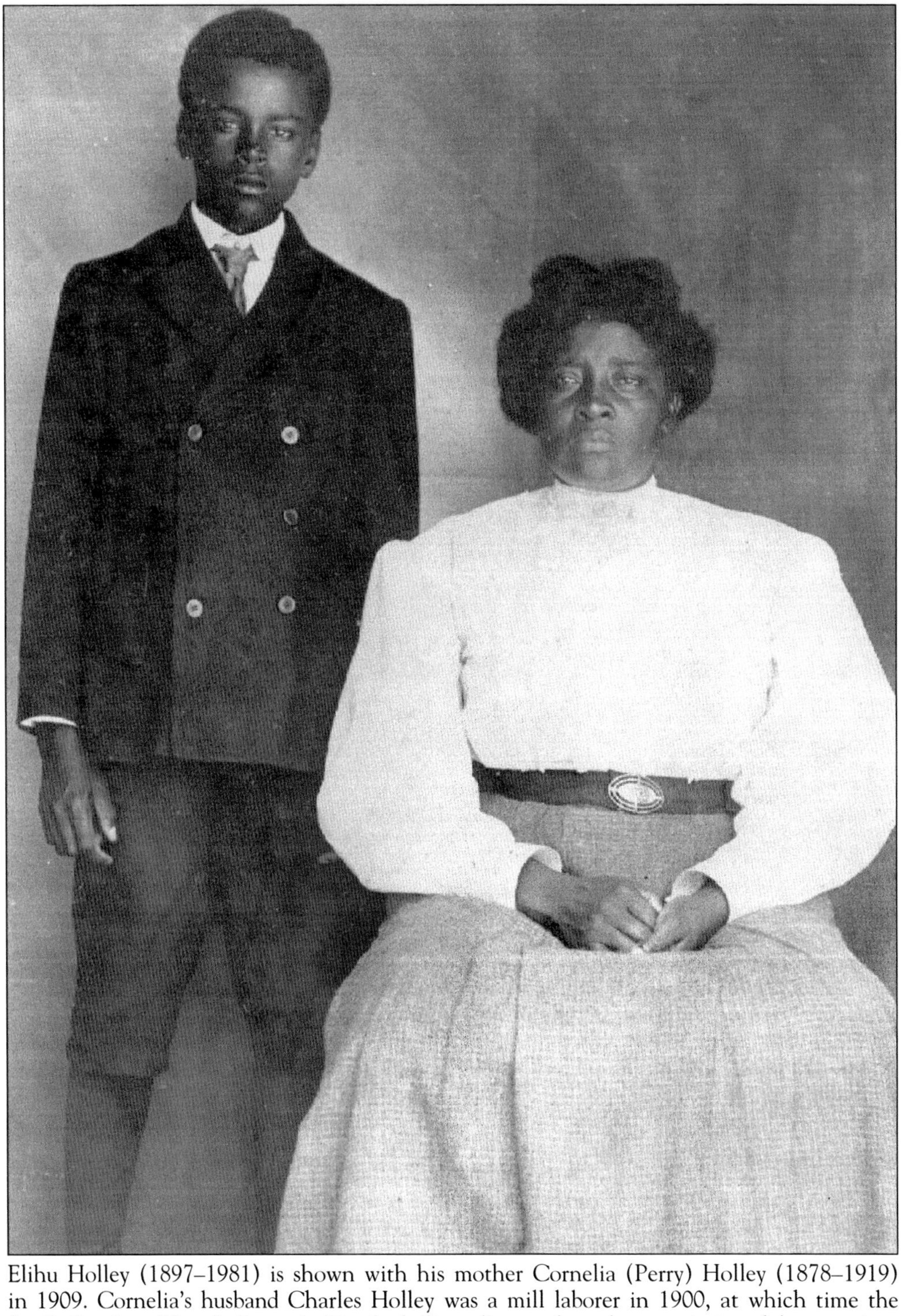

Elihu Holley (1897–1981) is shown with his mother Cornelia (Perry) Holley (1878–1919) in 1909. Cornelia's husband Charles Holley was a mill laborer in 1900, at which time the family lived on Church Street in Hertford. Cornelia may have been a victim of the notorious Spanish flu epidemic. Elihu grew up to follow in his father's footsteps, eventually becoming a mill foreman in Hertford. (Courtesy of Laura Hudson and Celestine Modlin.)

Two

AT SCHOOL

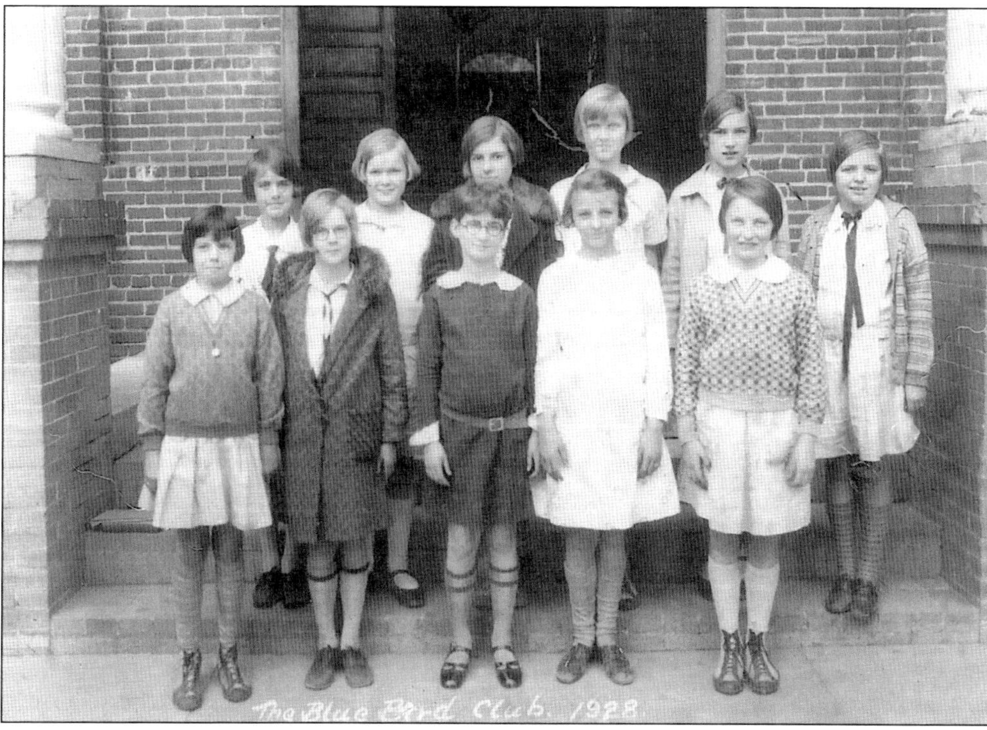

Members of the Blue Bird Club, shown here in 1928, were good friends all through their school years. They are, from left to right, (front row) Helene Nixon, Sarah Brinn, Frances King, Lillian Blanchard, and Leah Nachman; and (back row) Mary Lou Perry, Hattie Weaver Riddick, Kay Broughton, Carolyn Riddick, Hannah Margaret Stephens, and Eloise Broughton. (Courtesy of Helene Nixon.)

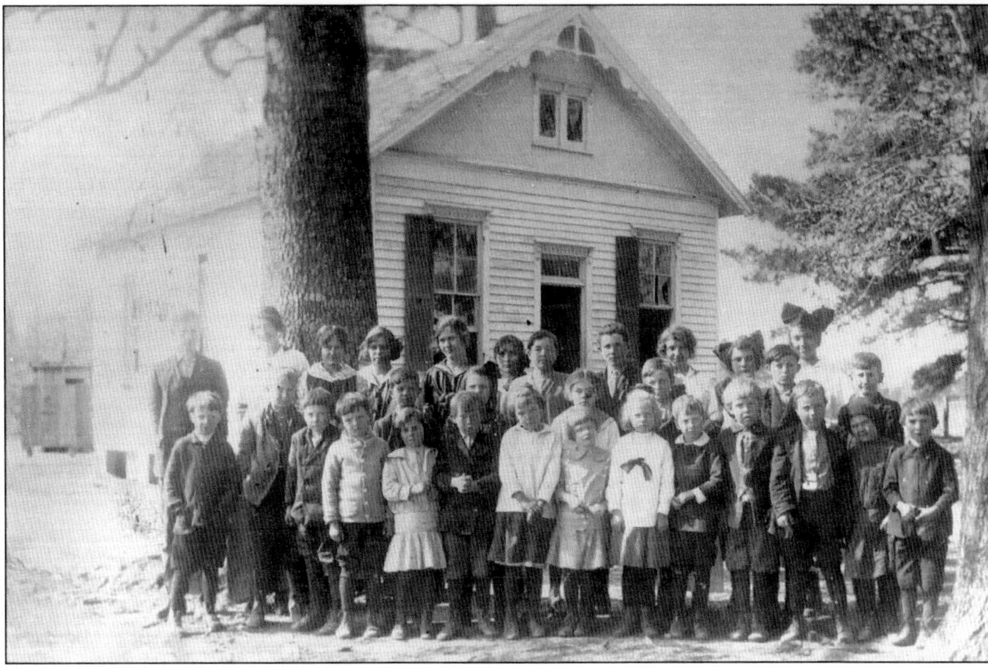

The Perry School in the Hunters Fork vicinity had a stylish Victorian facade. (Courtesy of Museum of the Albemarle.)

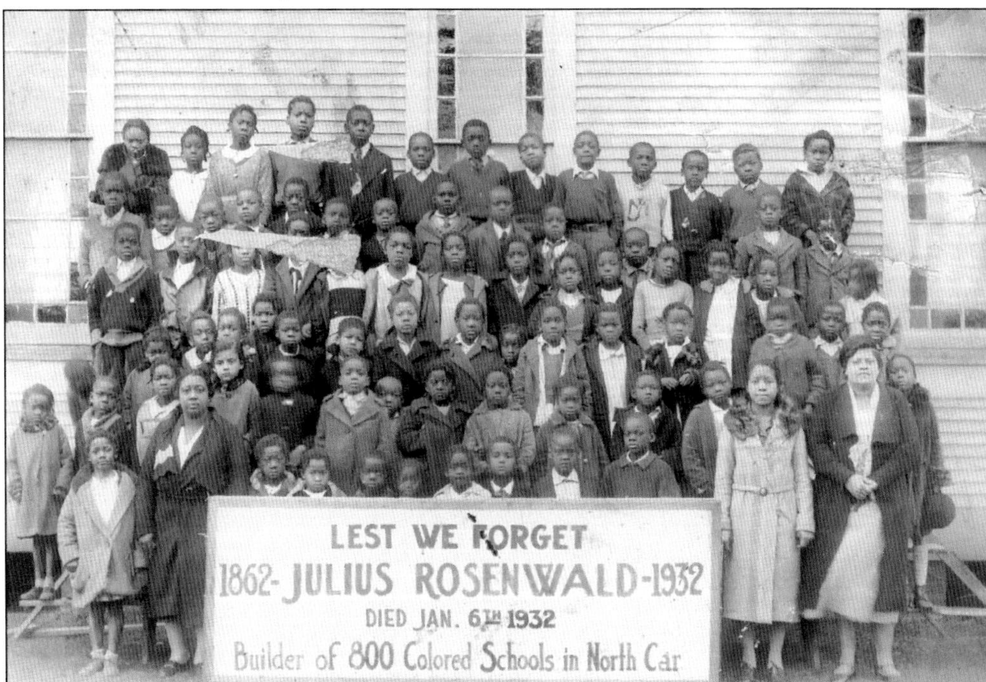

Students from Hertford Academy (black) gathered in 1932 to honor the late Julius Rosenwald. President of Sears Roebuck and Company, Rosenwald established a fund to build and support schools for black children. Two Rosenwald schools were built in Perquimans County. (Courtesy of Laura Hudson and Celestine Modlin.)

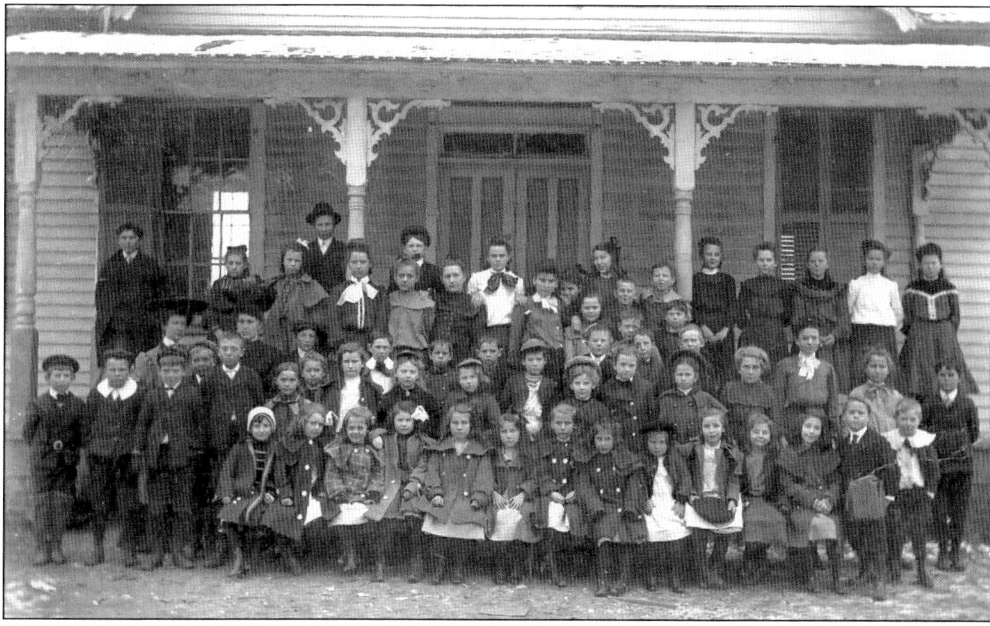

The Hertford Free School at the corner of Church and Dobbs Streets educated those town children who did not attend the private Hertford Academy. The children shown here c. 1900 include Archibald L. Riddick (far left), who became a noted surgeon and professor of surgery in Washington, D.C. (Courtesy of Raymond A. Winslow Jr.)

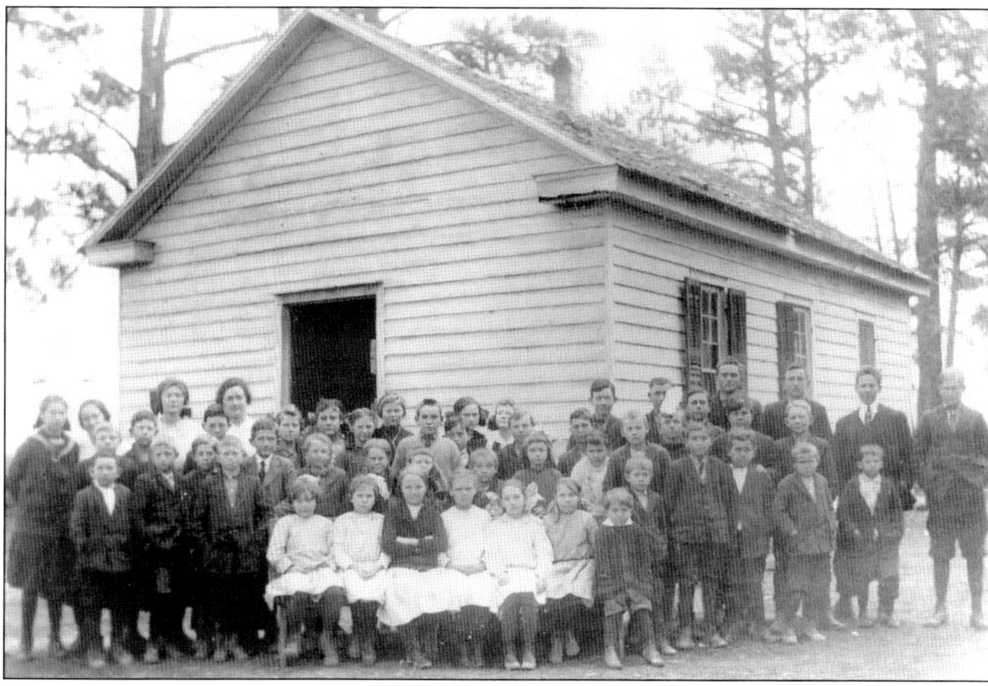

It took teachers with rare talents to instruct and discipline so many pupils in so small a school as the one at White Hat. In some schools, all grades were taught in a single room. Basic education was emphasized, and amenities were usually limited to a wood stove, a well or pump, and an outhouse. (Courtesy of Museum of the Albemarle.)

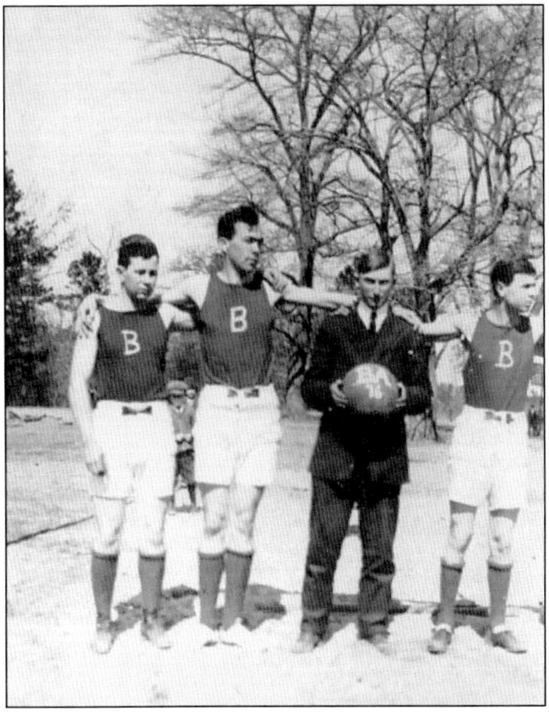

Timothy Jessup (second from left) has a height advantage over his teammates on the 1916 Belvidere Academy basketball team. (Courtesy of Thelma Chappell Riddick.)

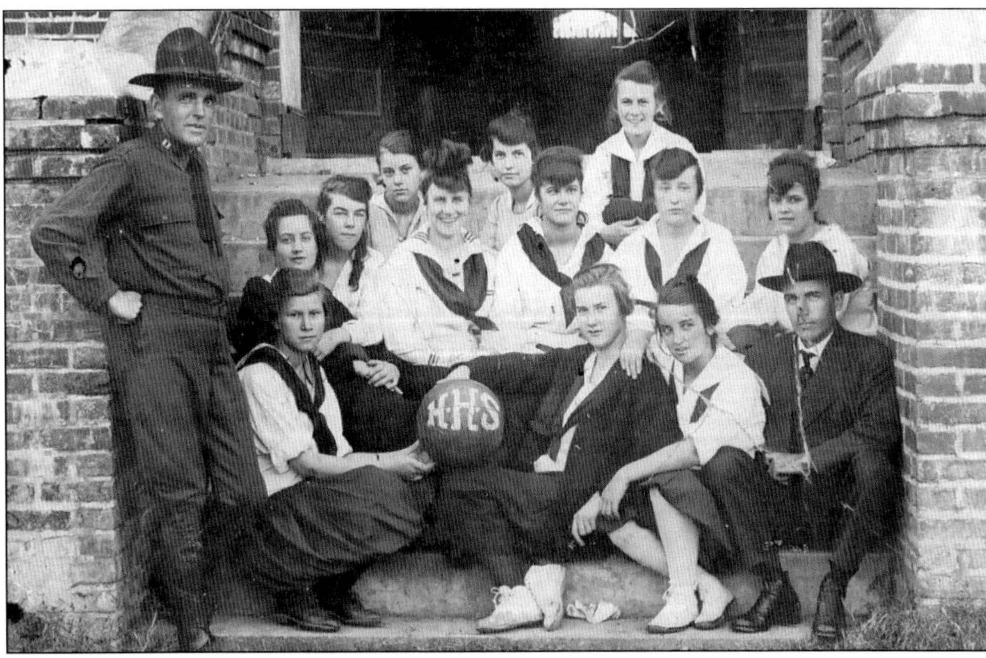

Organized sports for girls were uncommon in 1917, when this basketball team at Hertford High School played. Depicted, from left to right, are (front row) principal Louis R. Crawford, Louise Gaither, Glenmore Koonce, Annie Ruth Morgan, and coach Rev. Thomas Lawrence; (middle row) Alice Elliott, Hannah Mae Fleetwood, Mattie Newby, Dorothy Nixon, Eugenia Blanchard, and Marjorie Nixon; (back row) Marion Newby, Mary Sumner, and Helen Newbold. (Courtesy of Charles T. Skinner Jr.)

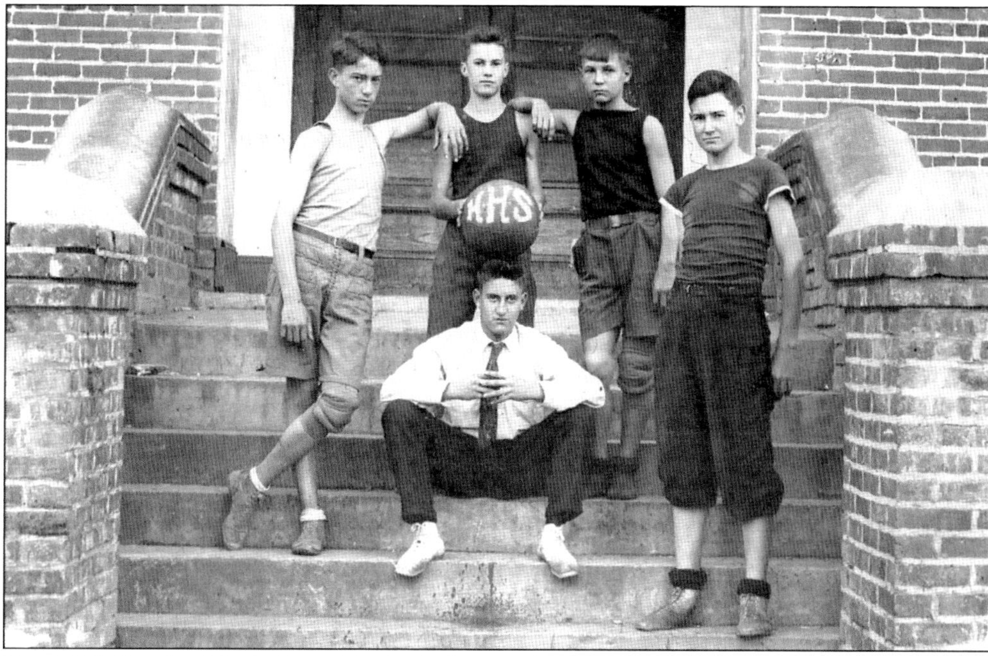

The 1917 Hertford High School basketball team does not have much in the way of uniforms, and Silas Whedbee (seated) is overdressed for sports. Holding the ball is Julian G. Nixon, who was killed in an automobile accident in 1926. (Courtesy of Dorothy Oakey Read.)

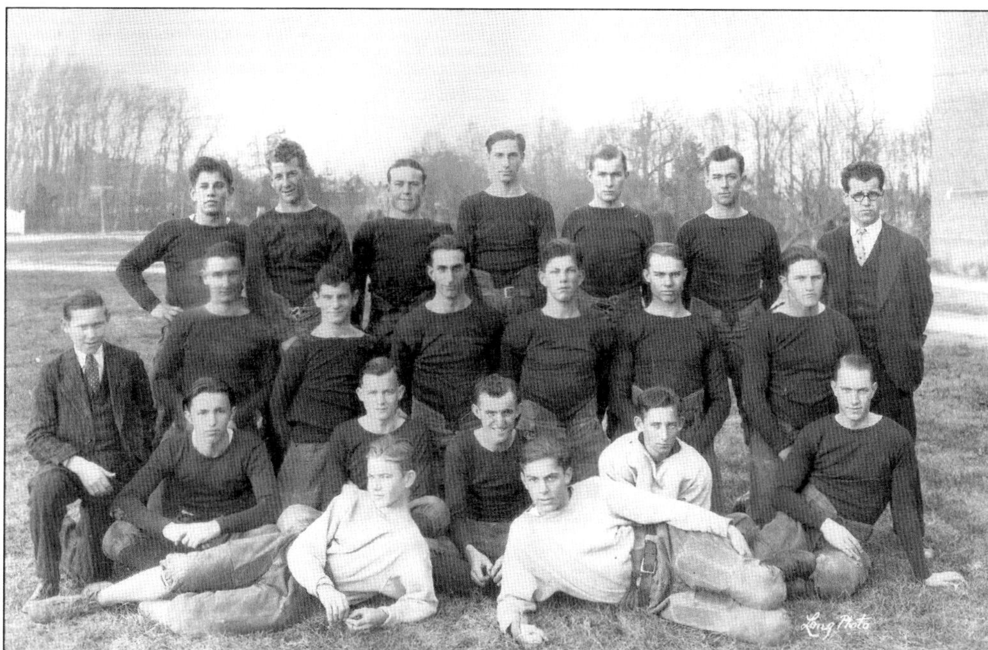

The 1928 football squad at Perquimans County High School finished third in the conference. Coach A.L. Eggers is in the back row, far right. (Courtesy of John V. Matthews.)

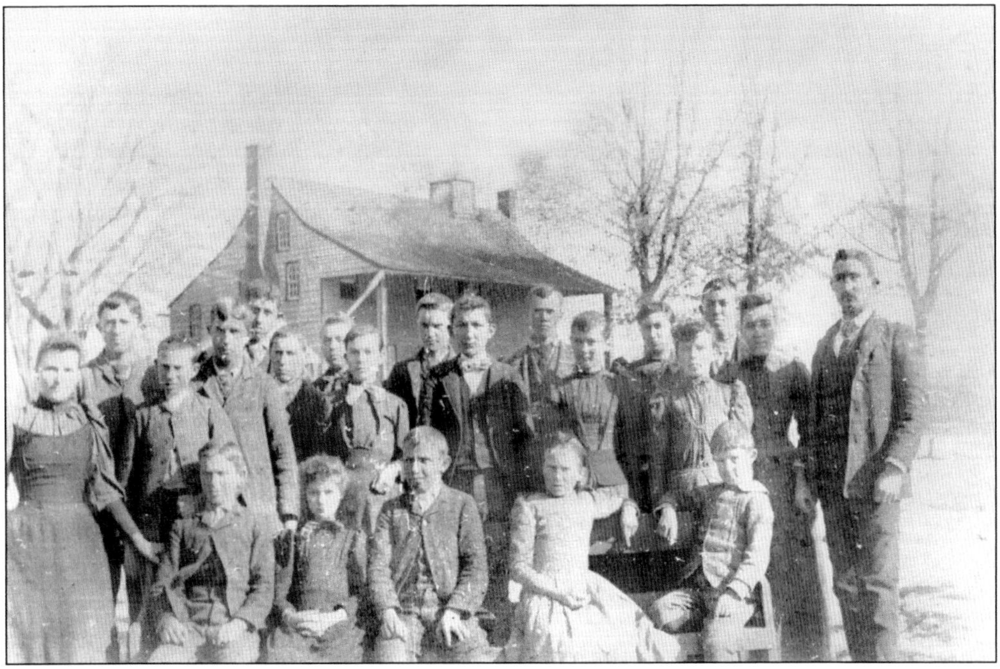

Belvidere Academy was opened by the Society of Friends in 1834. Originally a boarding school, it became one of the county's most important educational institutions. This c. 1880s photograph depicts students and faculty before the original academy building, which would be replaced in 1904. (Courtesy of Lynwood C. Winslow III.)

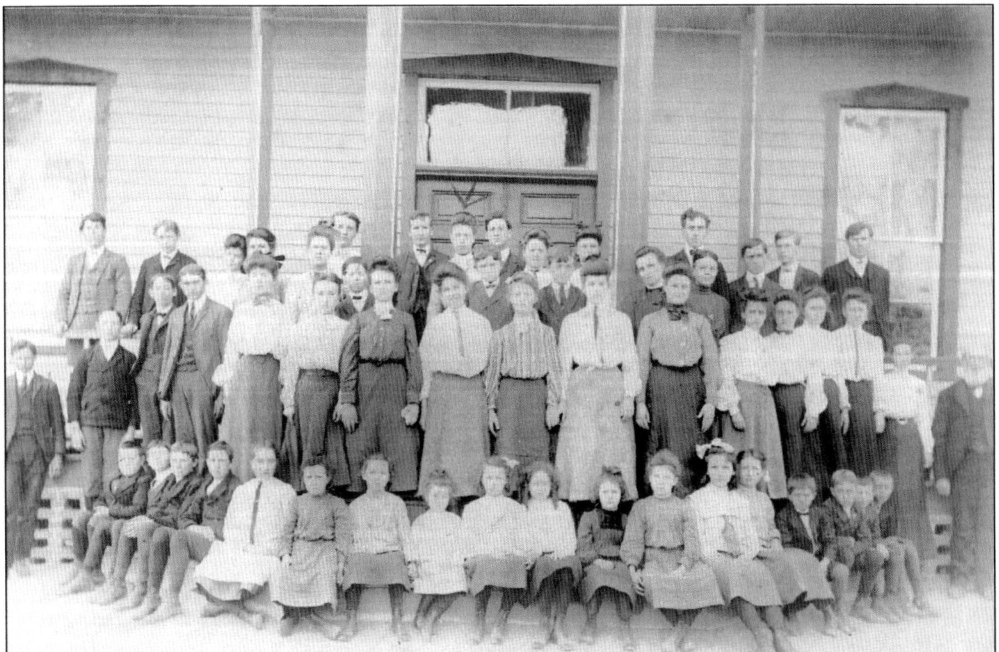

Belvidere Academy was still operated by the Society of Friends when these pupils were photographed c. 1910. In 1914, Piney Woods Monthly Meeting sold the property to the county board of education. (Courtesy of Thelma Chappell Riddick.)

William Gassaway Gaither (1848–1918) from Davie County came to Perquimans to teach at Hertford Academy and was later named principal. He also served as county superintendent of public instruction, Hertford postmaster, vestryman of the Episcopal church, agent for the Norfolk & Southern Railroad, and manager of the Perquimans River Steam Boat Line. (Courtesy of Bettie Gaither Stokes.)

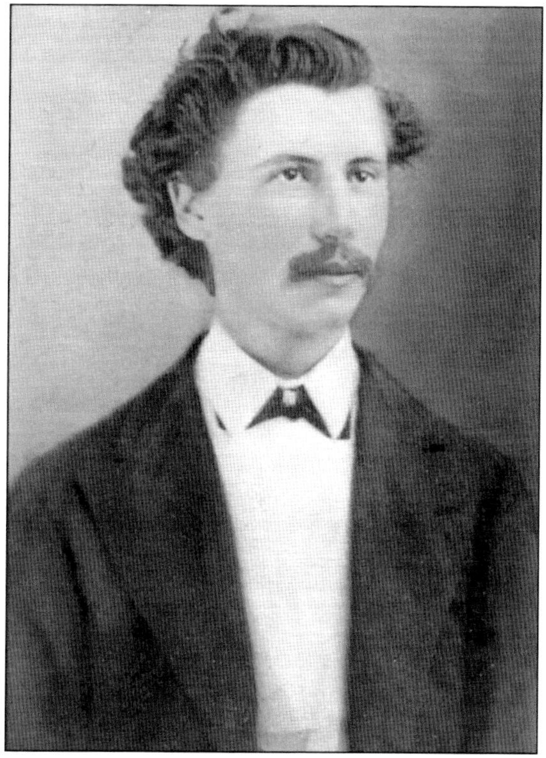

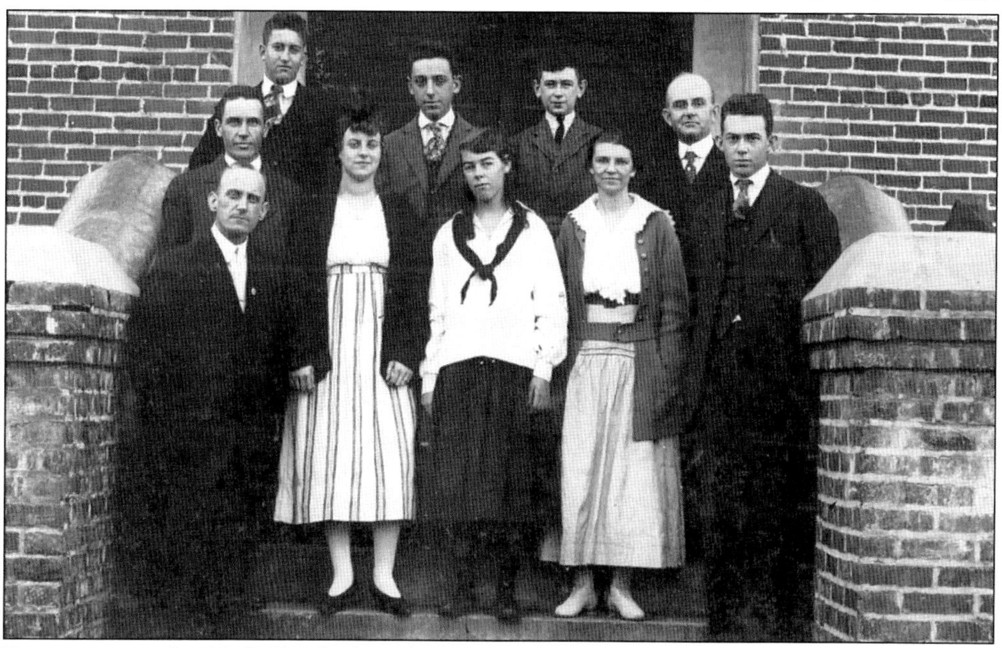

Experience on the 1917 Hertford High School Debating Team served these students well in law, education, and business. From left to right are (front row) school superintendent E. Hicks; (middle row) principal Elisha W. Joyner, Mattie Newby, Hannah Mae Fleetwood, Mae Wood Winslow, and James Stokes; (back row) Silas Whedbee, William Gaither, Edgar Newby, and Dabney White. (Courtesy of Charles T. Skinner Jr.)

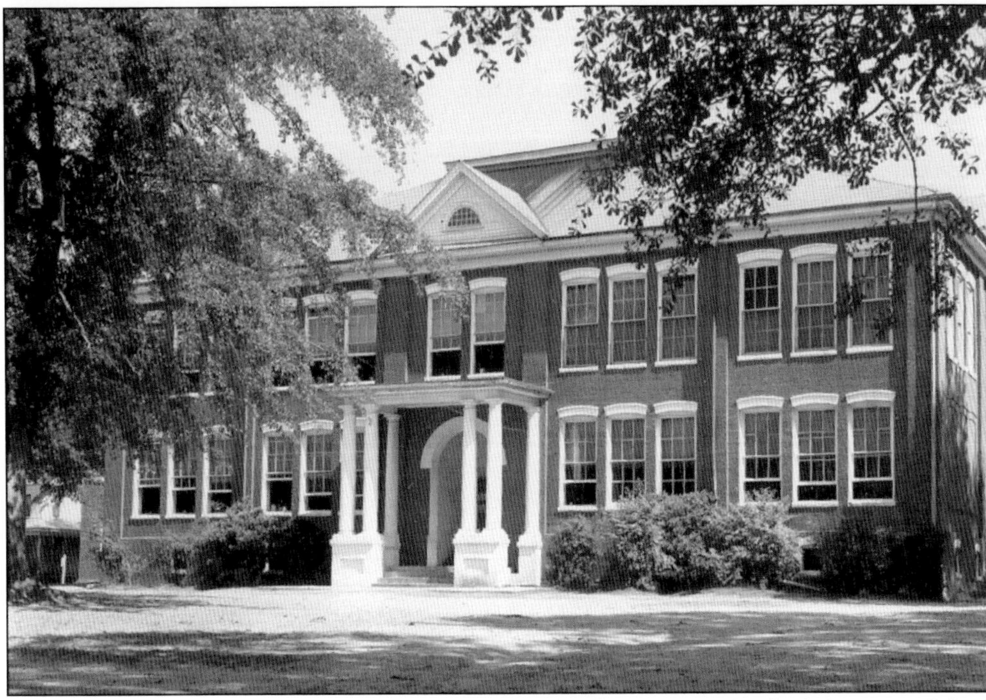

Framed by great oak trees that shaded its playground in later years, Hertford Grammar School served the community from 1907 to 1956. (Courtesy of Ruth Elliott Winslow.)

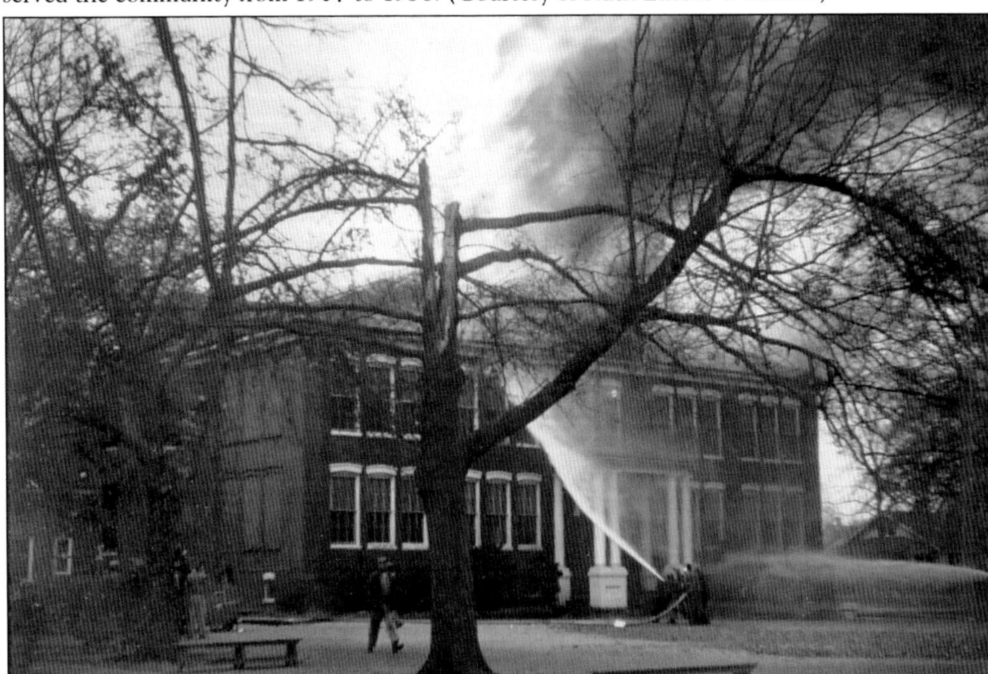

It was a great loss to the county when Hertford Grammar School was destroyed by fire on January 9, 1956. Fortunately, all students and teachers were evacuated from the building without injury. (Courtesy of Charles T. Skinner Jr.)

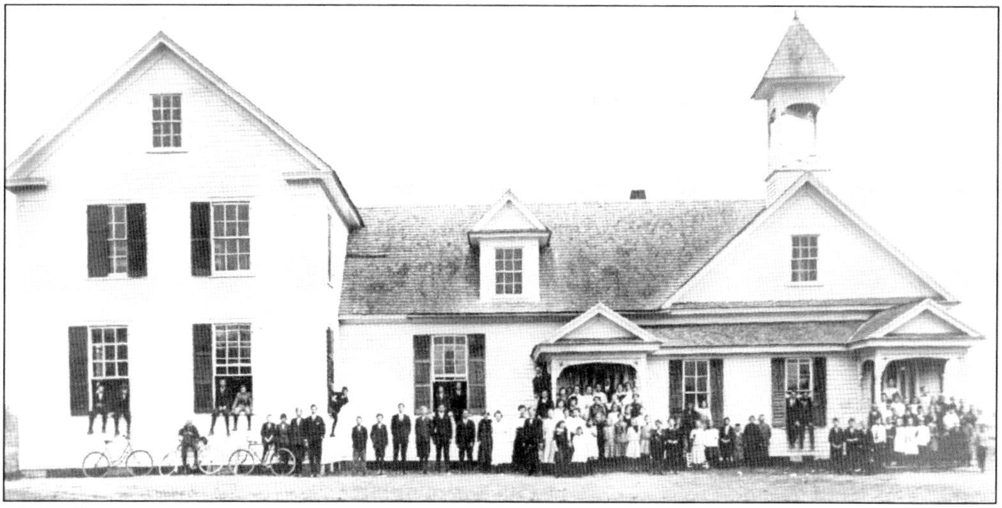

The Whiteston Graded and High School was built *c*. 1900. Seen here in the fall of 1915, it was both an elementary and a high school until 1925, and it continued to function as a grammar school until 1937. In addition to the regular graded curriculum, the school offered agriculture, Latin, and German. (Courtesy of Lynwood C. Winslow III.)

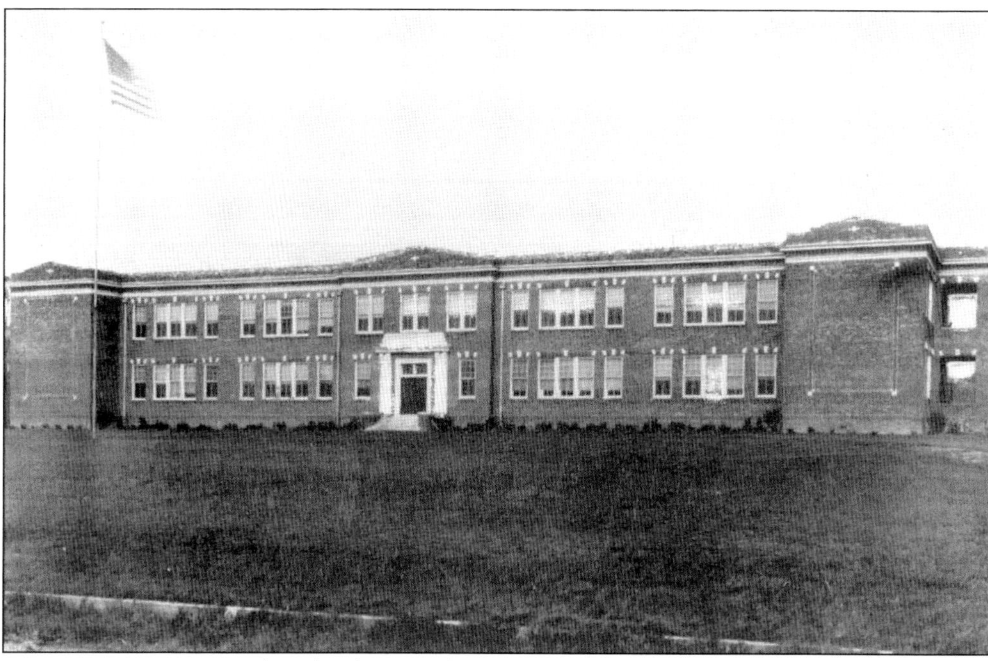

Perquimans County High School was only five years old when photographed for the 1929 yearbook, *Kilcokonen*. The wings on either end were removed decades later. (Courtesy of Raymond A. Winslow Jr.)

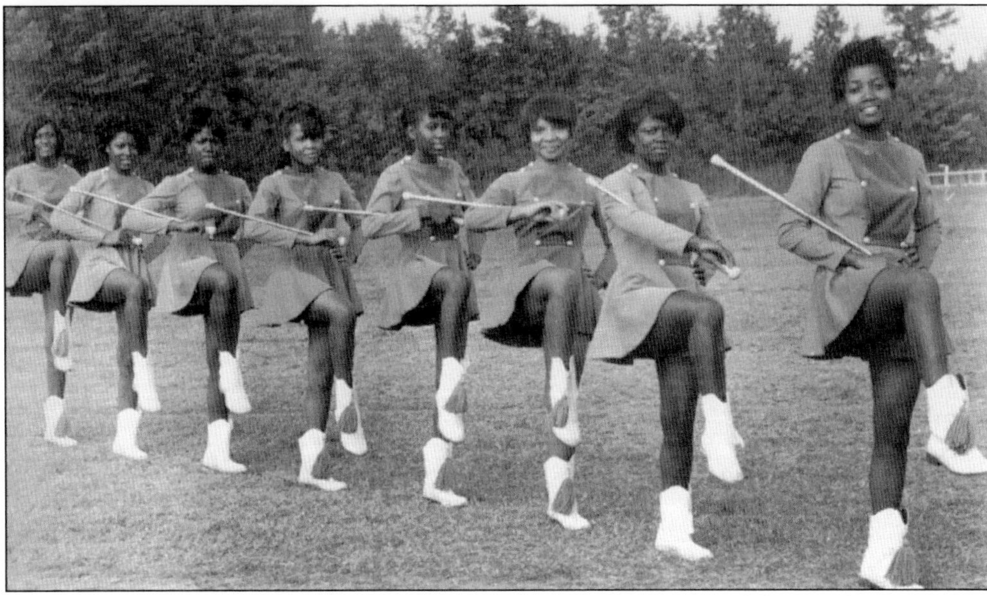

The majorettes at Perquimans County Union School in 1968, from left to right, were Doris James, Janet Smith, Darlene Jennings, Dianne Wiggins, Chrystal Mallory, Louvenia Felton, Carol Turner, and Constance Dunlap. (Courtesy of Evelyn Stubbins.)

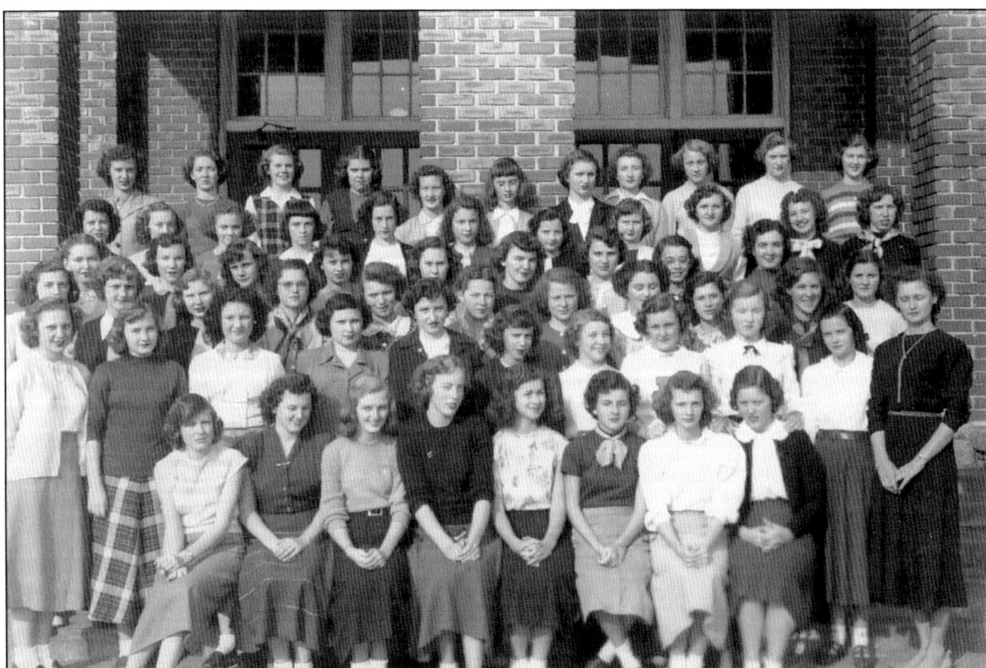

Anne Nowell taught the 1950–1951 Future Homemakers of America at Perquimans County High School. The expectation that most women would be homemakers was already declining. (Courtesy of Carolyn Lane.)

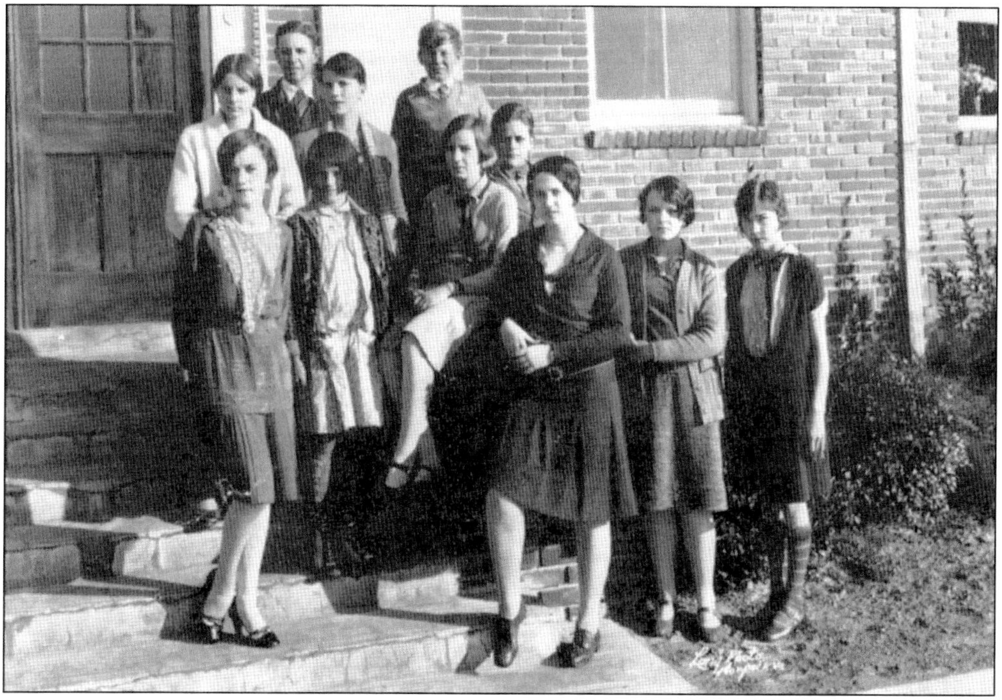

On the steps of Perquimans County High School stand the 1929 School News staff, with editor-in-chief Frances Fowler front and center. (Courtesy of Raymond A. Winslow Jr.)

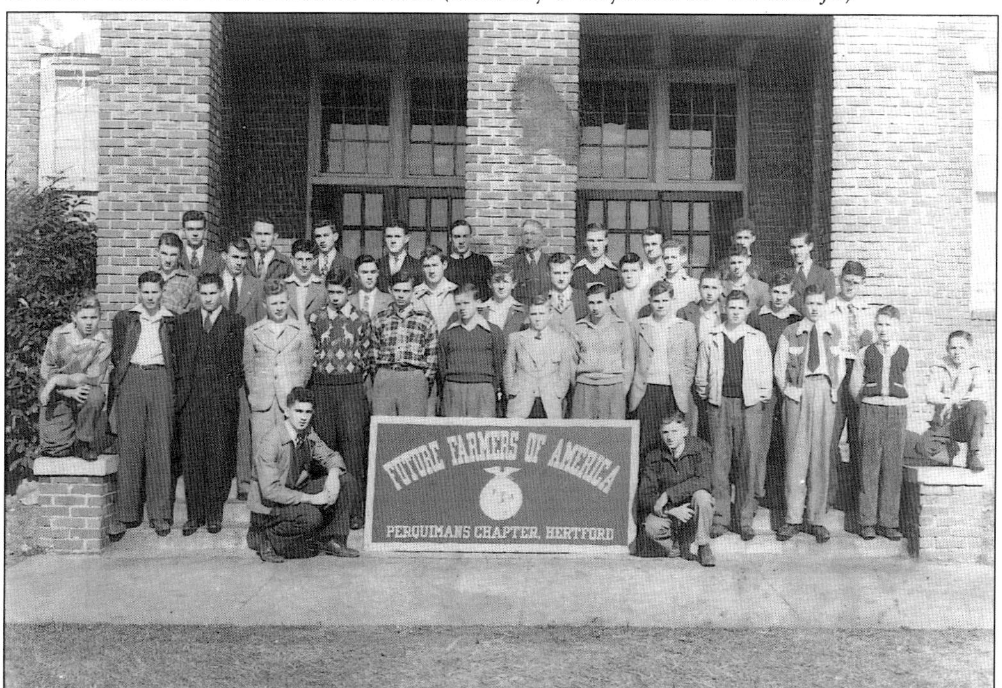

The 1947 Future Farmers of America at Perquimans County High School included agriculture students. The public schools offered instruction in farming, the occupation most young men in Perquimans would follow. (Courtesy of Prue Newby Reed.)

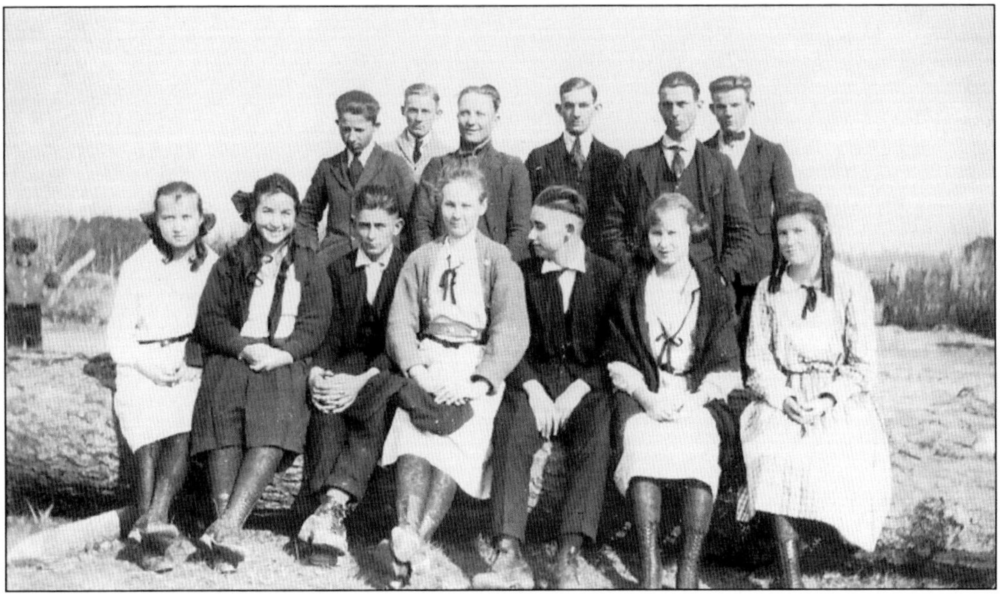

The 1922 eighth-grade class at Beech Spring School in Hertford Township found a convenient log for a prop. Nearly half the class were members of the Howell and Rogerson families. Local schools typically included interrelated families and were often close-knit groups. (Courtesy of Lynwood C. Winslow III.)

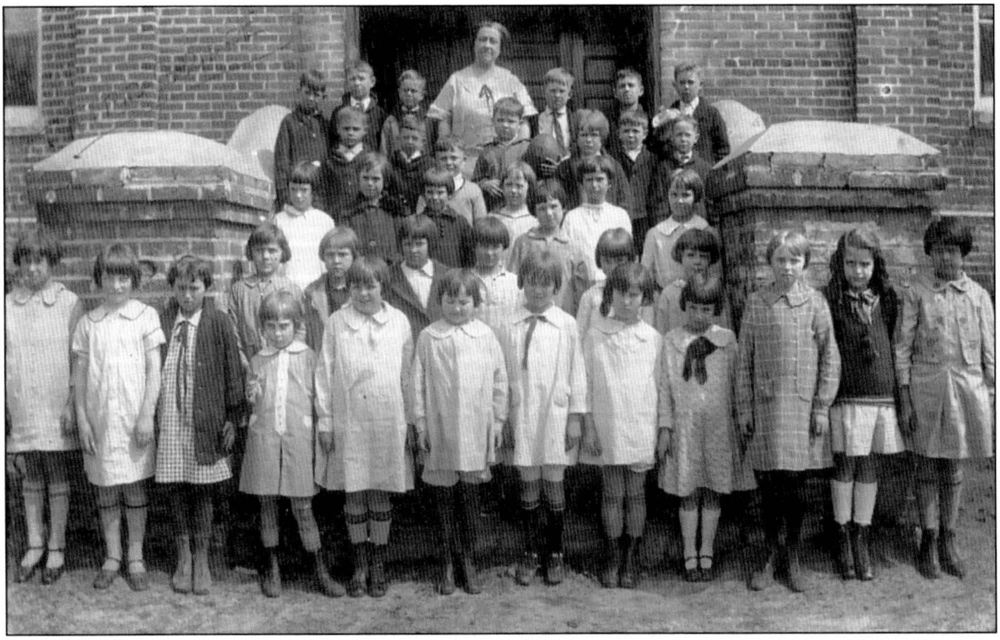

The third graders at Hertford Grammar School in 1926 seem a solemn lot in this photograph. Of course, many of us remember school teachers who could quell a class with a single look. In the front row (fifth from right) is Ruth Elliott, who would become a teacher at this school. (Courtesy of Ruth Elliott Winslow.)

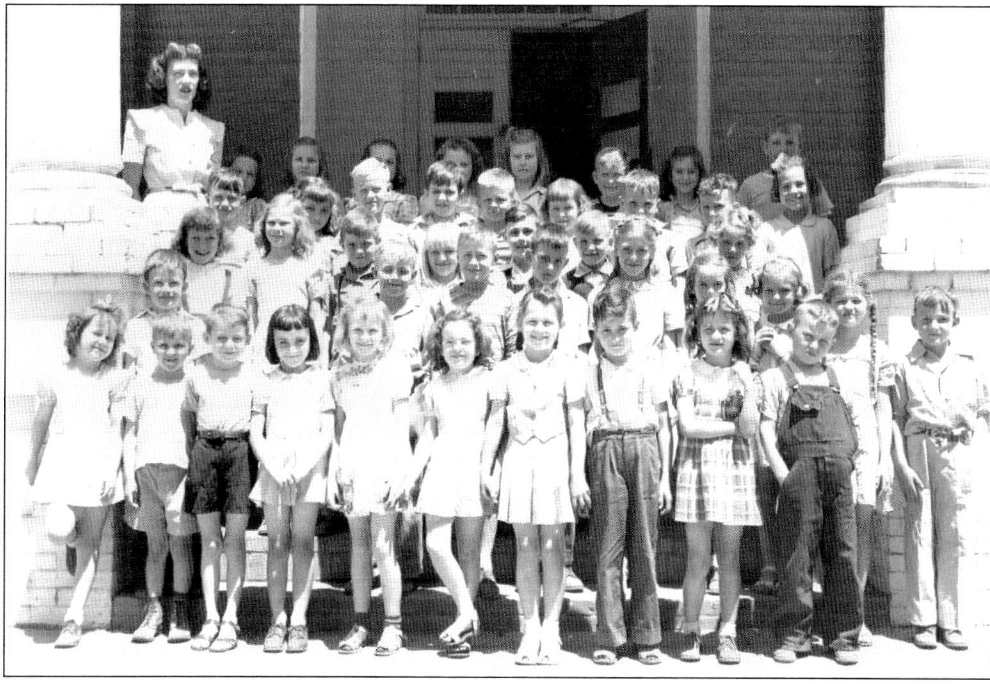

Ruth Elliott taught second grade at Hertford Grammar School for many years. She is shown here with a class, *c*. 1946. (Courtesy of Ruth Elliott Winslow)

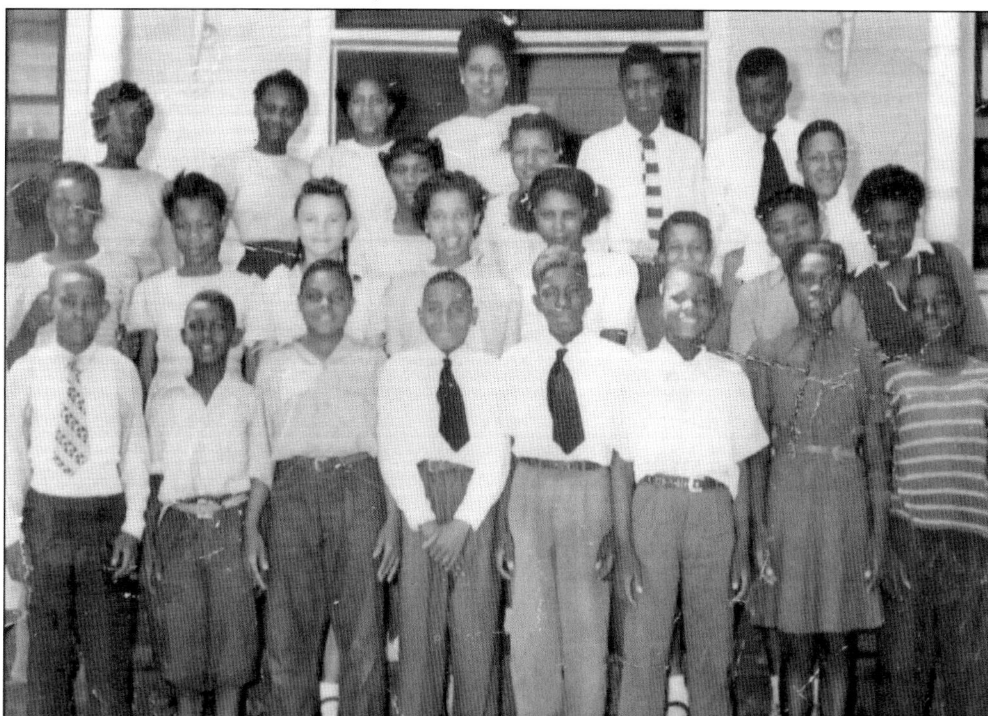

Mrs. Hazel Beamon (back row, center) posed with her eighth-grade class at Hertford High School in May 1948. (Courtesy of Lena Council.)

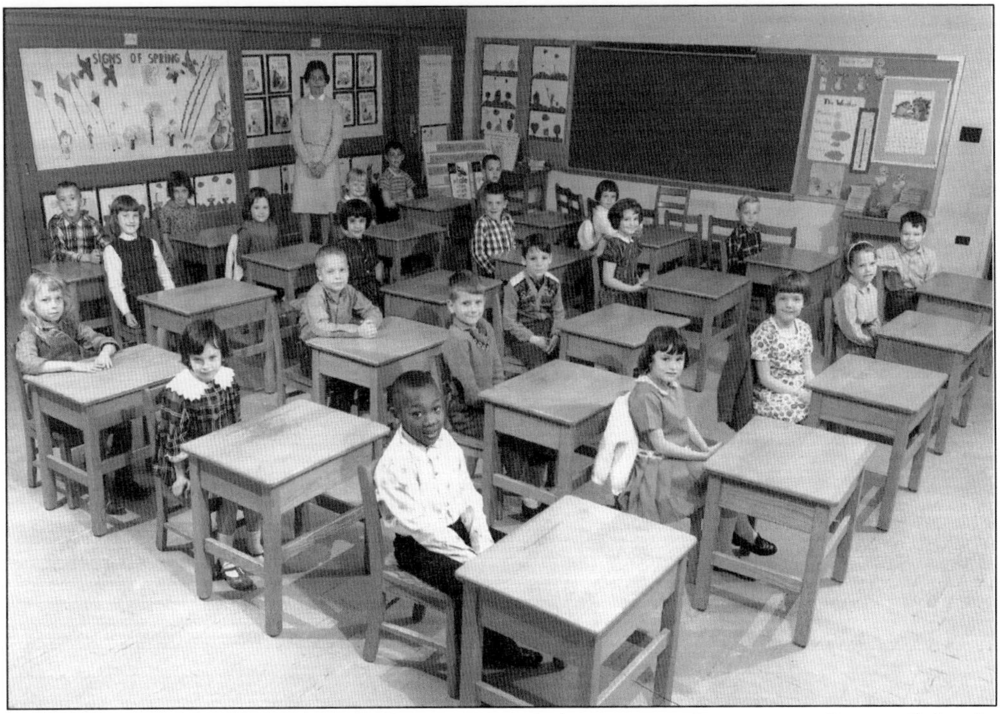

The 1965–1966 school year saw the first integrated classrooms in Perquimans County Schools. This is Helen Woodard's first grade class at Hertford Grammar School, with Phillip Harrell Jr. (front left) ready for the next assignment. (Courtesy of Shirley Wiggins.)

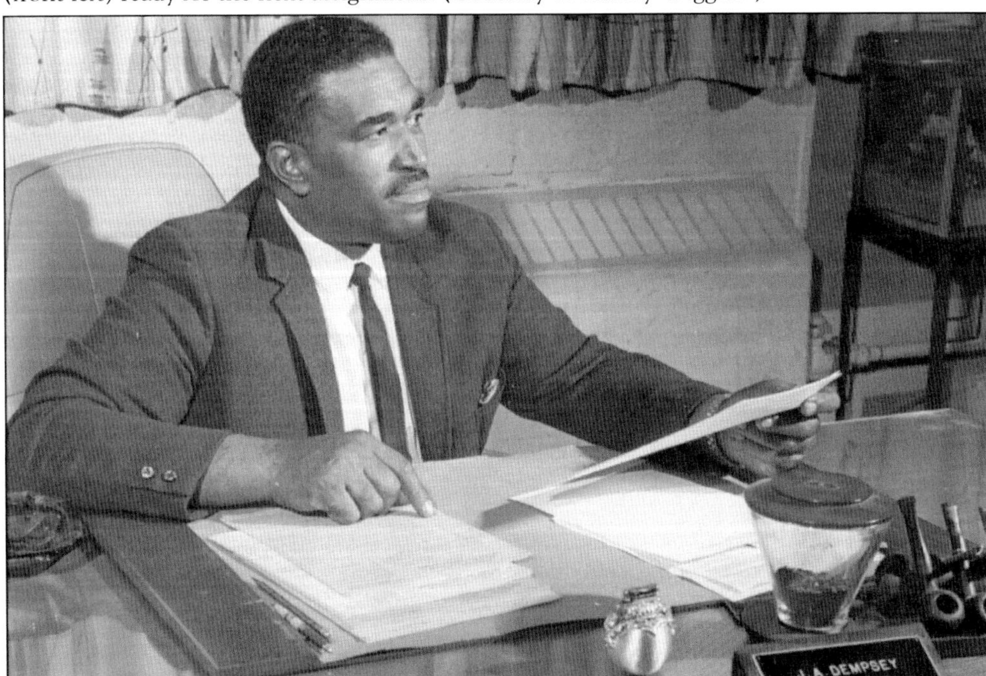

J.A. Dempsey, shown here in 1968, was principal of Perquimans County Union School. (Courtesy of Evelyn Stubbins.)

Mabel Stroud taught English at Hertford High School, *c*. 1947. The school, since demolished, stood on King Street. (Courtesy of Helen Thompson Shaw.)

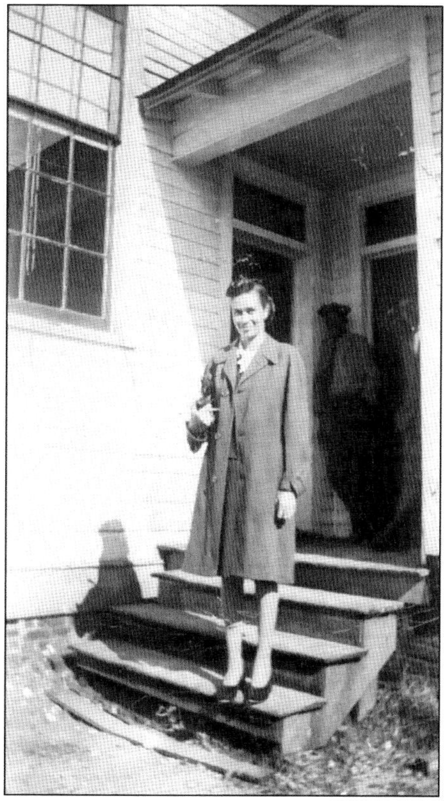

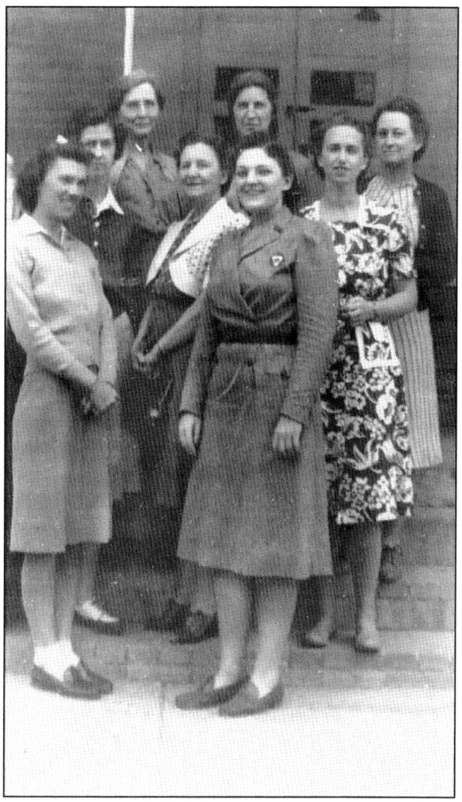

The faculty of Hertford Grammar School during World War II included, from left to right, (front row) Ruth Elliott and Mary Jane Spruill; (middle row) Mildred Reed, Inez White, and Frances Fowler; (back row) Mary Chappell, Mary Sumner, and Etta Walters. (Courtesy of Ruth Elliott Winslow.)

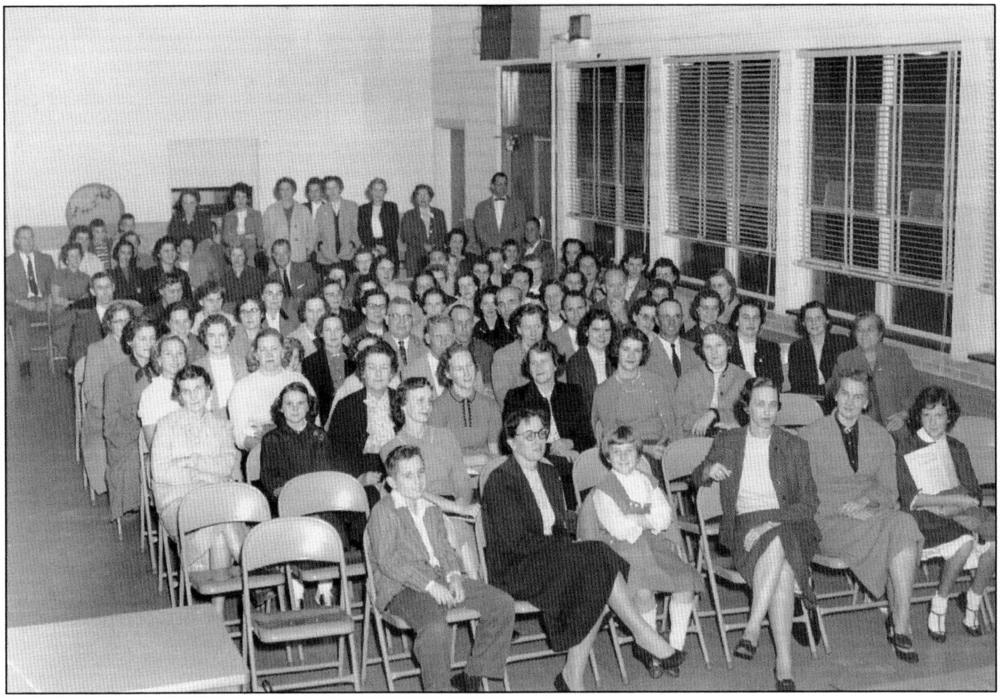

Parent-Teacher Associations have long been a significant support for local schools. Here is a Hertford Grammar School PTA group in the late 1950s. (Courtesy of Ruth Elliott Winslow.)

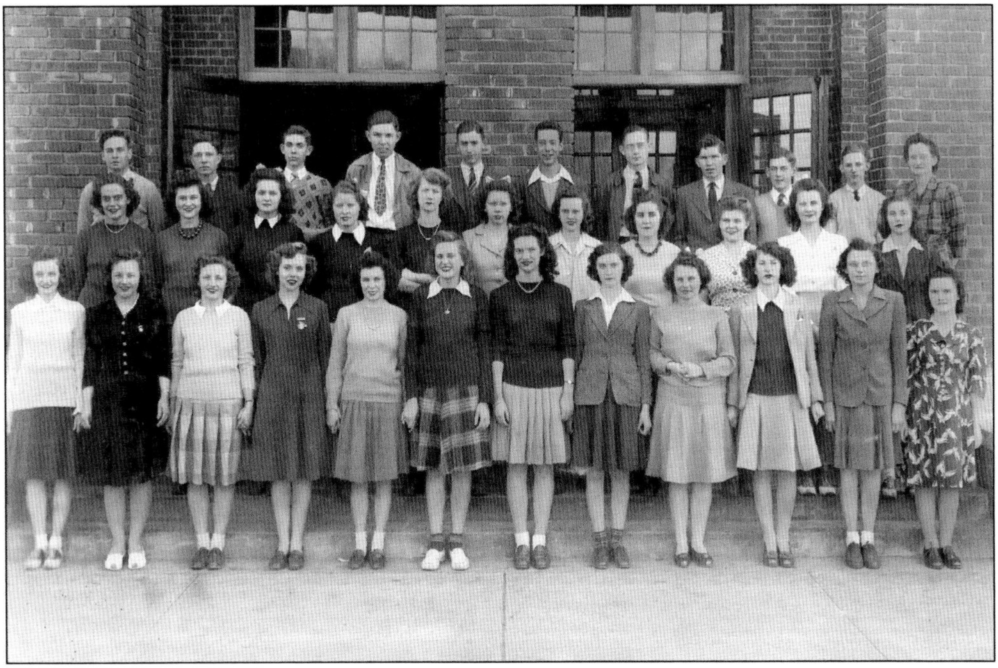

Girls outnumbered boys in the 1944 graduating class at Perquimans County High School. Dorothy Oakey (front row, seventh from left); Sybil Skinner (middle row, far right); and Charlie Skinner (back row, next to Miss Esther Evans, teacher, at far right) have contributed a great deal to the community over the years. (Courtesy of Dorothy Oakey Read.)

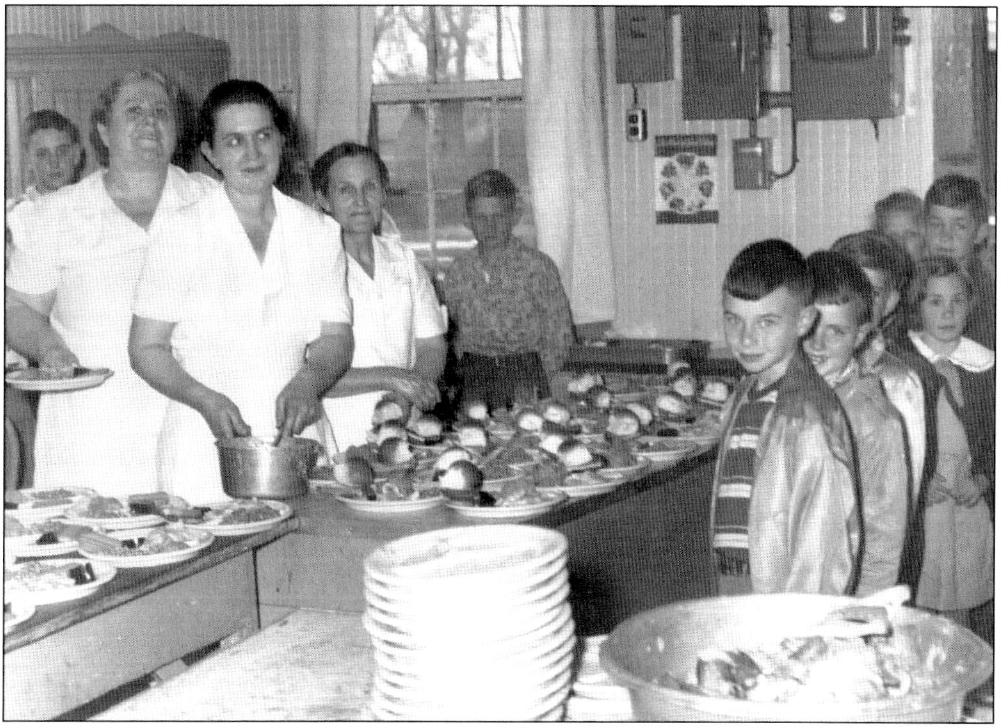

The Hertford Grammar School lunchroom was located in a separate building shared with the public library. Regardless of the weather, students marched from the school to the lunchroom and back again, but the excellent food was worth it. The building is now home to the Perquimans County Senior Citizens Center. (Courtesy of Ruth Elliott Winslow.)

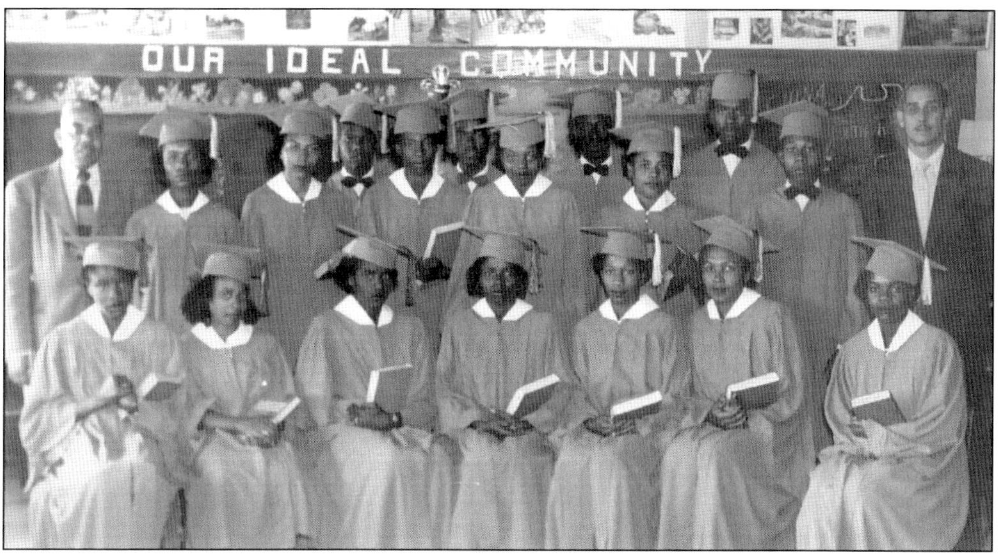

The 1951 class at Perquimans County Training School in Winfall is ready for graduation. In the back row are Principal Richard Kingsbury (left) and teacher Walter Privott (right.) Valedictorian Shirley Wiggins (front row, standing fourth from left) studied nursing, rose to the rank of captain in the U.S. Navy, and served as the first woman on the Perquimans County Board of Commissioners after returning home. (Courtesy of Shirley Wiggins.)

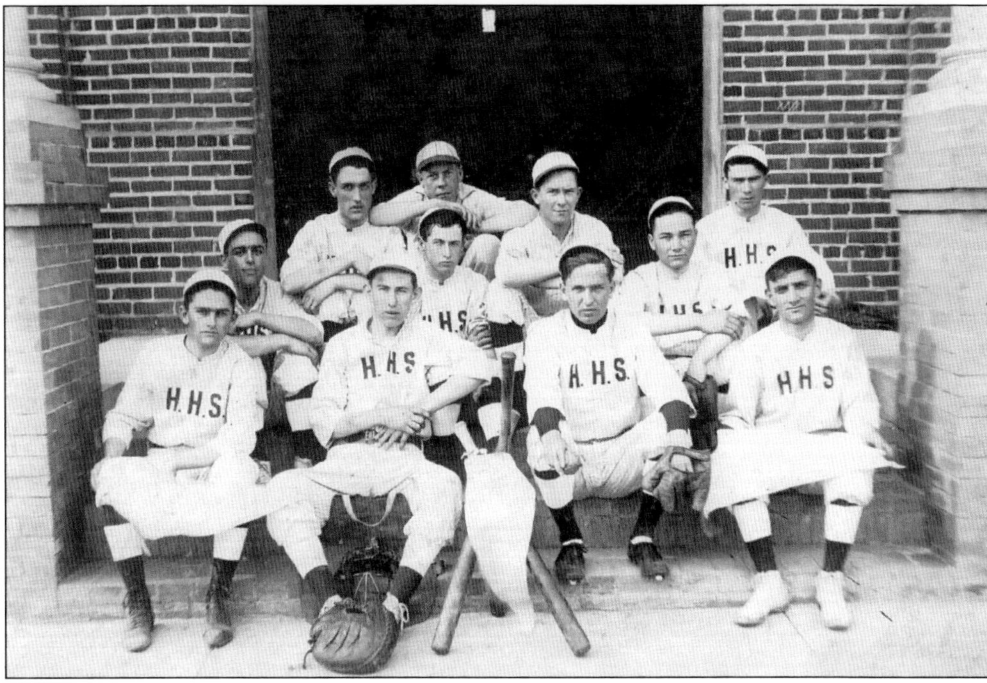

Hertford High's 1915 baseball team won the championship of northeastern North Carolina. Players are, from left to right, (front row) John Ward, Shelton Newbold, Thomas Sumner, and William Elliott; (middle row) Emmett Winslow, Thach Everett, and Carlton Cannon; (back row) Don Campen, Ashley Fleetwood, Herman Winslow, and E. Young Berry. (Courtesy of Charles T. Skinner Jr.)

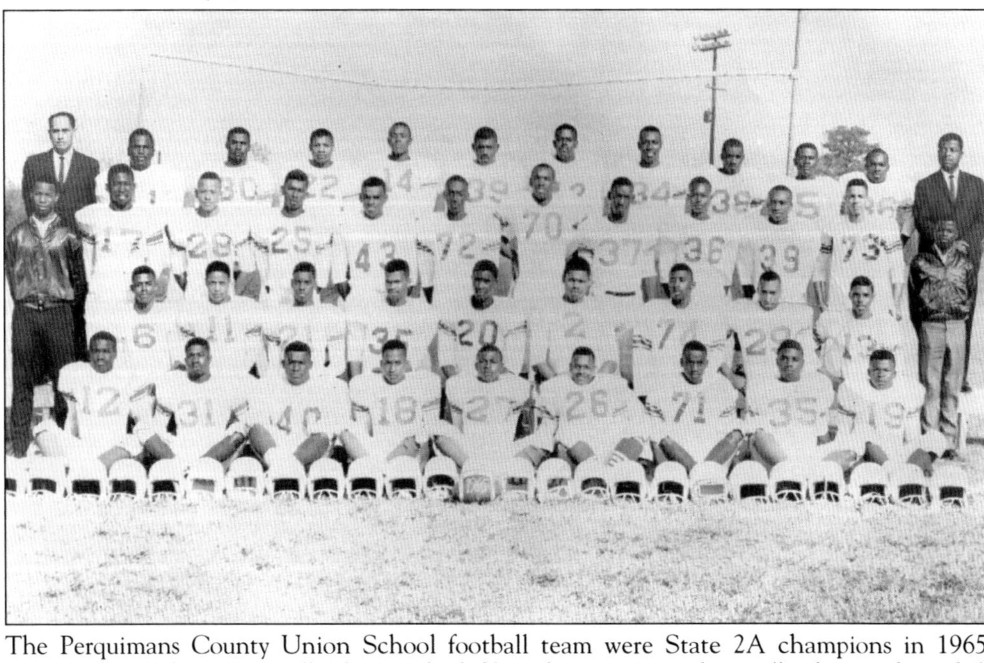

The Perquimans County Union School football team were State 2A champions in 1965, coached by Walter Privott (back row, far left) and James S. Midgette (back row, far right). (Courtesy of Joe Winslow.)

James Augustus "Catfish" Hunter (1946–1999) may be the only Perquimans native whose name is recognized around the world. He made baseball history and was elected to the Baseball Hall of Fame in 1987. He is shown here early in his baseball career. (Courtesy of Sidney Eley.)

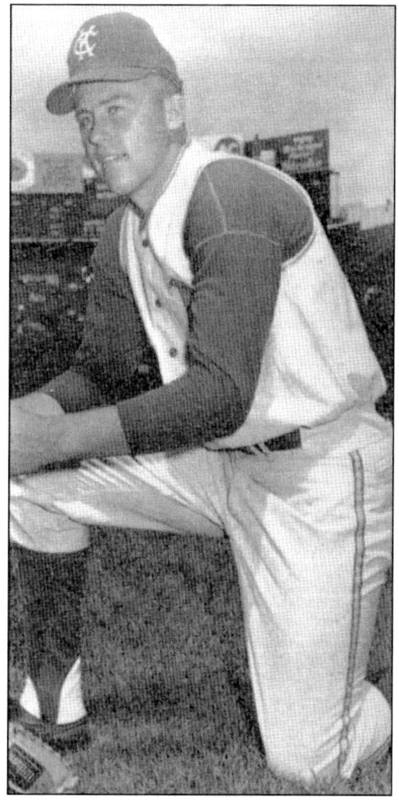

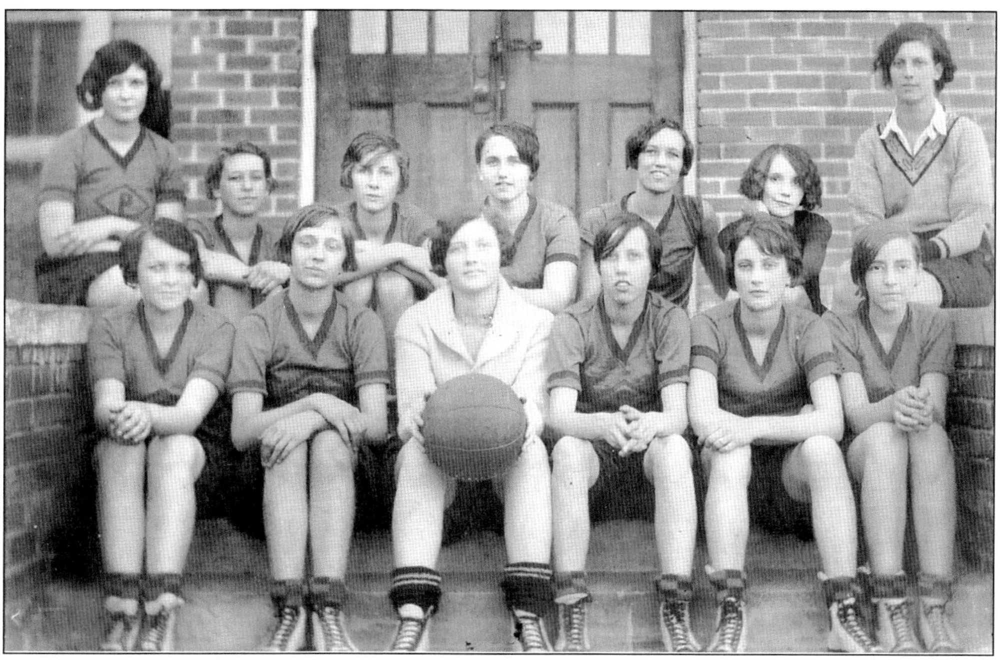

The 1928–1929 girls' basketball team takes time out on the steps of Perquimans County High School. At top right is coach Dorothy White, who taught at the school for many years. (Courtesy of Mary Barbee Corprew.)

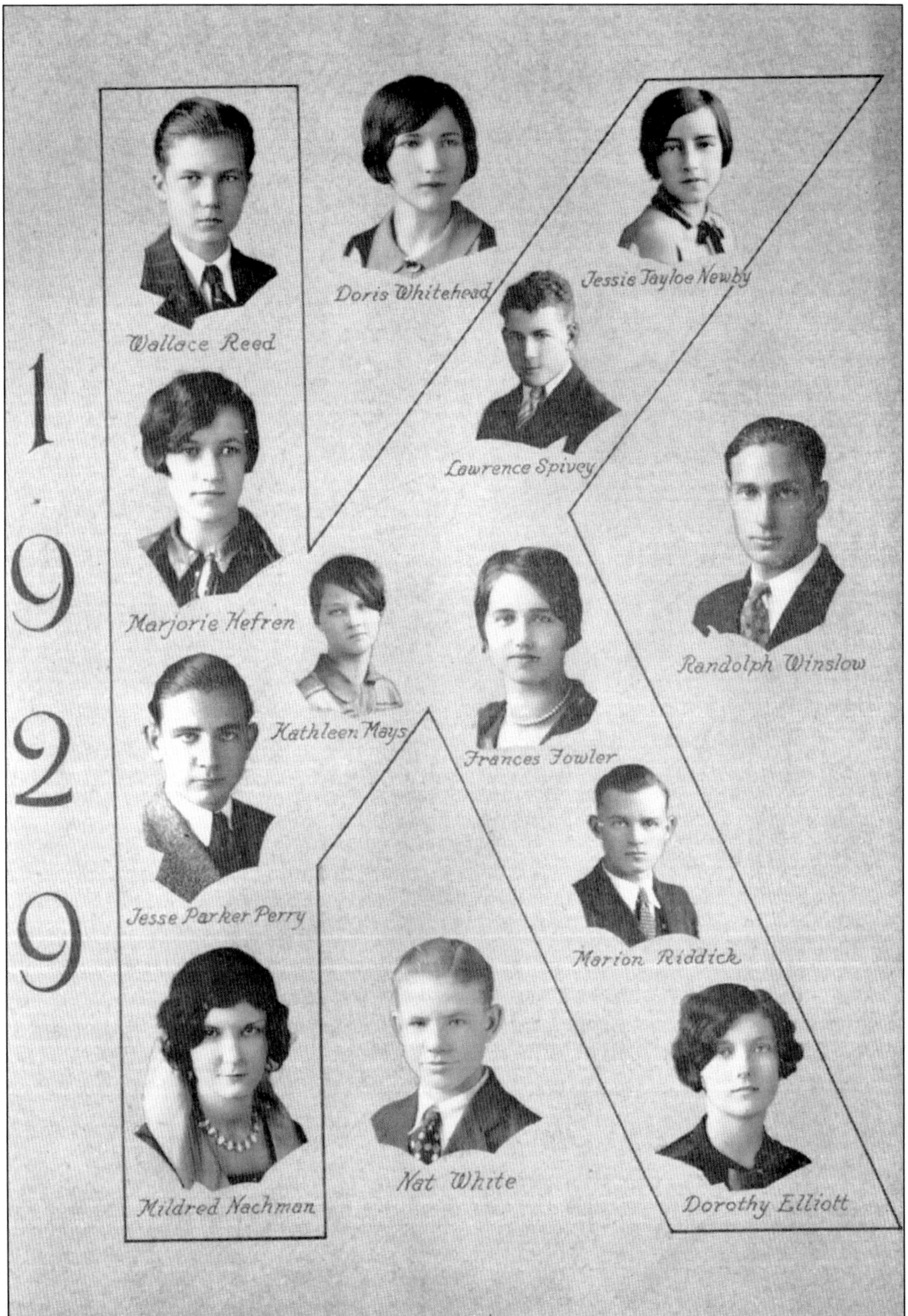

Doris Whitehead was editor-in-chief of the 1929 *Kilcokonen*, Perquimans County High School yearbook, and is shown here with the yearbook staff. (Courtesy of Raymond A. Winslow Jr.)

Three

AT WORK

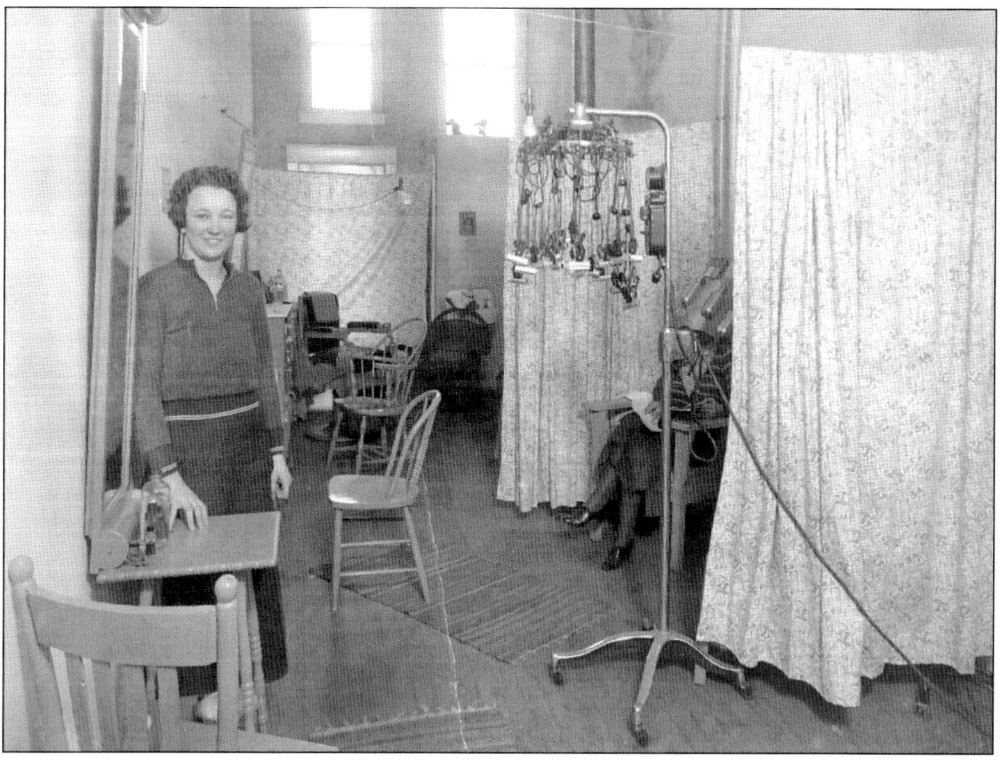

It was a brave woman who would allow the device pictured in the center to be fastened to her hair, but Ililda Ainsley Matthews (left) was a skilled beautician whose beauty parlor served decades of Hertford ladies (and an occasional gentleman). This view dates from c. 1931. Her daughter Marta carries on the hairdressing tradition today. (Courtesy of Marta Matthews Colson.)

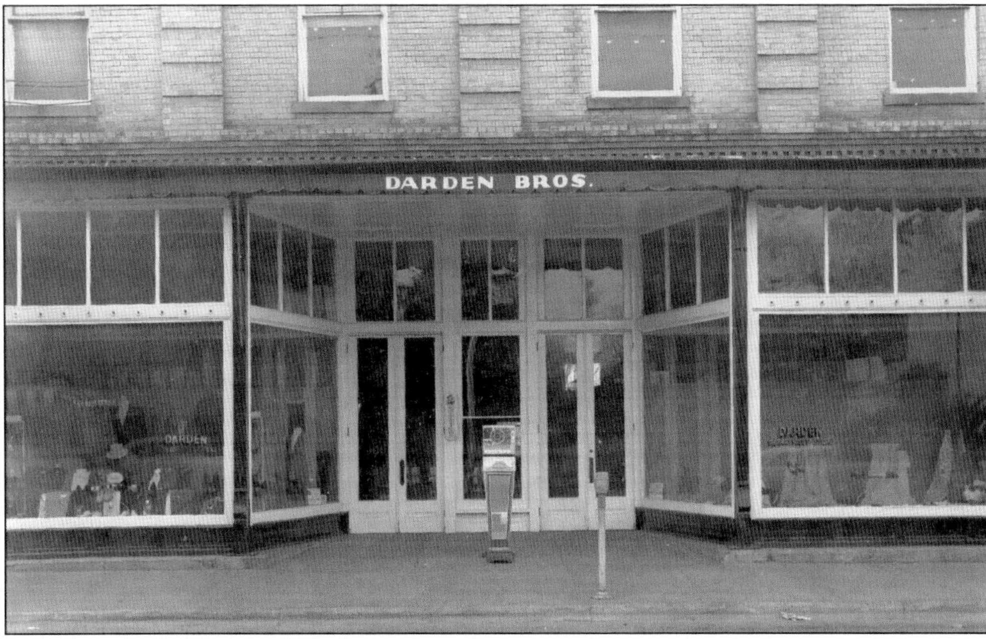

In this building erected by Anderson and Isaac White *c.* 1909, brothers Vivian and Douglas Darden opened a department store prior to 1920. Darden's was one of Hertford's leading businesses for decades. Significantly altered, the building is now called Hall of Fame Square and houses a number of small business enterprises. (Courtesy of John Christensen.)

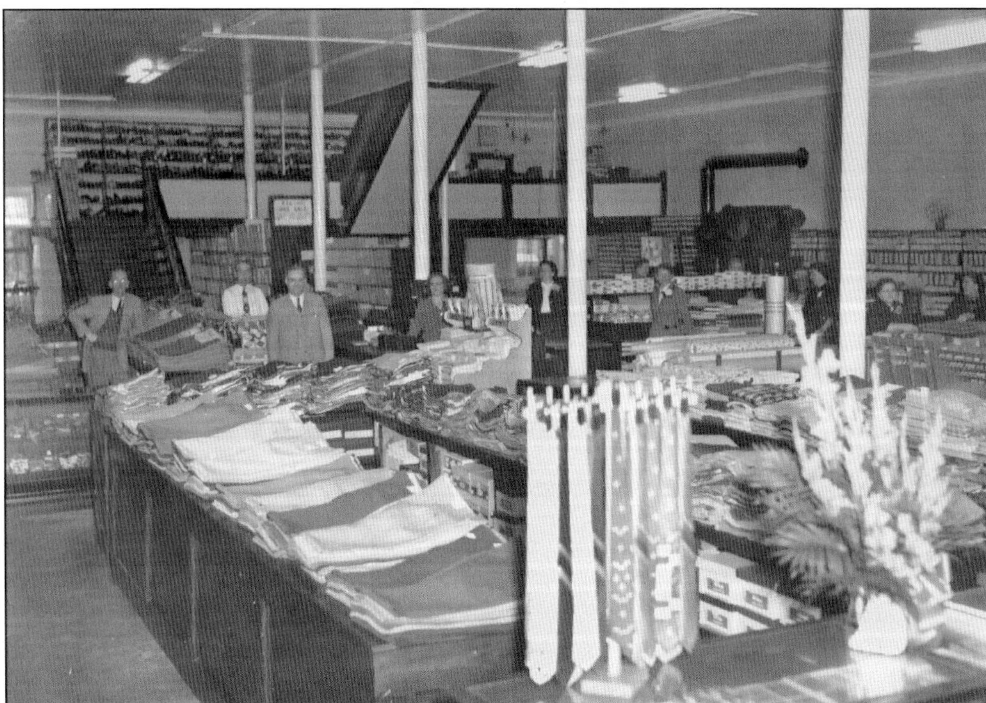
The men's clothing section and sewing goods section of Darden Department Store are shown here. (Courtesy of John Christensen.)

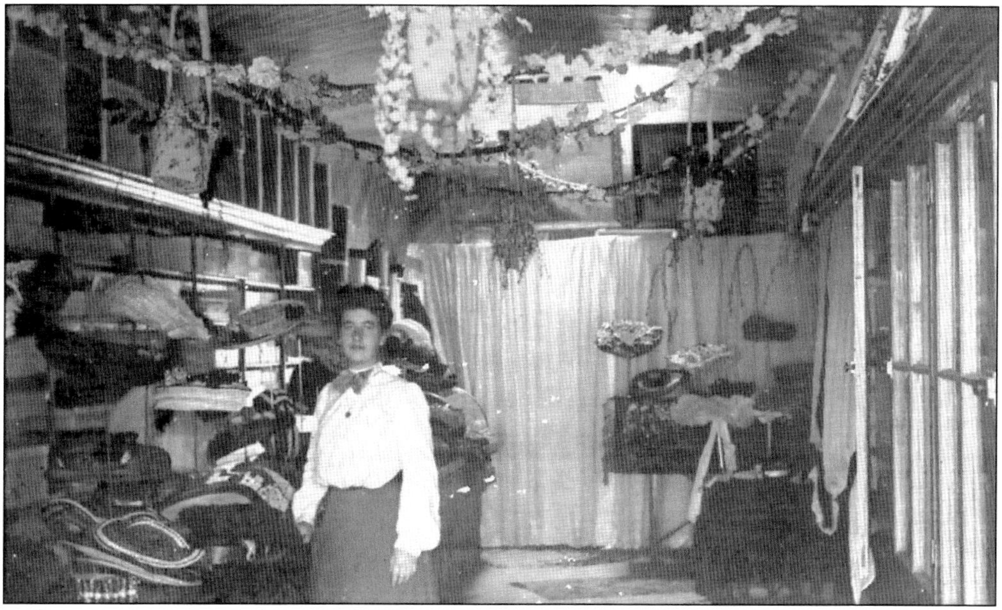

Millinery was one of the few businesses considered respectable for Victorian women to operate. Albertice (White) White Hawkins (1867–1939) is seen here on the opening day of her millinery store, which stood where RBC Centura Bank now is located. (Courtesy of Mary Barbee Corprew.)

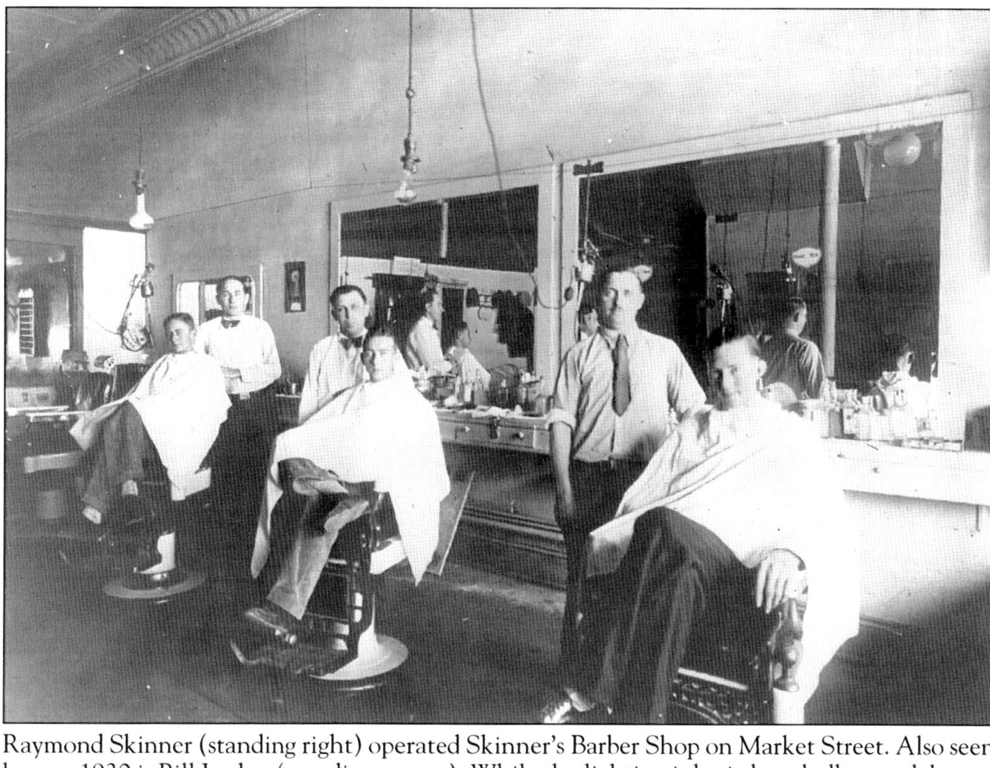

Raymond Skinner (standing right) operated Skinner's Barber Shop on Market Street. Also seen here *c*. 1930 is Bill Jordan (standing center). While the lighting is basic bare bulbs, an elaborate pressed-tin ceiling lends an air of elegance. (Courtesy of Sybil Skinner.)

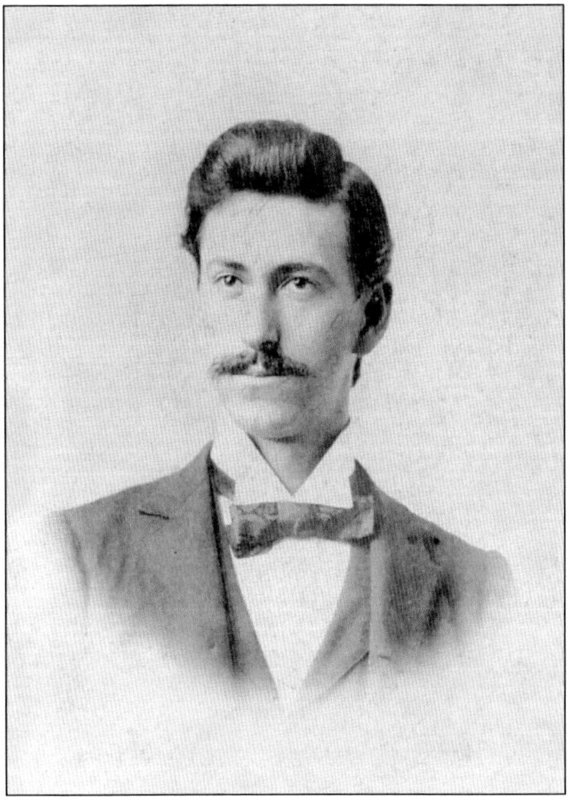

Arthur Nereus Winslow (1874–1946) sat for the famed photographer Zoeller in 1897, while a student at Belvidere Academy. He became a farmer and merchant, an active member of Up River Friends Meeting, a justice of the peace, and a stalwart Republican. He was the census taker for Nicanor precinct in 1910 and 1930. (Courtesy of Raymond A. Winslow, Jr.)

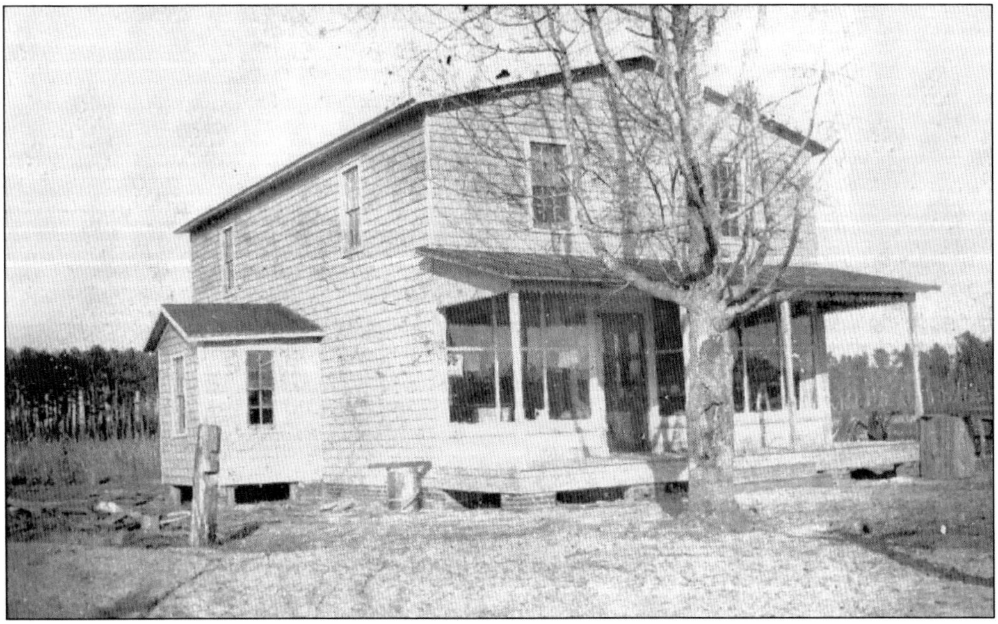

Arthur N. Winslow operated this general store in the Up River vicinity for nearly 50 years. Most daily necessities were stocked, and customers frequently paid with eggs, chickens, or other commodities. Some neighbors called the store "Little Baltimore," as manufactured items were frequently ordered from that city. (Courtesy of Raymond A. Winslow Jr.)

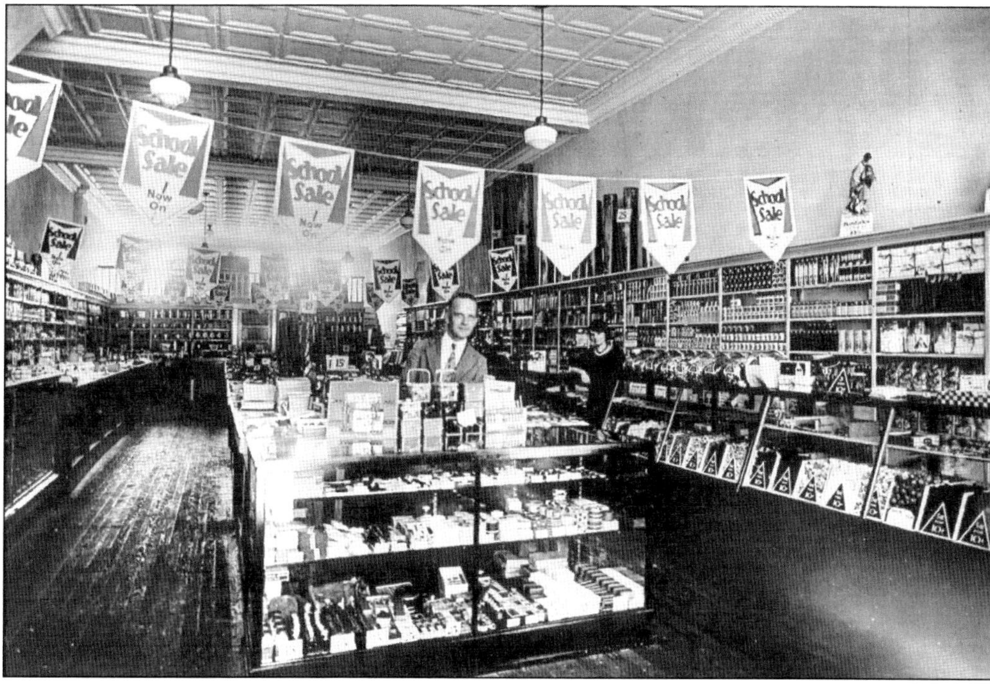

Gregory's, one of Hertford's most enduring family businesses, is seen here in the early 1920s, with "School Sale Now On" banners. Mark Judson Gregory (1892–1965) appears in the center of his 5-and-10-cent store. (Courtesy of Margaret Ainsley Brewin.)

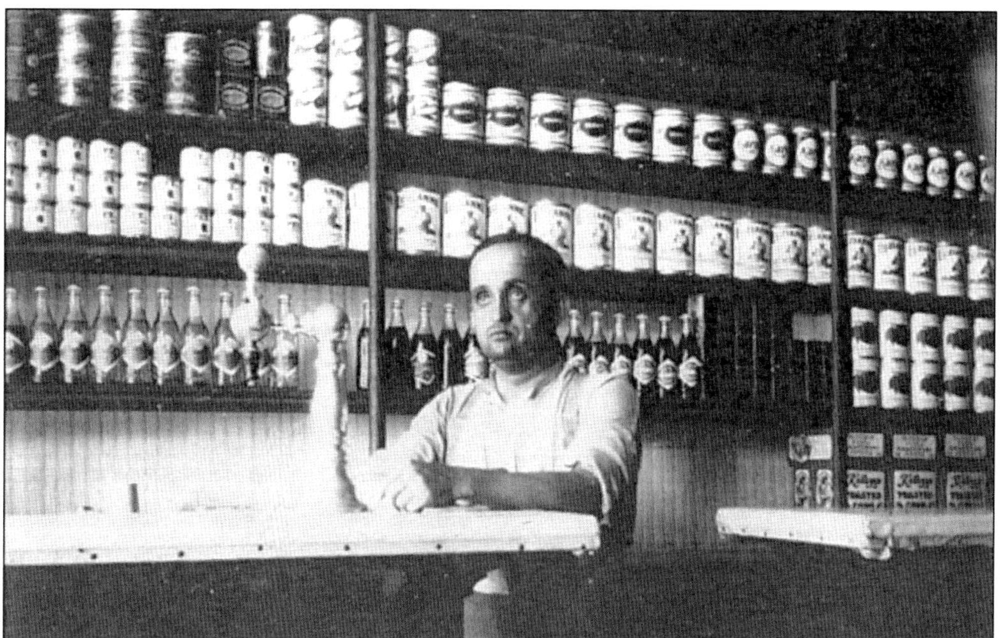

Pennsylvania-born James V. Keenan (1876–1948) looks pensive in his store in Hertford, perhaps wondering how to move all those canned goods in a town with so many stores and so few people. Keenan worked from an early age in a variety of retail establishments. (Courtesy of Charles T. Skinner Jr.)

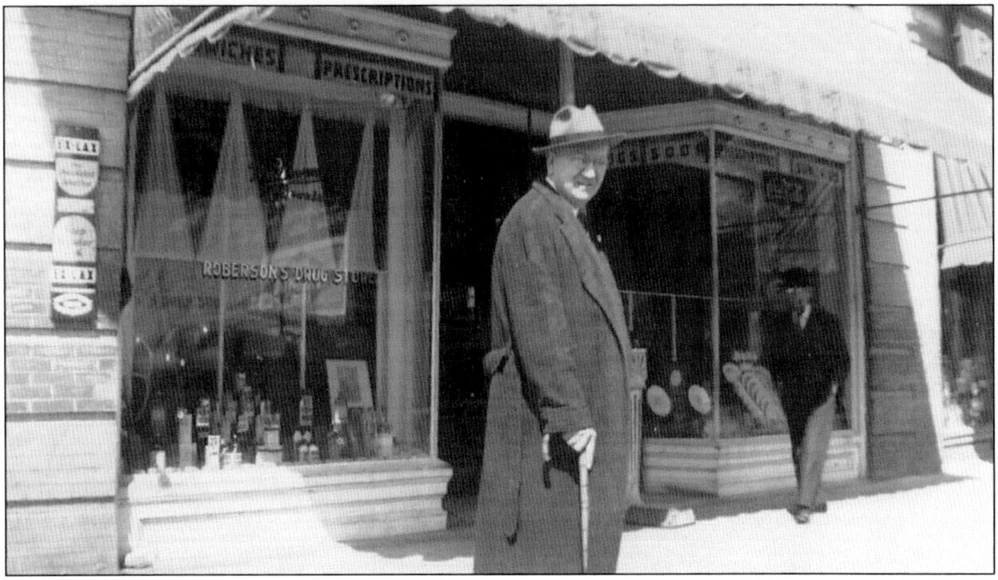

Pharmacist John Glenn Roberson (1891–1940) strolls past his drugstore on Church Street. Under several names and owners, a drugstore has occupied those same premises ever since Dr. Robert W. Smith erected the building in 1911; it is now called Woodard's and is famous for its 50¢ ice cream dip. (Courtesy of John V. Matthews.)

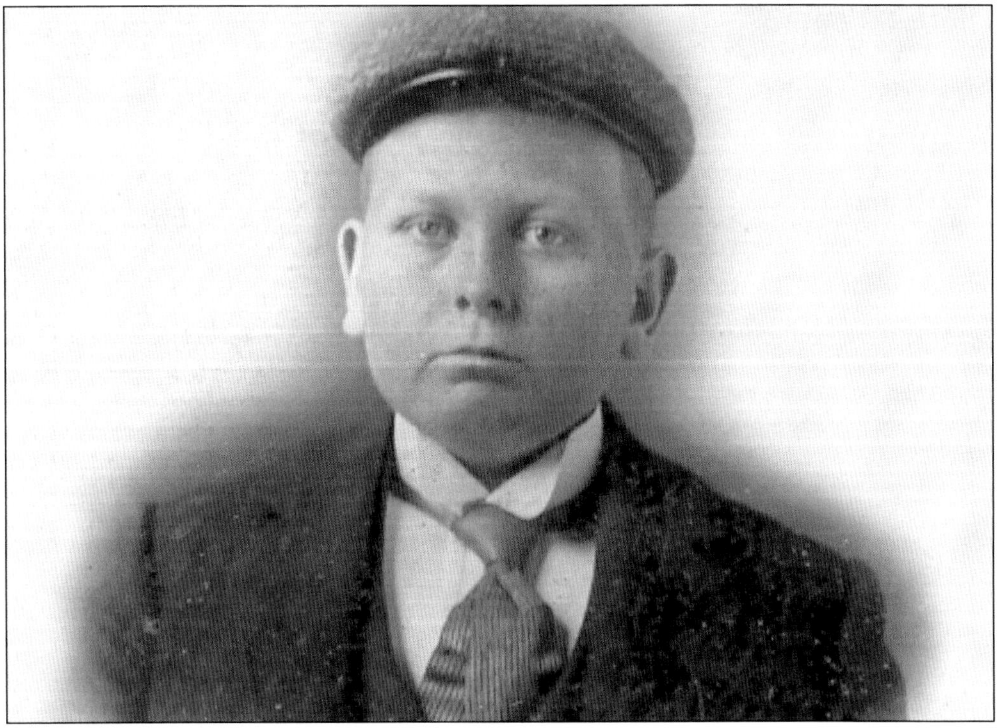

William Oscar Saunders (1886–1940), born in Perquimans County, won fame as editor of the unique newspaper *The Independent* of Elizabeth City. He was an indefatigable supporter of progress and reform, as well as an inveterate nagger of corrupt politicians and hypocritical preachers. (Courtesy of Mary Barbee Corprew.)

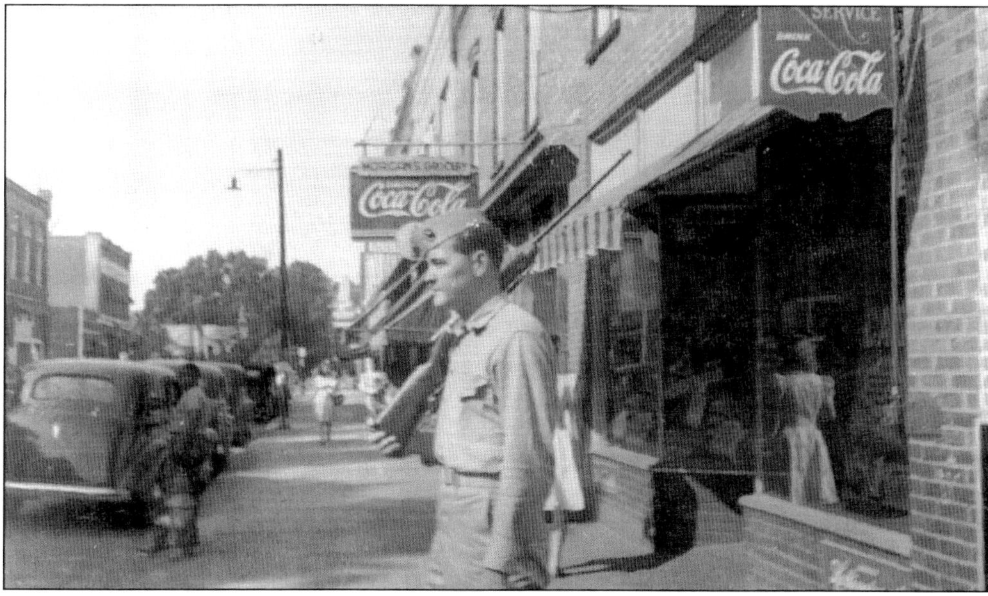

Home on leave from Cherry Point, Emmett Landing shouldered his weapon in downtown Hertford in June 1943. He served more than seven years in the Marine Corps and Marine Corps Reserves. In the center background is a sign for Morgan's Grocery. (Courtesy of Charles T. Skinner Jr.)

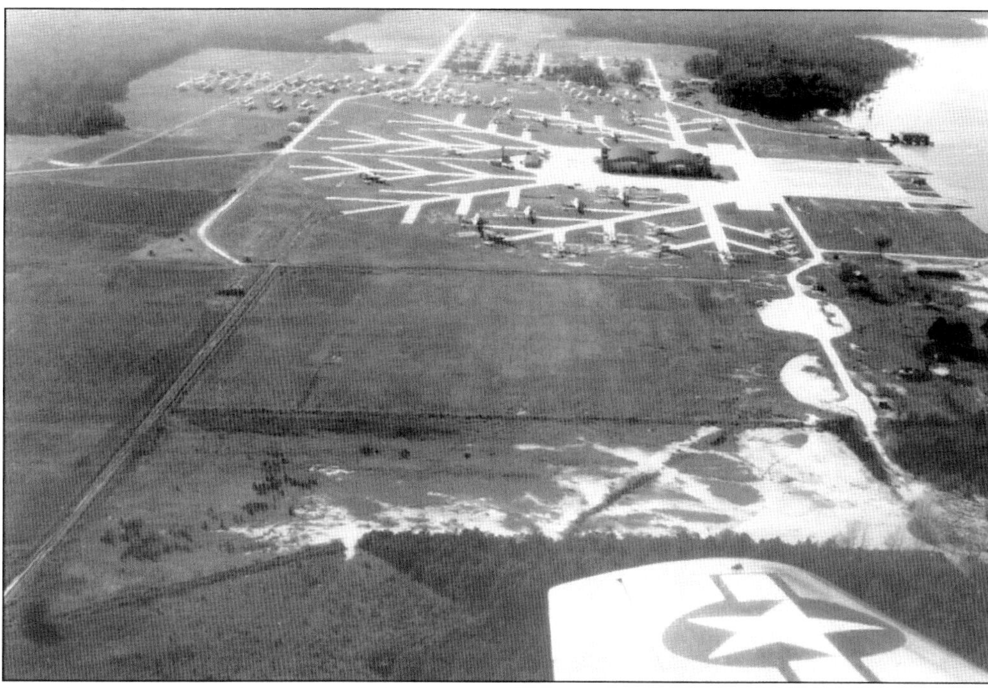

Seen here in an aerial view *c.* 1945, the naval station at Harvey Point was a major factor in wartime Perquimans life. The U.S. Navy, in March 1943, acquired more than 1,200 acres between Perquimans River (right) and Albemarle Sound, including historic Belgrade and Ashland plantations. The site is now the Harvey Point Defense Testing Activity. (Courtesy of Museum of the Albemarle.)

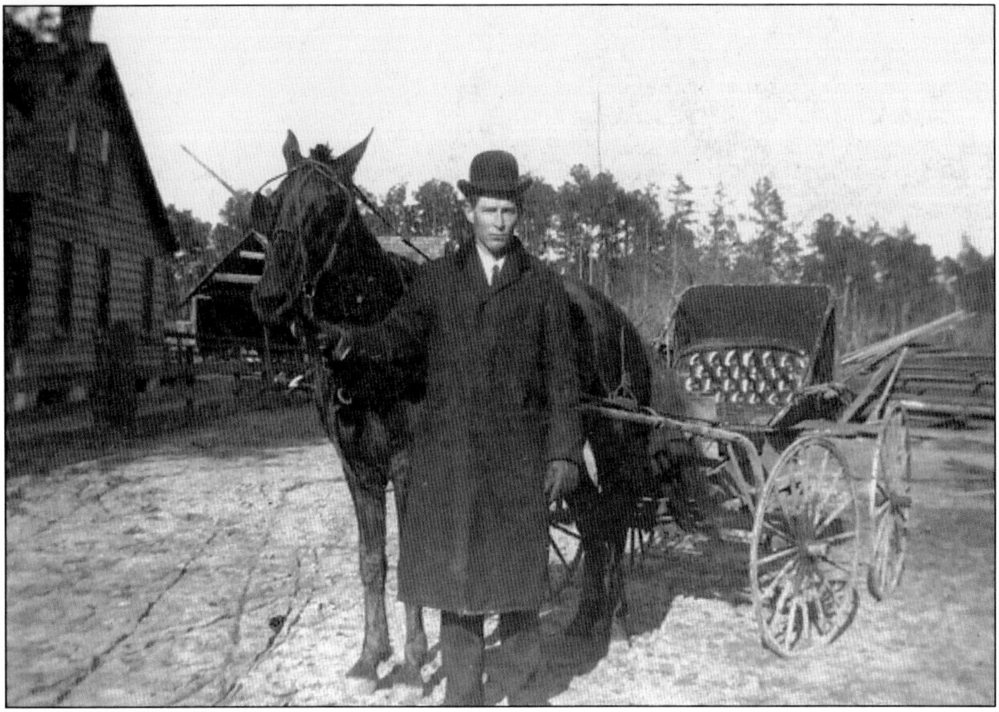

William T. Smith was the first rural mail carrier for Belvidere Post Office, serving 28 years. He often made his rounds in a sturdy road cart, rather than the buggy shown here. (Courtesy of Peggy Lane.)

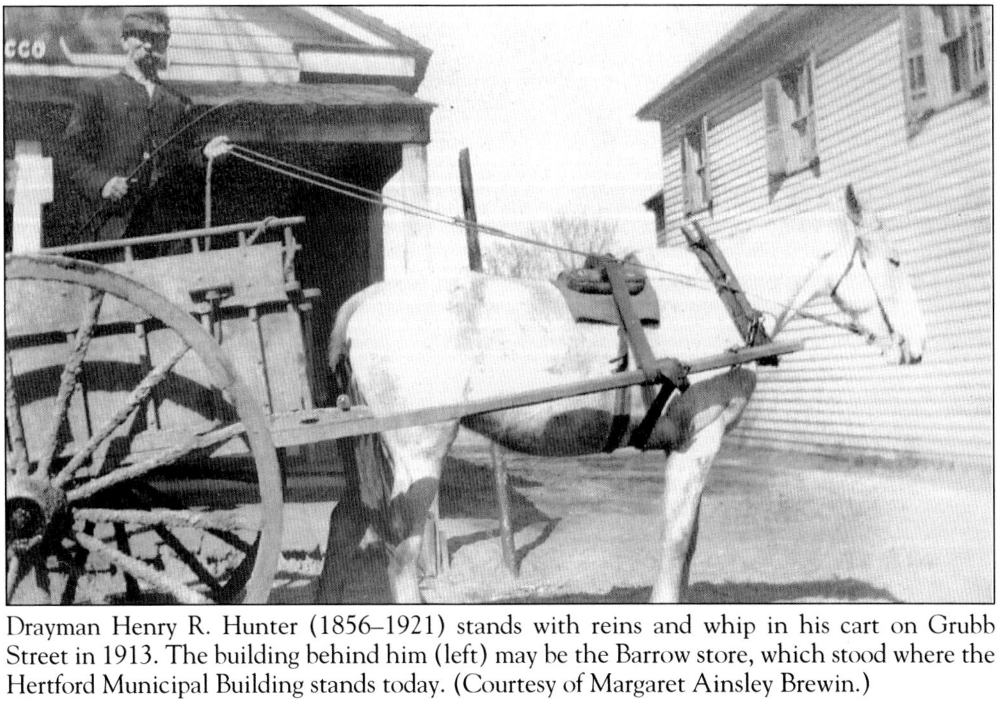

Drayman Henry R. Hunter (1856–1921) stands with reins and whip in his cart on Grubb Street in 1913. The building behind him (left) may be the Barrow store, which stood where the Hertford Municipal Building stands today. (Courtesy of Margaret Ainsley Brewin.)

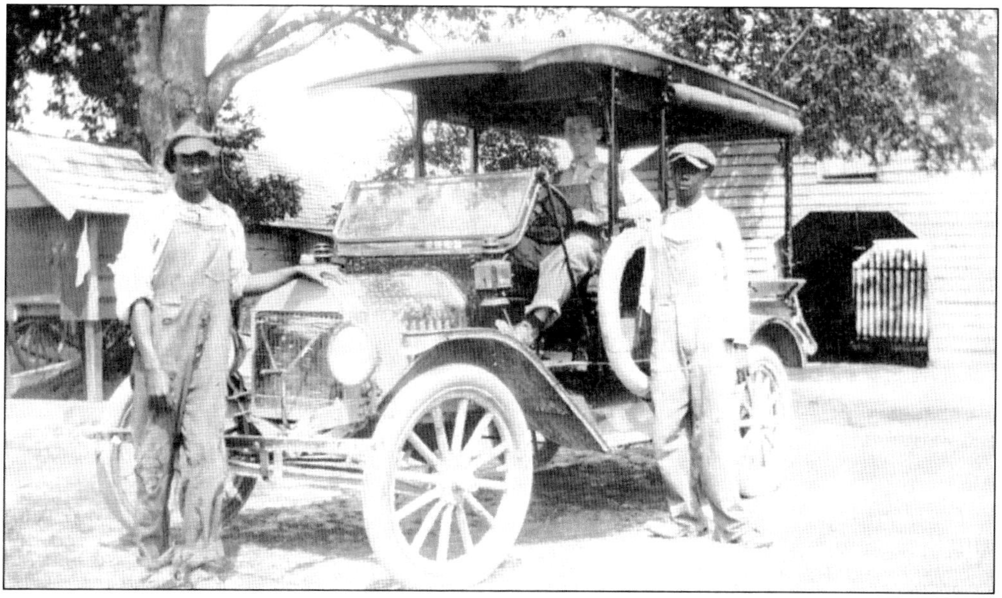

Huckster John J. Chappell Jr. (center) sold local chickens and eggs in Norfolk, Virginia. Seen with him in this early 1920s photograph are Tom Jordan (left) and Irvin Eason (right). (Courtesy of Thelma Chappell Riddick.)

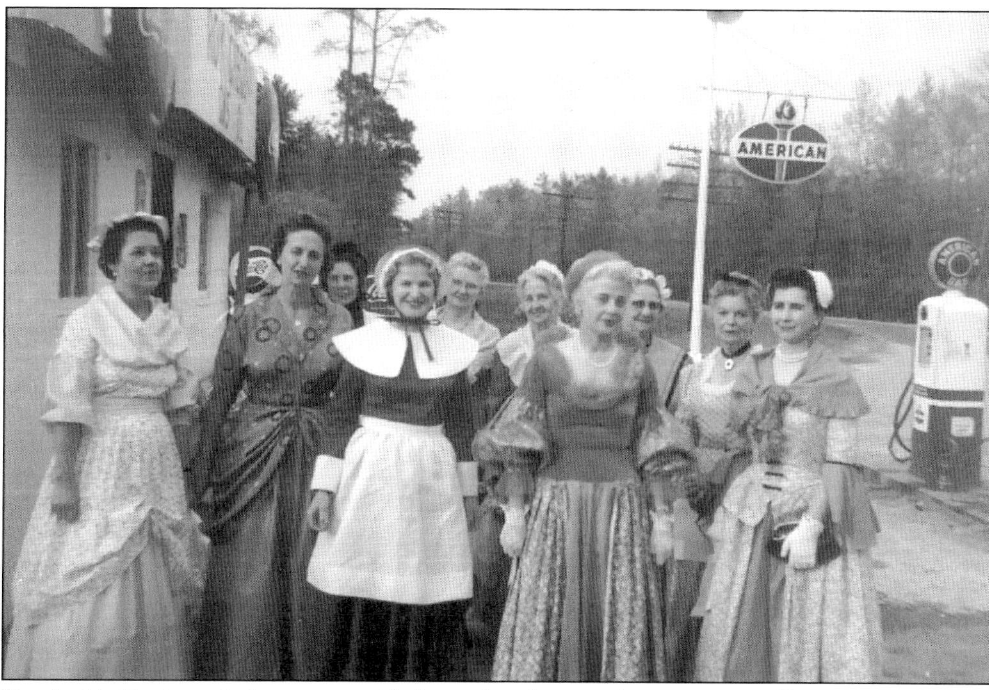

Hertford ladies in period costume guided state legislators to historic sites of Perquimans in 1963, celebrating the Carolina Charter Tercentenary. From left, they are Roxanna Jackson, Frances Monds, Mary Edwards, Polly Hollowell, Lenna Griffin, Mildred Whitley, Lucille Winslow, Helen Skinner, Cornelia Jessup, and Lois White. (Courtesy of Charles T. Skinner Jr.)

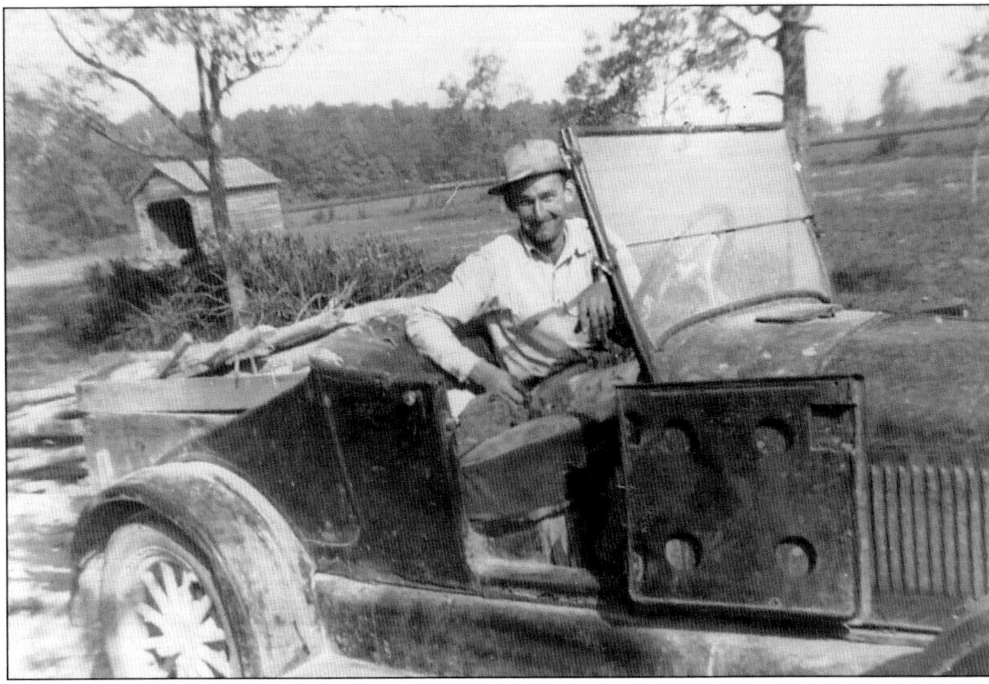

Wallace Hobbs halts his Model T Ford for the camera, *c.* 1939. (Courtesy of Joyce Hobbs.)

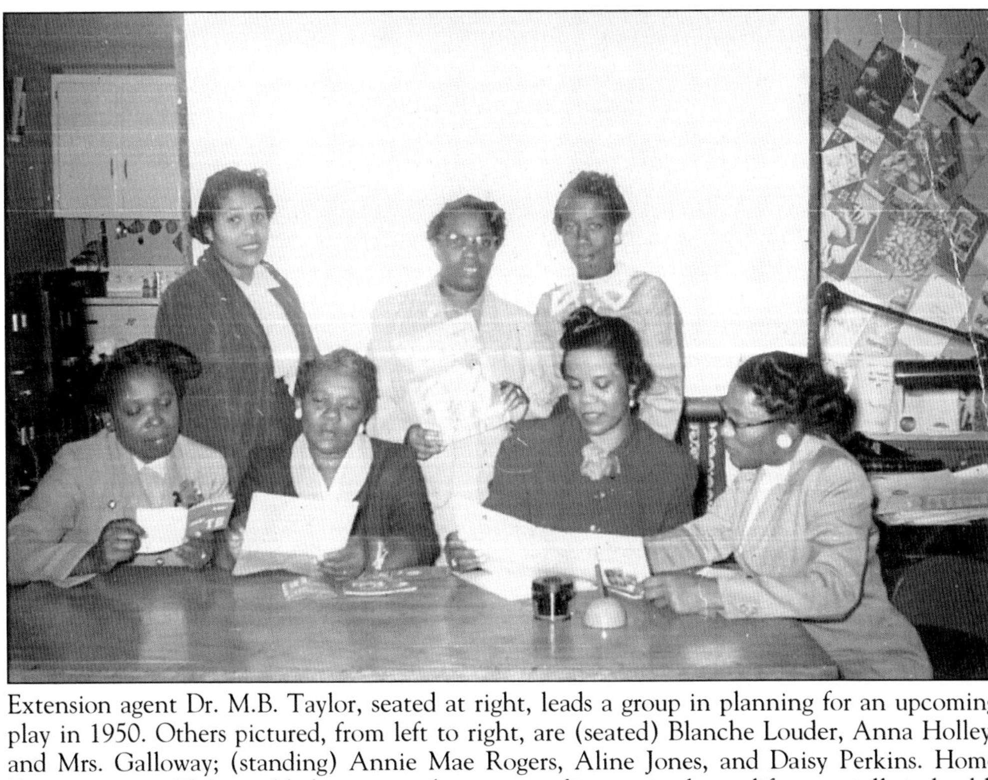

Extension agent Dr. M.B. Taylor, seated at right, leads a group in planning for an upcoming play in 1950. Others pictured, from left to right, are (seated) Blanche Louder, Anna Holley, and Mrs. Galloway; (standing) Annie Mae Rogers, Aline Jones, and Daisy Perkins. Home Demonstration Clubs enabled women to learn ways of improving home life, especially in health and nutrition. (Courtesy of Laura Hudson and Celestine Modlin.)

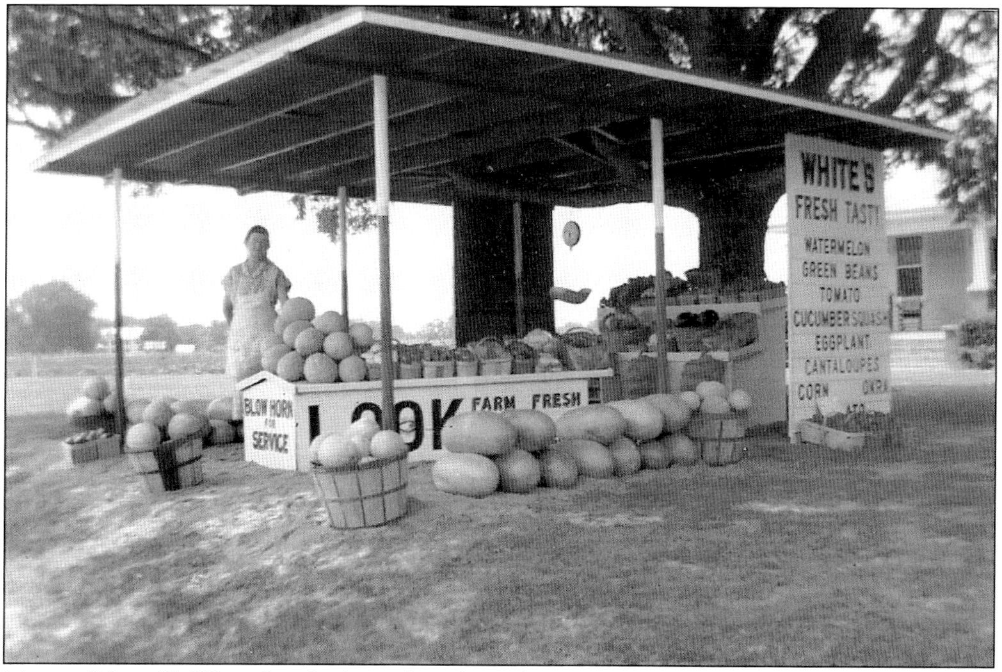

Maggie (Howell) White has fresh produce from the family farm for sale by the roadside in this 1960 photograph. Roadside produce stands are a familiar summer sight to this day. (Courtesy of Ann Carol White and Barbara White.)

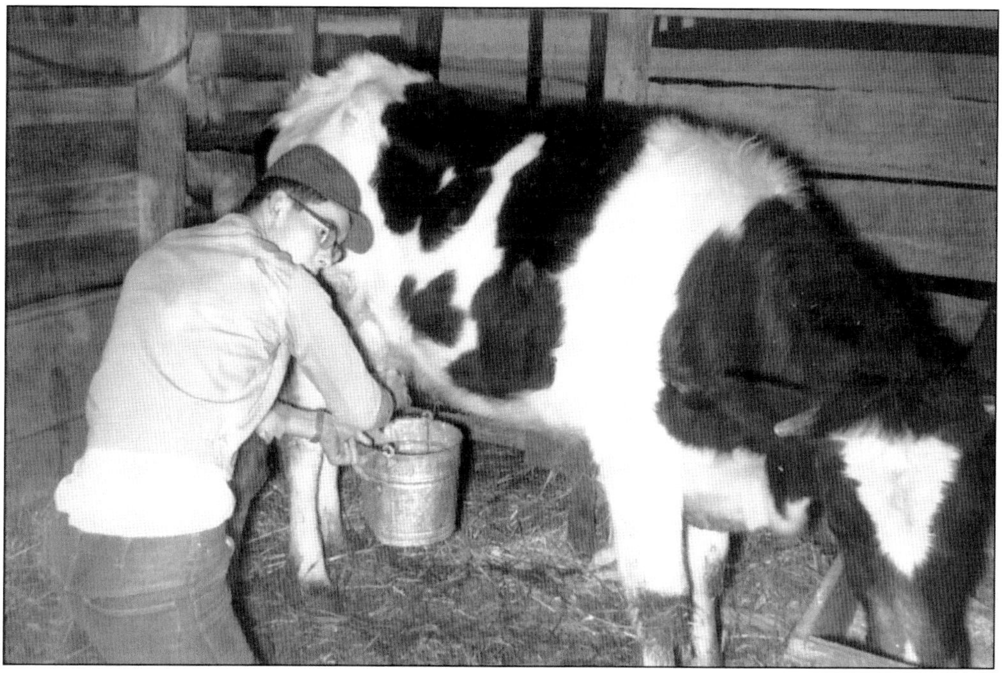

John Hobbs milks a family cow in 1965 at Bethel. With dairy farming growing more mechanized and less profitable, milk cows have become a rare sight in Perquimans County. (Courtesy of Joyce Hobbs.)

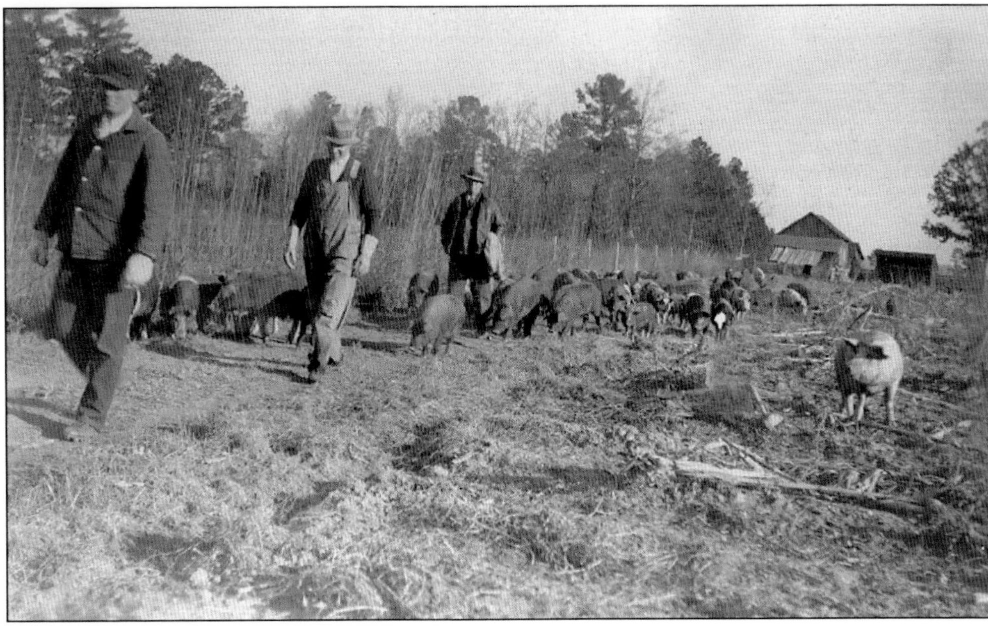

Pigs, like these shown in Layden's field at Belvidere in the late 1920s, have been a staple of Perquimans agriculture and diet for 350 years. The county is famed for its pork barbecue. (Courtesy of Lynwood C. Winslow III.)

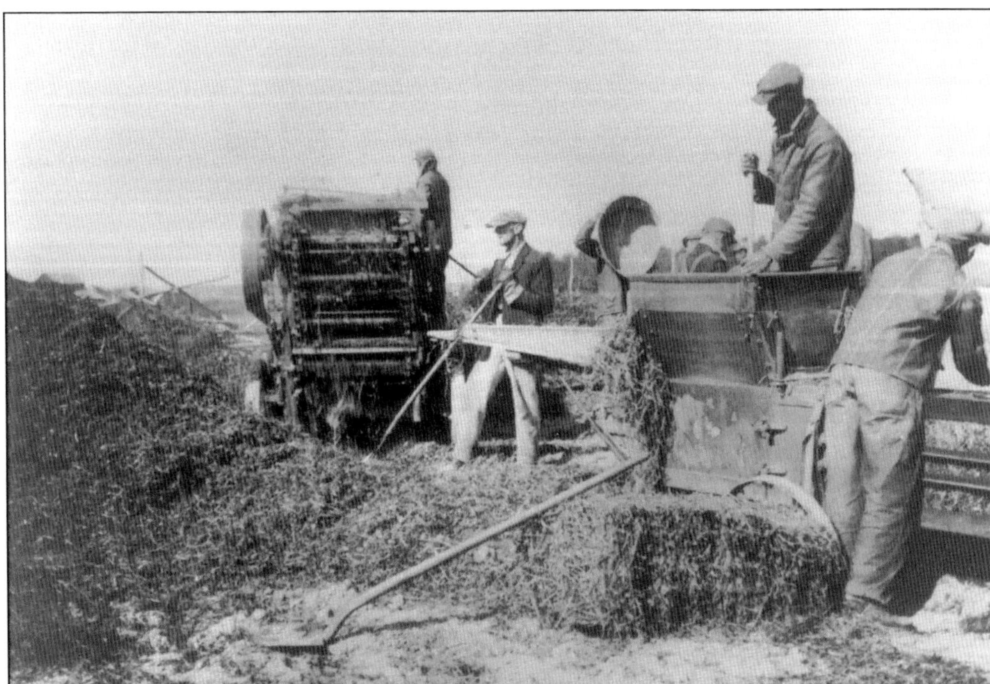

Early in the mechanized era, peanut harvesting still required a great amount of hand labor. (Courtesy of Prue Newby Reed.)

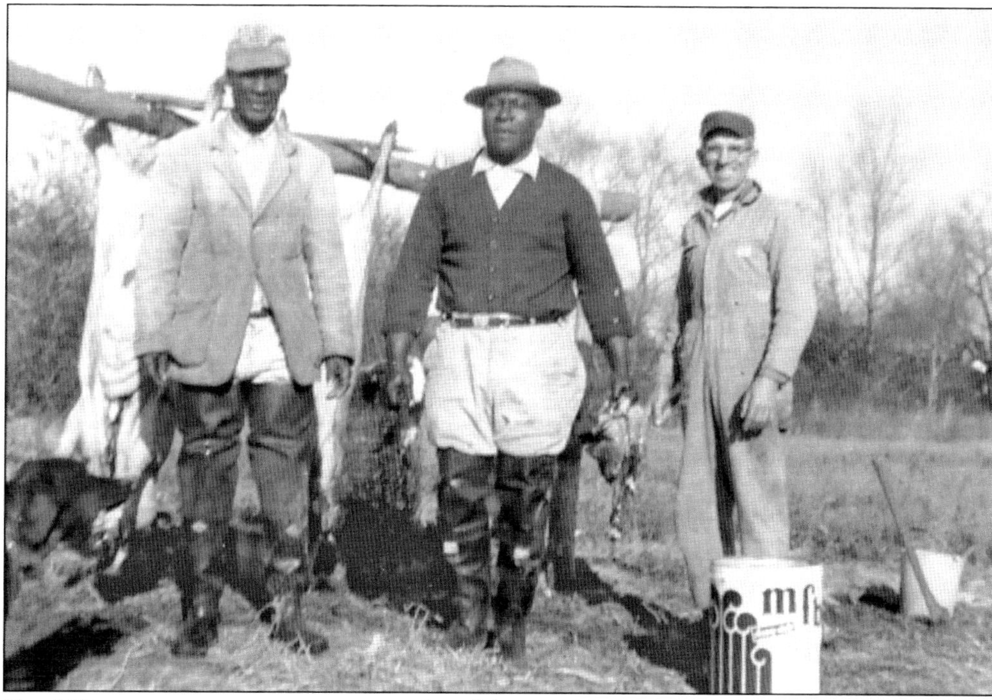

Hog killing was an important event in farm life, guaranteeing a supply of meat for the family. In 1960, from left to right, Leroy Billups, his brother Louis Billups, and Travis White butchered hogs at the Cox Farm. (Courtesy of Lenora Rouse.)

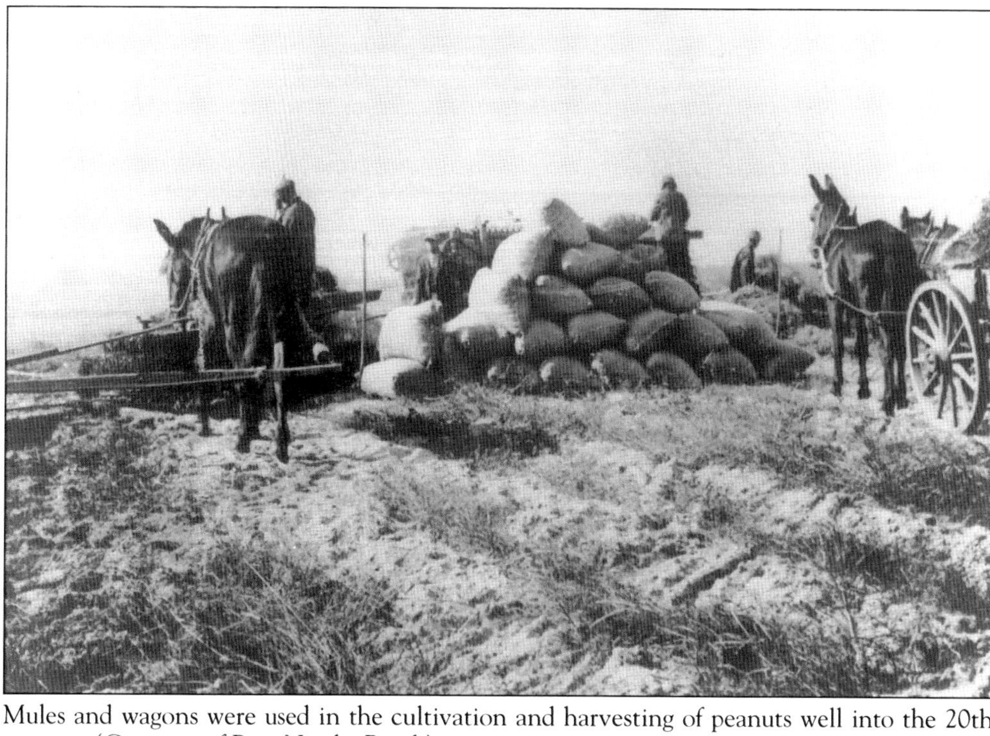

Mules and wagons were used in the cultivation and harvesting of peanuts well into the 20th century. (Courtesy of Prue Newby Reed.)

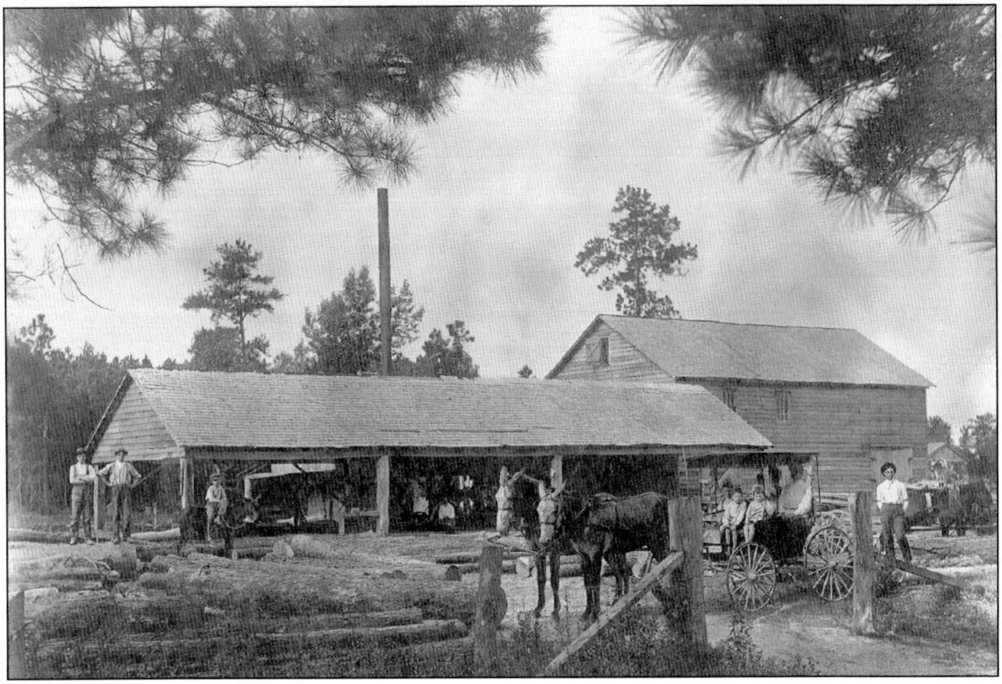

At the turn of the 20th century, Perquimans had many small-scale logging and sawmill operations, such as the one shown here, that supplied lumber for local use. (Courtesy of Alice Jeanne Ward.)

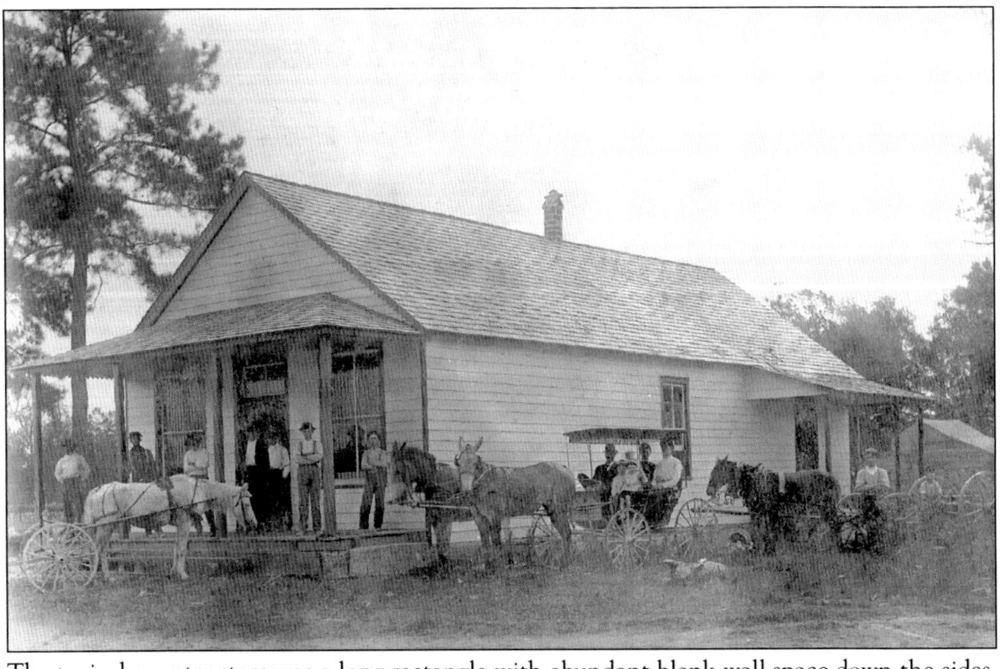

The typical country store was a long rectangle with abundant blank wall space down the sides. A small flue invariably served a pot-bellied stove. Presumably, the group in the surrey (center) are the owner and his family. At the right are two pairs of wheels that probably served to carry logs and lumber. (Courtesy of Alice Jeanne Ward.)

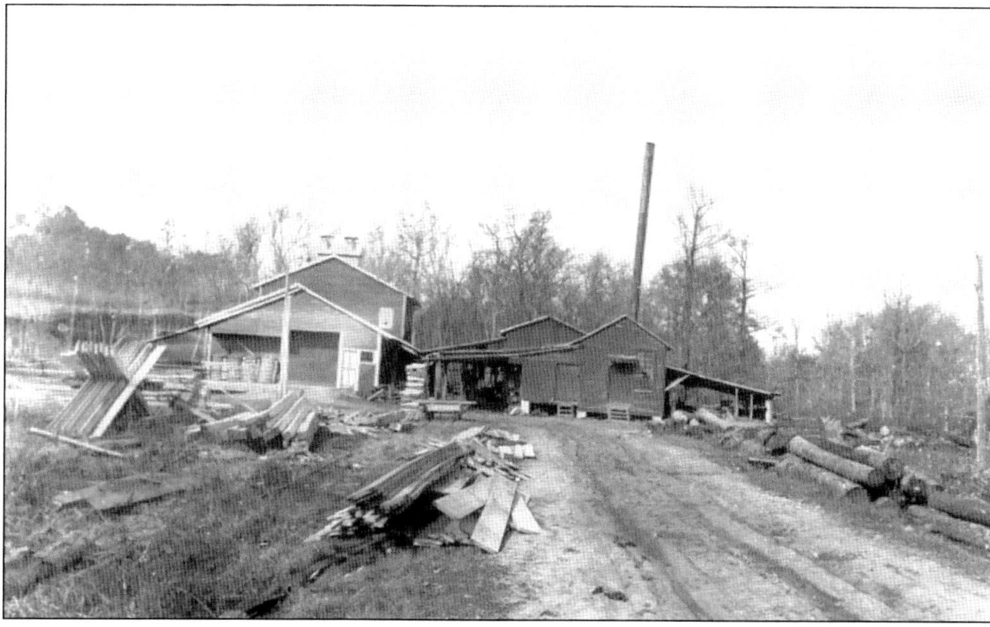

Dating from *c.* 1913, Fernando C. White's mill complex at Belvidere included sawmill, gristmill, cotton gin, lumberyard, blacksmith shop, machine shop, and general store. It is depicted here in the late 1920s. (Courtesy of Lynwood C. Winslow III.)

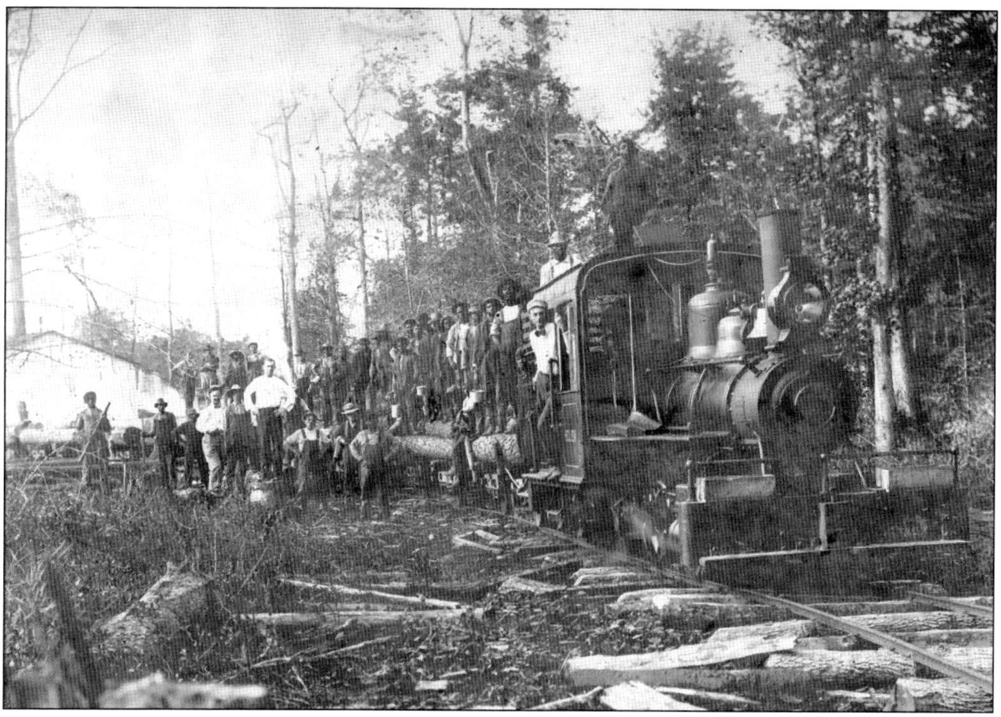

When the railroad reached Perquimans County in 1881, a new era of industry opened. Logging became a major enterprise and many lumber companies had railroad spur lines reaching into large tracts of woodland. A logging train and the crew that felled the trees for transport to sawmills were captured in this photograph. (Courtesy of Prue Newby Reed.)

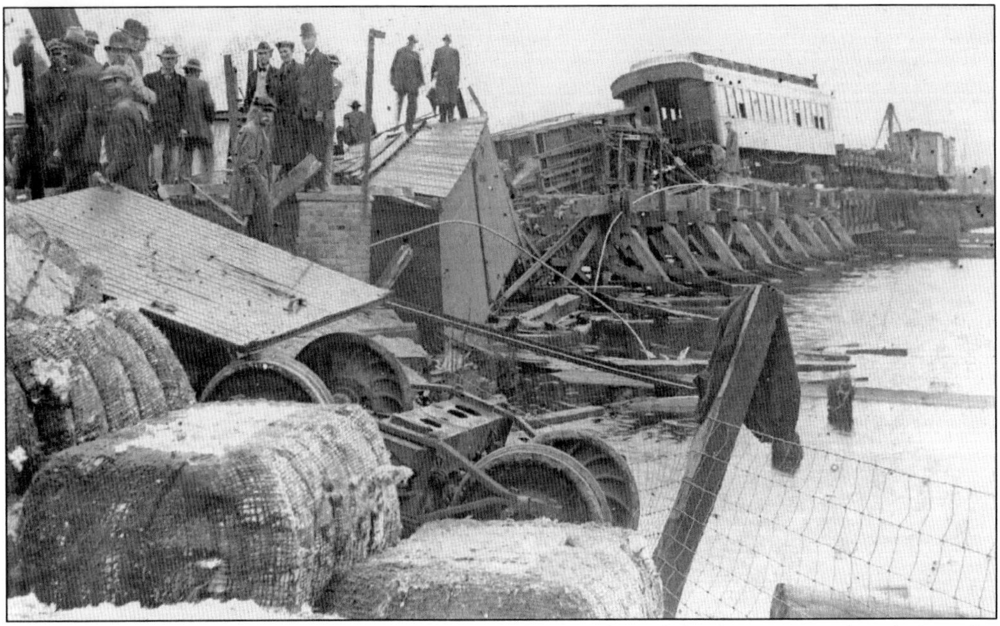

Disasters attract crowds and several locals survey the wreckage left when a train derailed on the railway bridge between Hertford and Winfall in 1923. Cotton bales, parts of boxcars, and bridge debris litter the shore. (Courtesy of Charles T. Skinner Jr.)

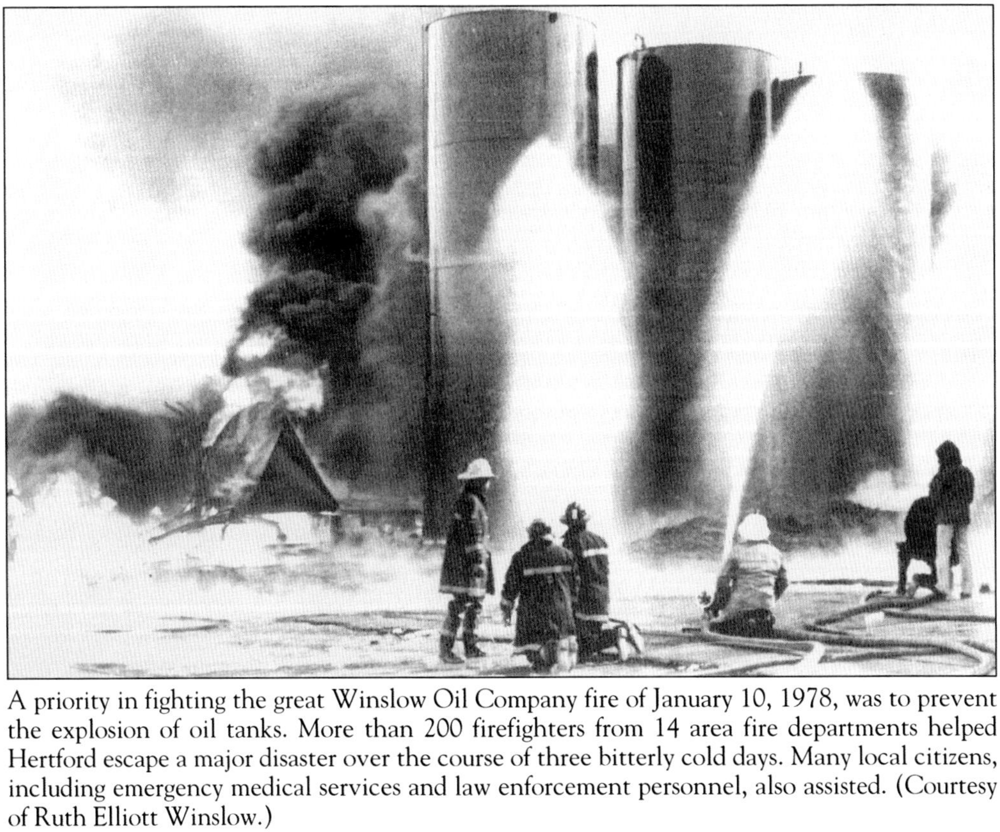

A priority in fighting the great Winslow Oil Company fire of January 10, 1978, was to prevent the explosion of oil tanks. More than 200 firefighters from 14 area fire departments helped Hertford escape a major disaster over the course of three bitterly cold days. Many local citizens, including emergency medical services and law enforcement personnel, also assisted. (Courtesy of Ruth Elliott Winslow.)

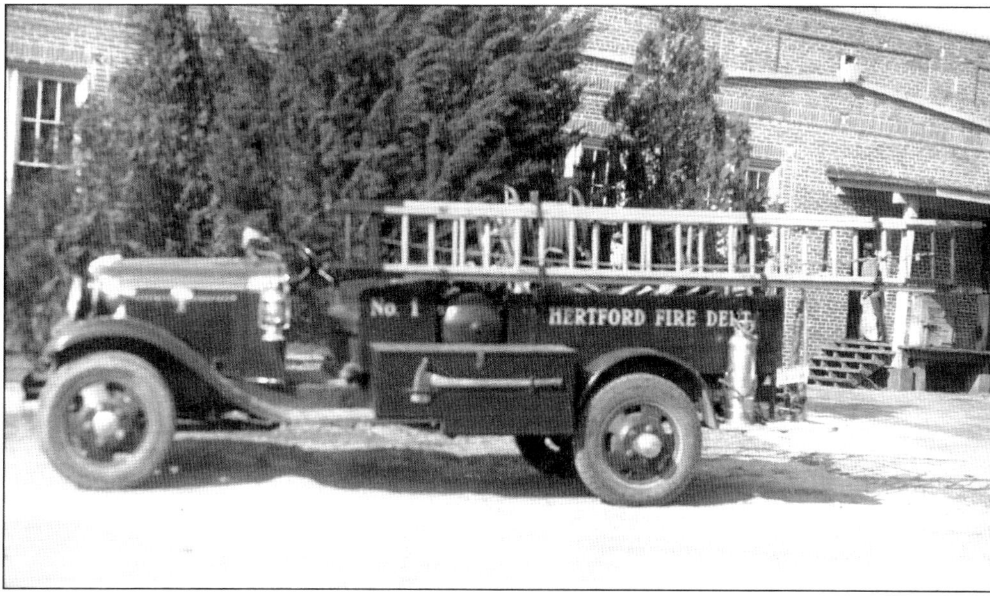

The new ladder truck of the Hertford Fire Department in 1934 is parked before the town ice plant. The V-8 Ford was equipped with soda/acid tank, ladders, and a hand-cranked siten, but no windshield. (Courtesy of Charles T. Skinner Jr.)

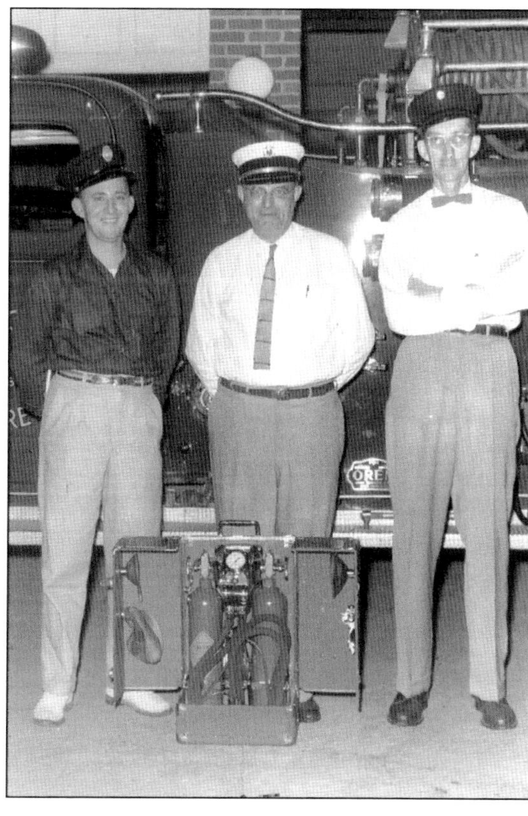

Displaying the Hertford Fire Department's new respirator in 1955, from left to right, are Capt. Charles Skinner, Chief (and town mayor) Vivian Darden, and Capt. Henry Clay Sullivan. (Courtesy of Charles T. Skinner Jr.)

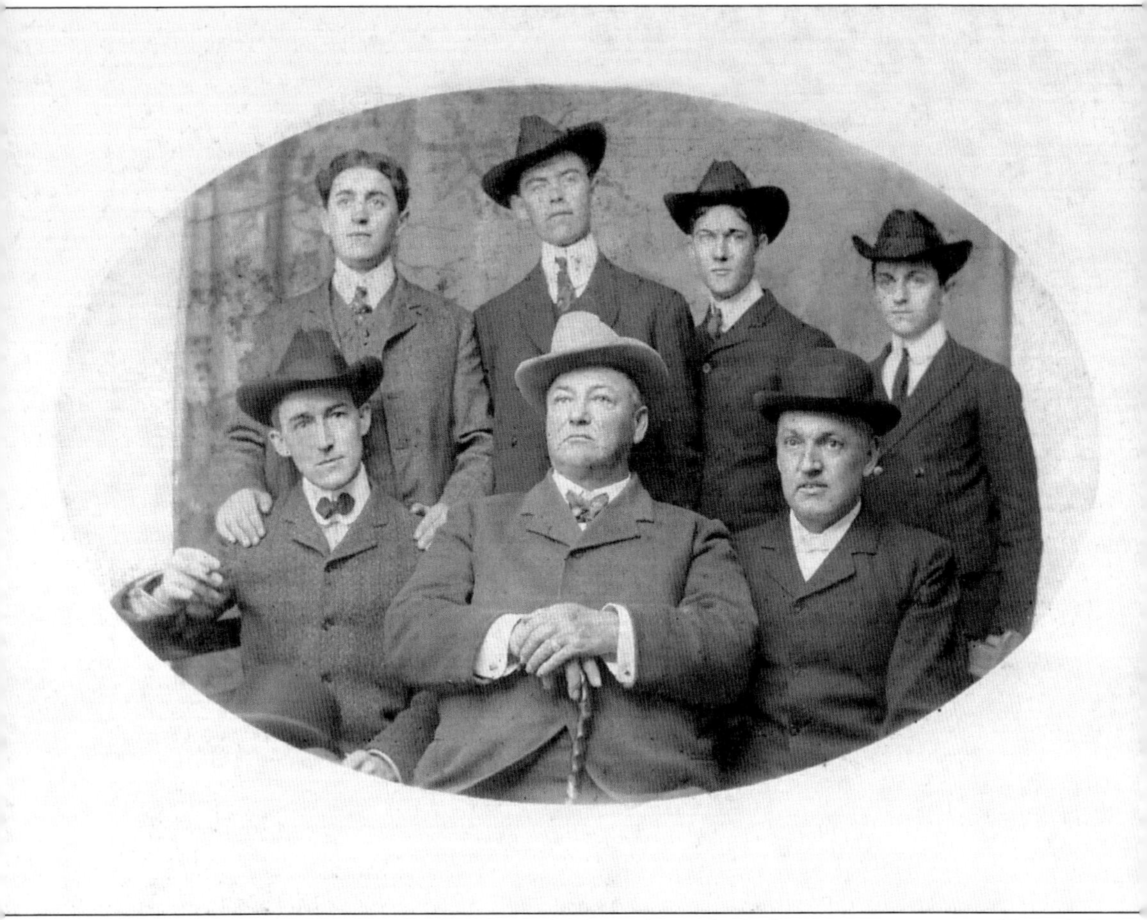

This *c*. 1910 photograph includes major leaders of Hertford's business community. From left to right, they are: (front row) landowner and cotton gin operator Charles Wood; Matthew H. White; and bank cashier and county treasurer Louis B. Norman; (back row) Nicholas Rutenberg; landowner and social organizer Barrow Fleetwood; lumber mill manager William B. Hudson; and Simon Rutenberg. White (1851–1913) had perhaps the most varied business interests in Perquimans, including general merchandise, real estate, agriculture, grist and saw mills, an ice company, cotton oil processing, horse trading, and horse racing. He also constructed rental houses in the town and made significant improvements to the public road that passed through one of his farms. The Rutenberg brothers, clothing store operators, were from Odessa, Russia, and were leaders of the small Jewish community in Hertford. Hudson was a native of New Jersey. (Courtesy of Charles T. Skinner Jr.)

Four

AT PLAY

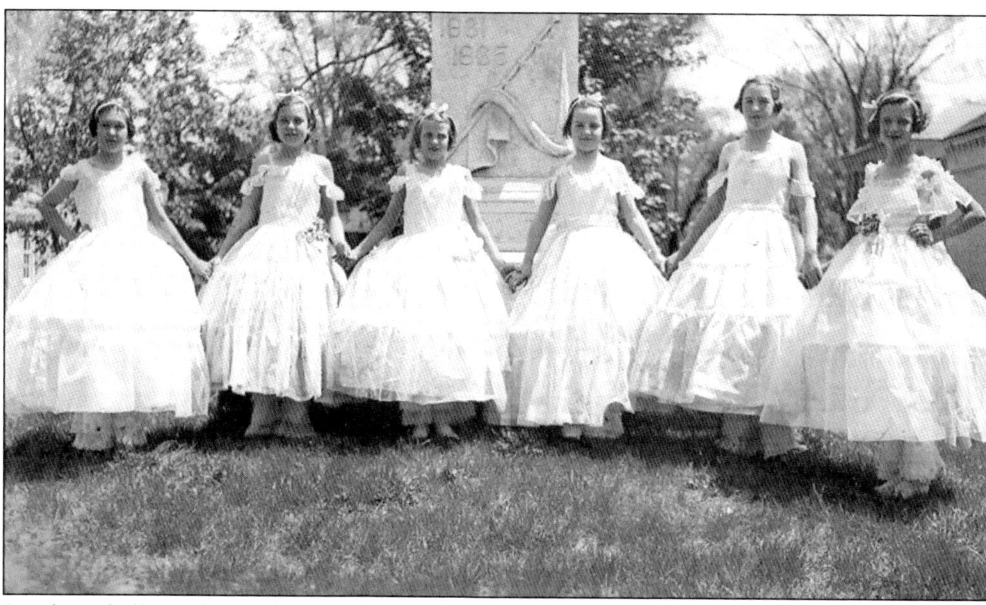

Southern belles in hoop skirts and pantaloons on the courthouse green in May 1932 are, from left to right, Marjorie Buck, Katherine Jessup, Anne Felton, Nancy Darden, Lila Budd Stevens, and Florence Darden. (Courtesy of Florence Darden Christensen.)

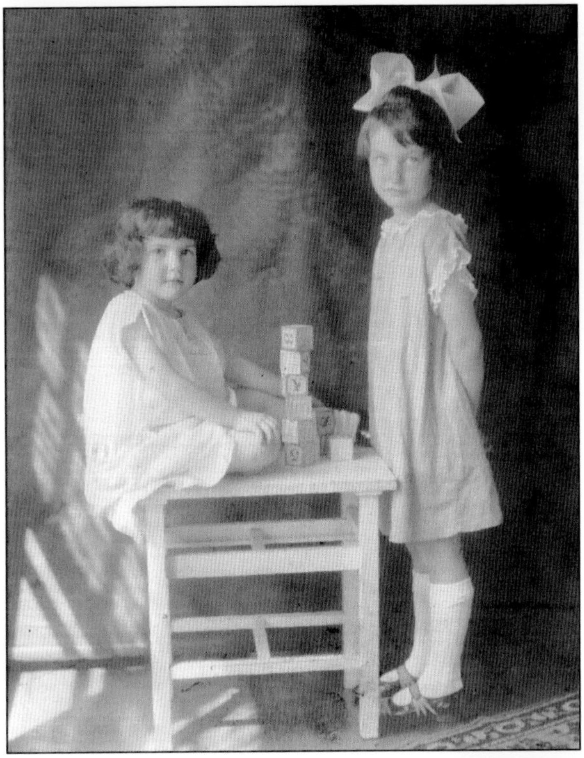

Ruth Nachman (left) has a precarious perch under the watchful eyes of big sister Leah, *c.* 1925. (Courtesy of Mary K. Vidaurri.)

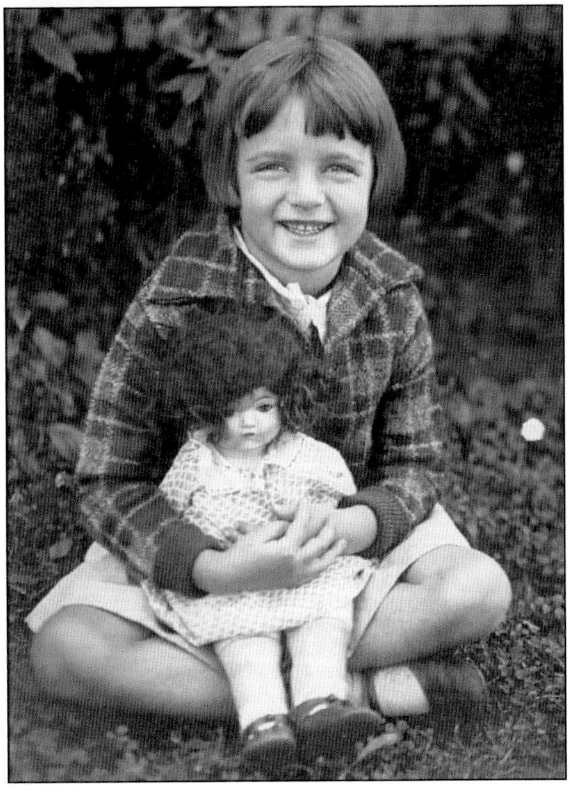

Sometimes a girl's best friend is her dolly, or so it seems to little Florence Darden. (Courtesy of Florence Darden Christensen.)

Lena (Felton) Lloyd is dressed for a special occasion, *c.* 1940s. Gown, lace, jewelry, and corsage suggest a formal dance may await her. (Courtesy of Lena Council.)

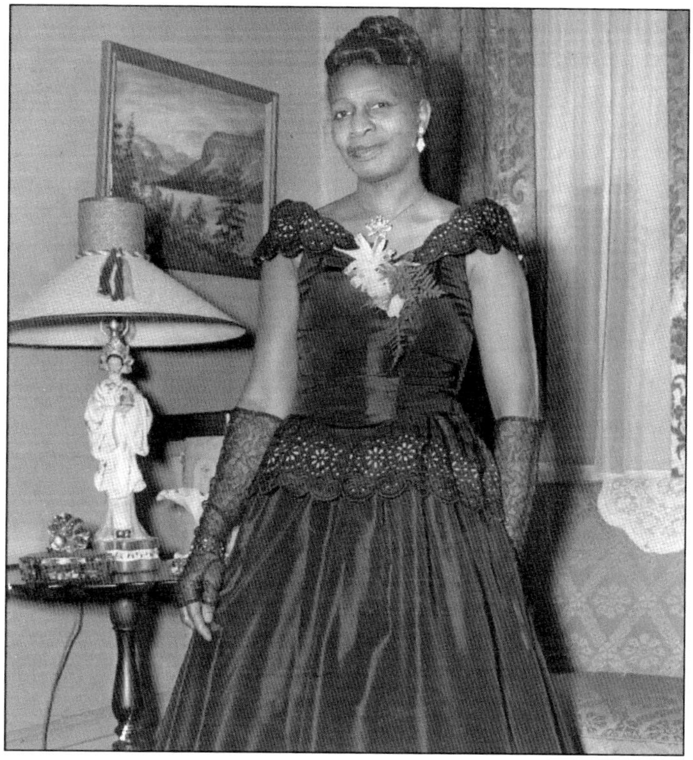

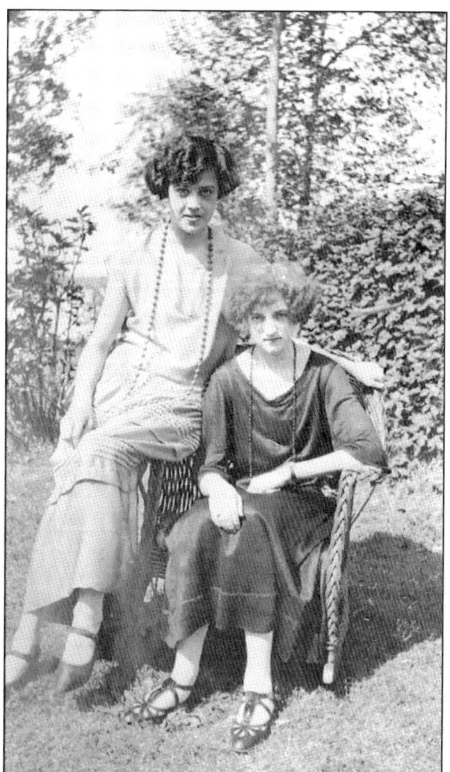

These young women are more suitably dressed for an afternoon in the parlor, but their photographer needs sunlight for his picture, so they pose on Front Street in the 1920s. (Courtesy of Claudia Brinn Bunch.)

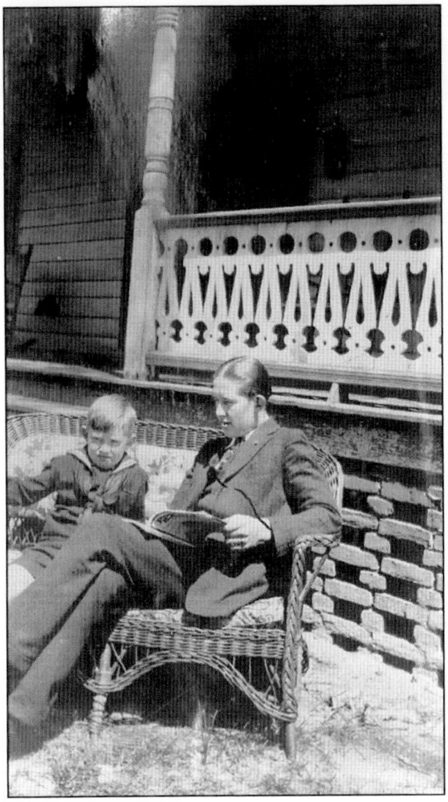

Mothers hoped their boys were doing this: Claude Brinn (left) and big brother Robert read together on a wicker loveseat in the front yard, *c.* 1923. (Courtesy of Claudia Brinn Bunch.)

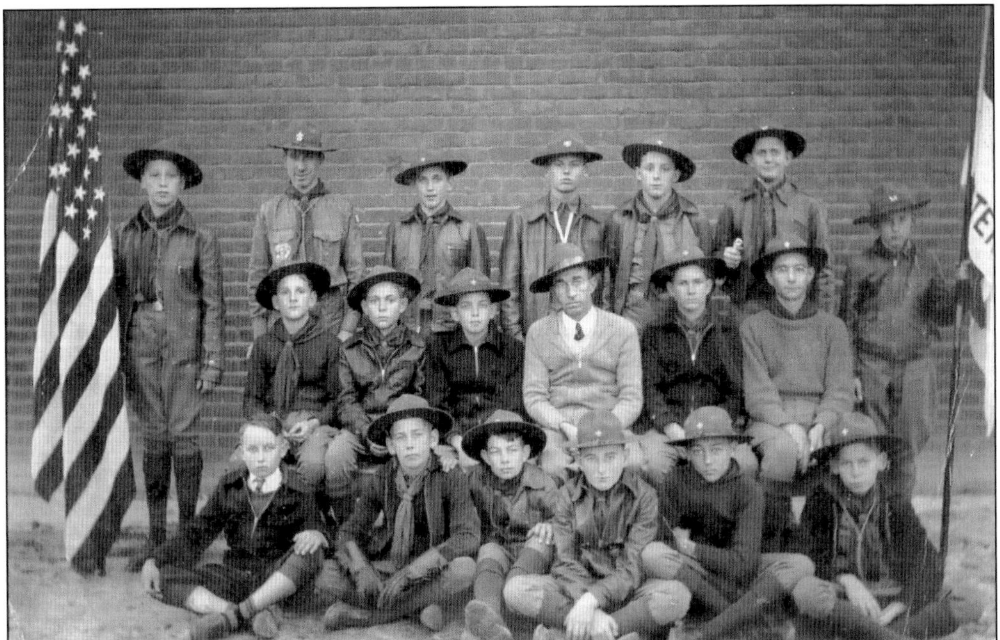

Hertford's Boy Scouts were prepared, of course, for this *c.* 1939 group picture. In the back row, second from right, is Julian Broughton, who would serve as sheriff of Perquimans County longer than anyone else in the history of that office. (Courtesy of Gene Boyce.)

This is what boys were really doing: James Evart Newby (center, front) and his pals likely have some mischief in mind, c. 1920. (Courtesy of Claudia Brinn Bunch.)

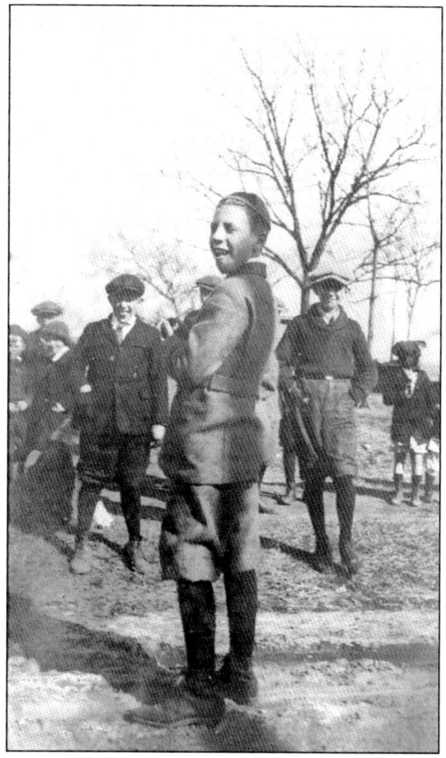

Fred T. Riddick, agriculture teacher at King Street Elementary School (below, far left), also served as scout leader. He is shown with a scout troop in the early 1960s. From left to right are (front row) Walter Rogers, Horace Bembry, Larry Broady, and James Brickhouse; (back row) Louis Harvey, George White, Raymond Jones, and Linwood Welch. (Courtesy of Hattie T. Riddick.)

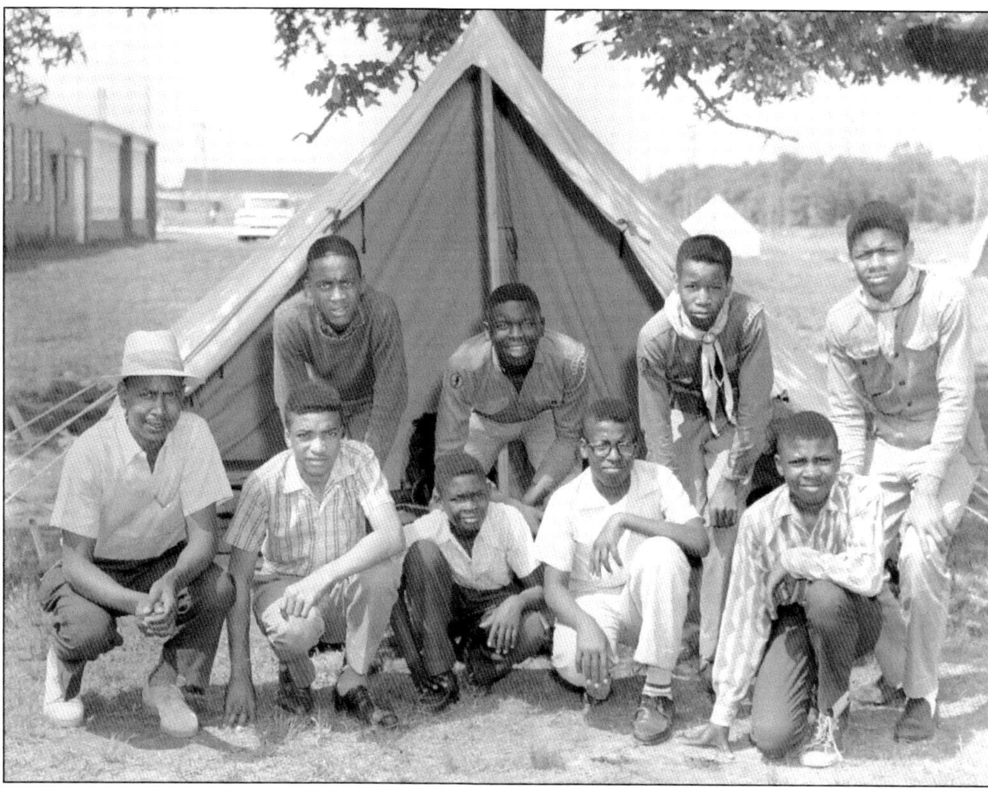

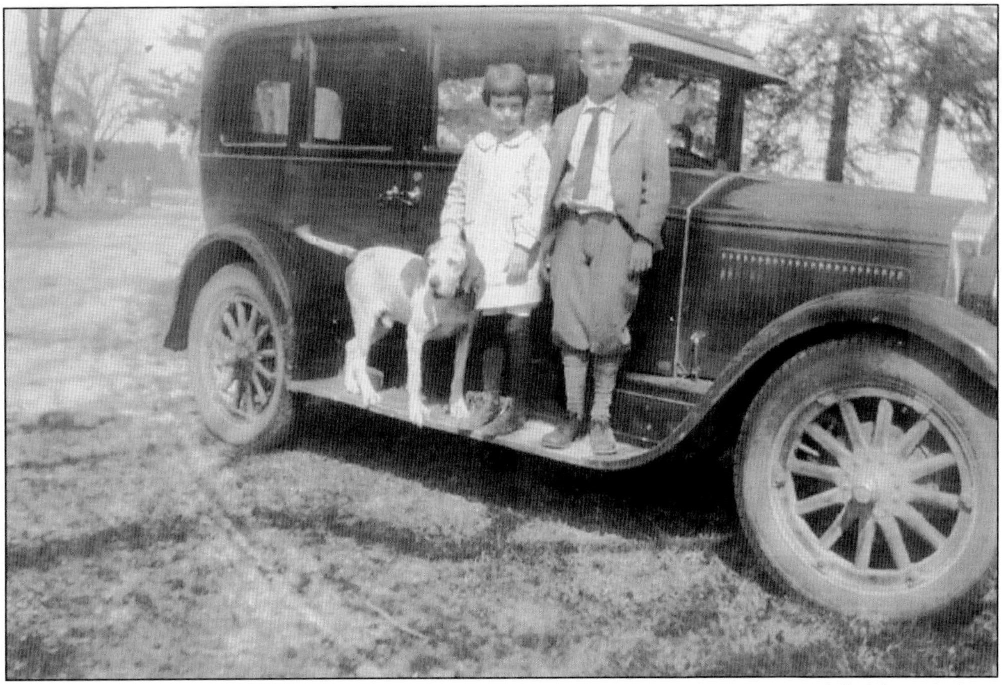

Pausing from their travels, from right, are Roy Reed, his cousin Florence Litchfield, and their old friend Spot. The car's running board was a fun—albeit dangerous—perch for short rides. (Courtesy of Prue Newby Reed.)

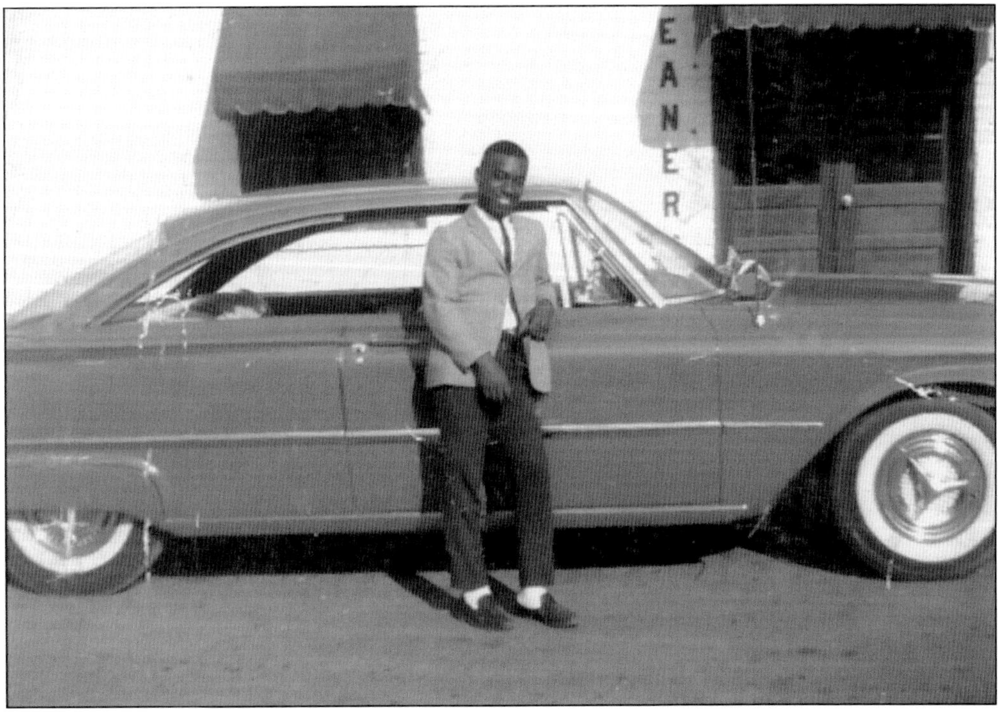

Howard Blanchard proudly leans on a 1961 Ford Starliner in front of Roberson's Cleaners on Edenton Road Street. (Courtesy of Brenda Dillard.)

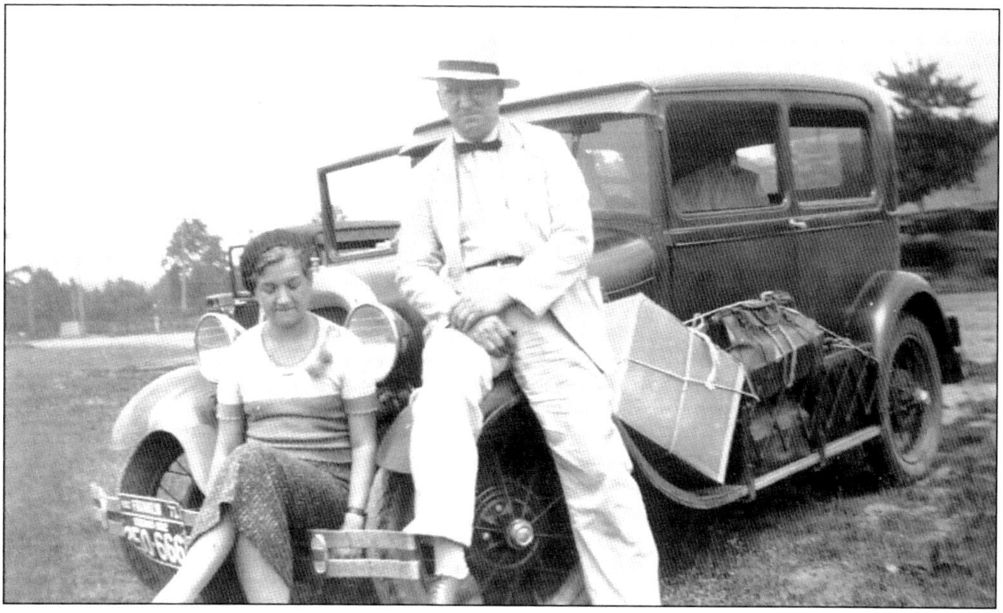

Spivey Roberson sits on the bumper while her father Glenn Roberson gets the better seat on the fender. The running board is full of luggage, making it difficult to use the driver's door. (Courtesy of Kay Matthews Whedbee.)

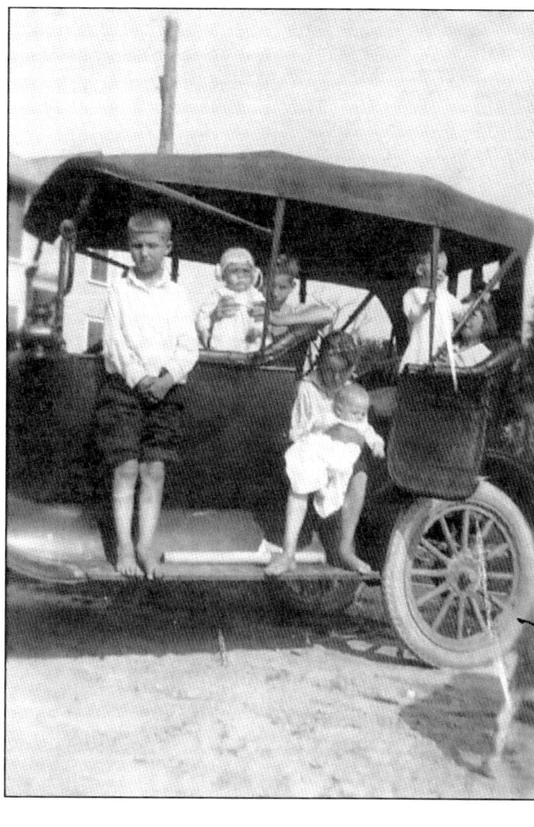

Wallace and Roy Reed are shown with several of their cousins. The boys in the middle probably are not happy to be holding babies. (Courtesy of Prue Newby Reed.)

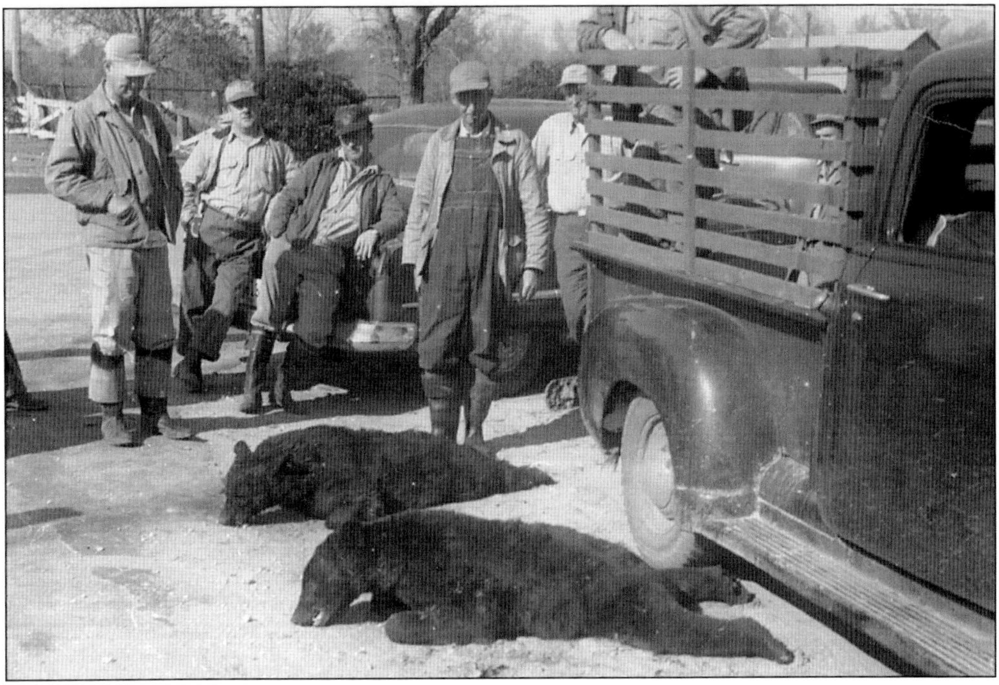

Bears are no longer the menace to livestock and people they once were, but bear hunting has remained a popular pastime for generations. These bears were taken on the fringes of the Dismal Swamp near Whiteston. (Courtesy of Lynwood C. Winslow III.)

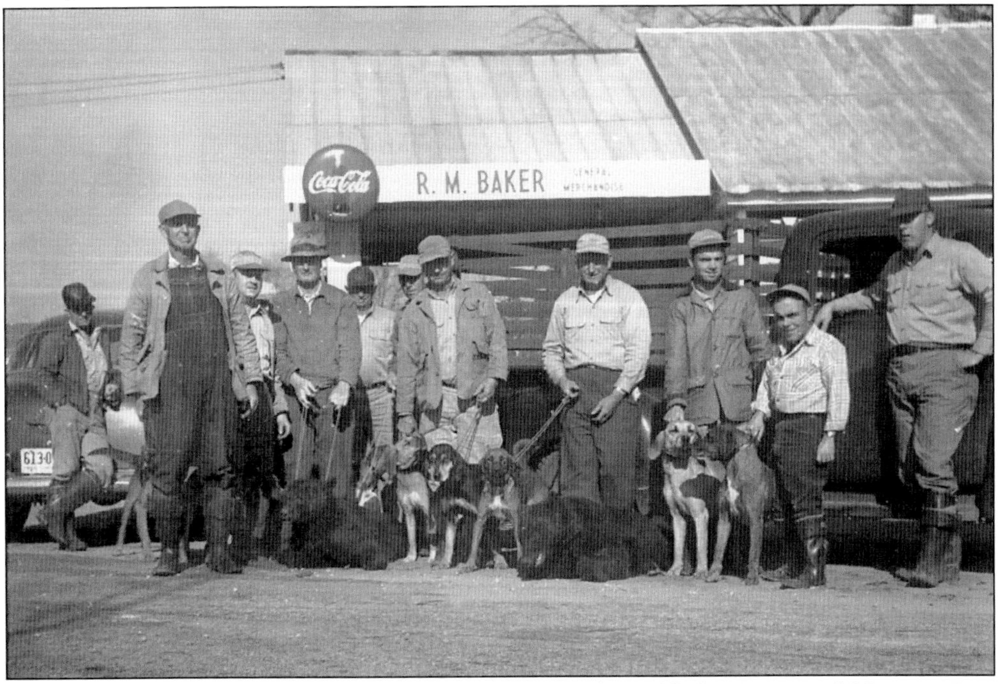

Hunters and dogs rendezvous at Baker's Store, formerly Riddick's Store and Nicanor Post Office. The cry of hounds will soon echo through nearby woods. (Courtesy of Lynwood C. Winslow III.)

Vivian Matthews holds two fish worth keeping before the Hertford Town Pier at the end of Grubb Street, *c.* 1940. At left is the pavilion; at right is the bathhouse. (Courtesy of Kay Matthews Whedbee.)

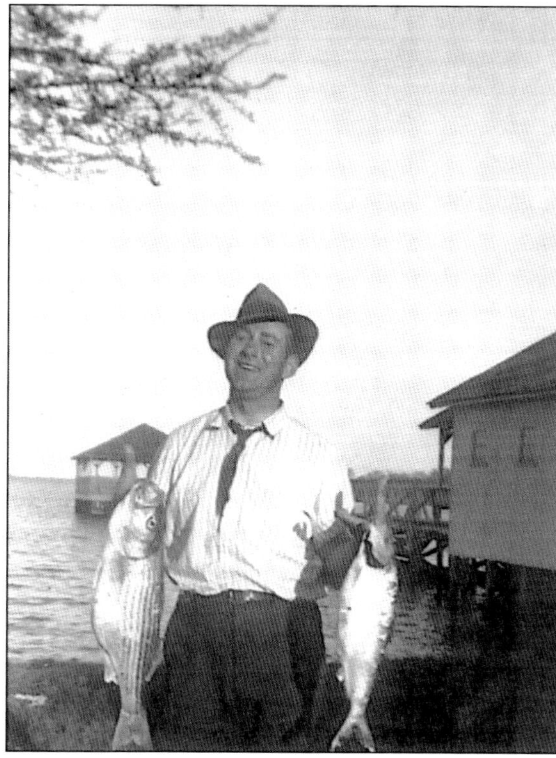

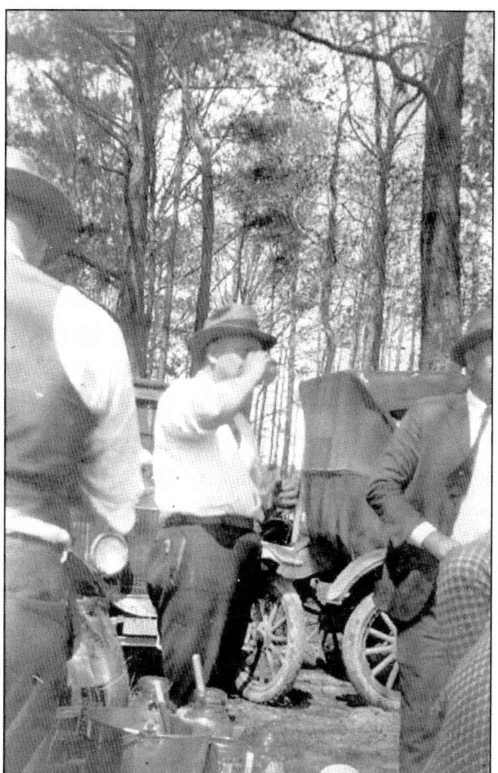

Were these gentlemen snapped at a church picnic, a family reunion, a hunt, or a sampling of home brew? (Courtesy of Kay Matthews Whedbee.)

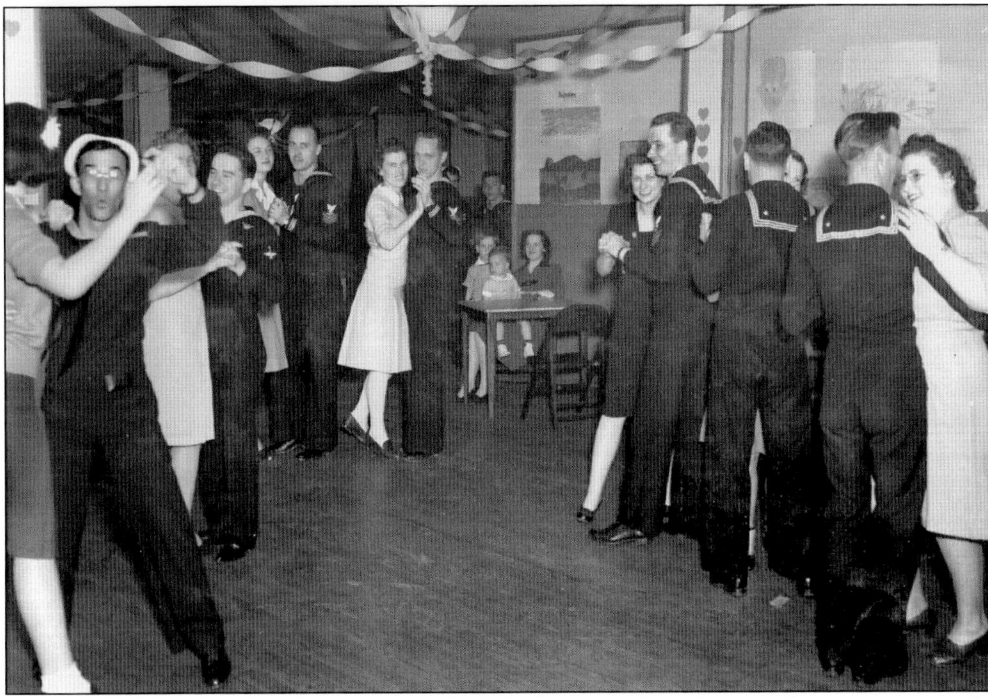

The couple at far left look as if they could break into a jitterbug at the USO on Grubb Street during World War II. There was dancing upstairs and dining downstairs in the building now occupied by Hertfordshire Antiques and The Tin Rabbit gift shop. (Courtesy of Ruth Elliott Winslow.)

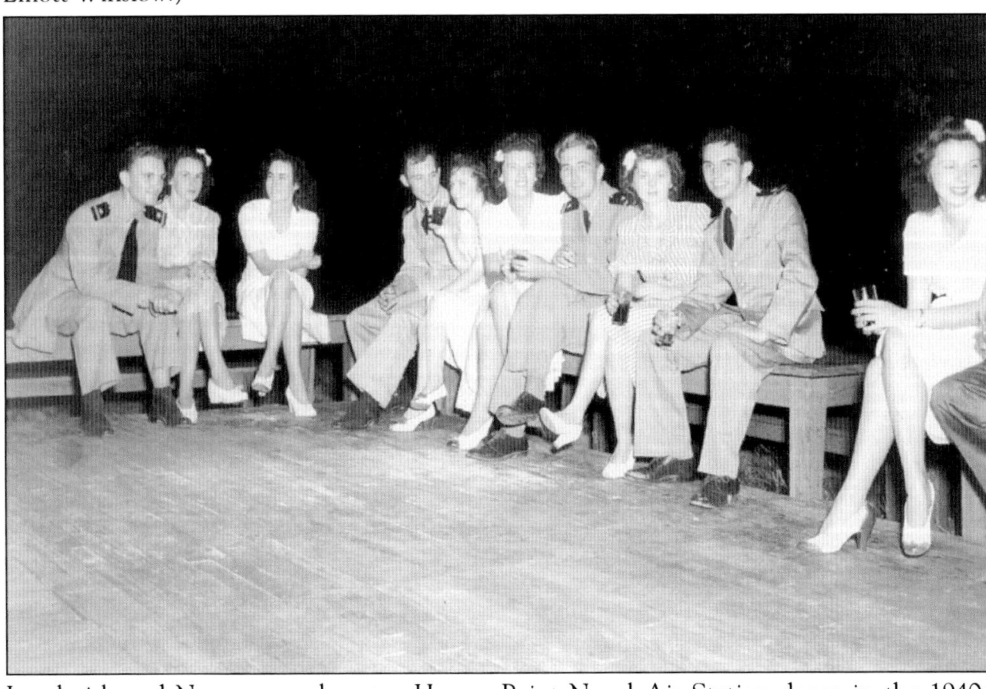

Local girls and Navy men relax at a Harvey Point Naval Air Station dance in the 1940s. (Courtesy of Ruth Elliott Winslow.)

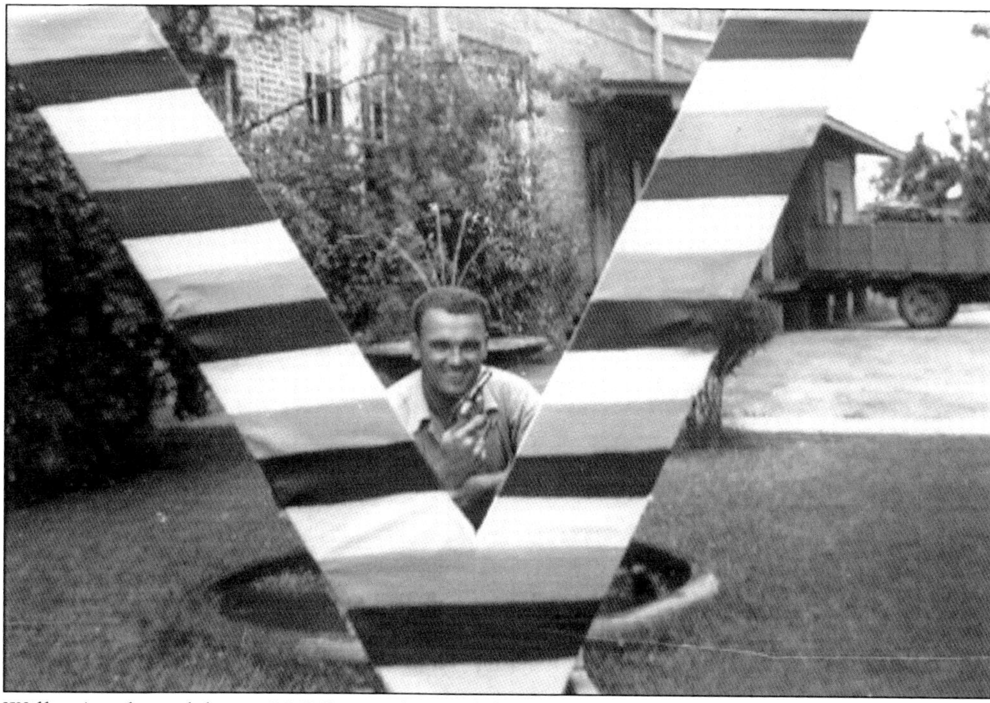

Willie Ainsley celebrates V-E Day in front of the Hertford ice plant in May 1945. (Courtesy of Margaret Ainsley Brewin.)

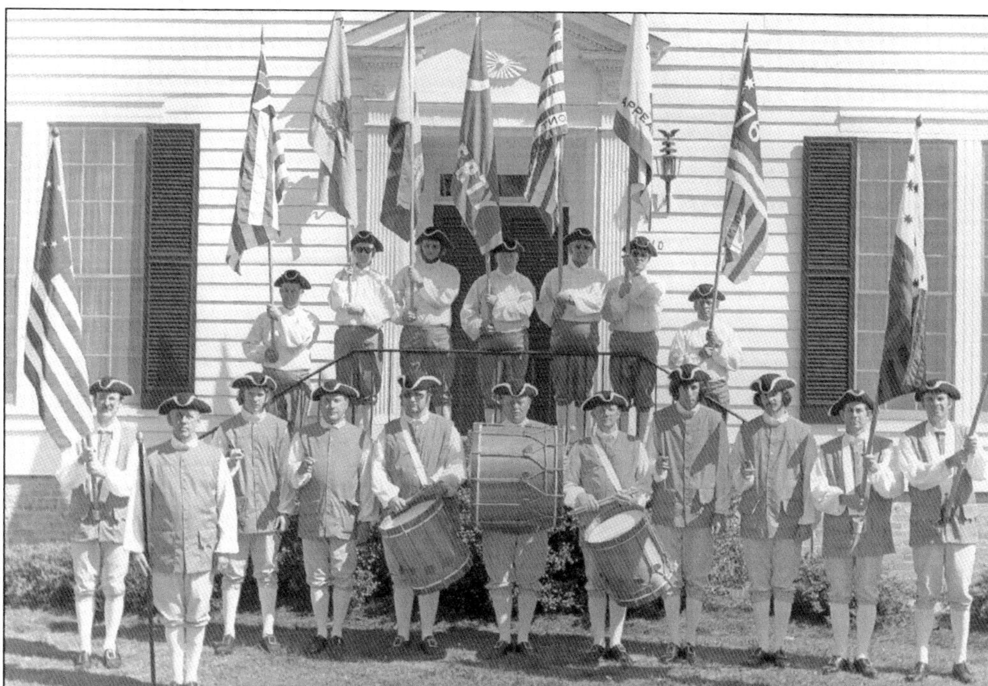

The Hertford Fife and Drum Corps, shown here in bicentennial array in 1976, offers an inspiring musical uplift at civic and patriotic gatherings. Drum major William A. White stands in the left foreground. (Courtesy of Sidney Eley.)

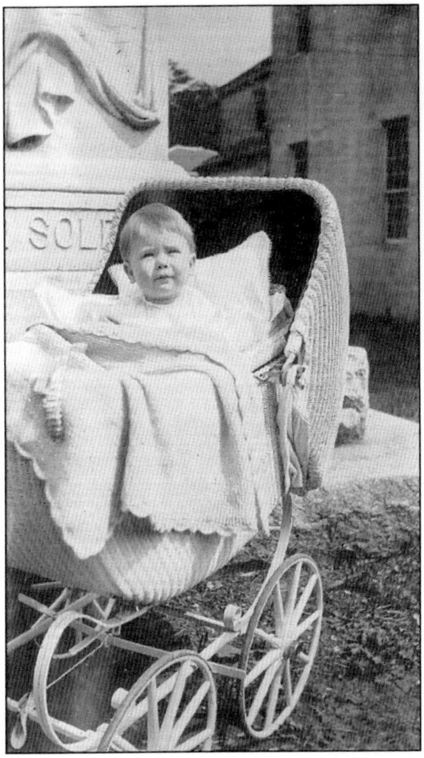

Baby Layden's carriage ride has been interrupted for a photograph at the Confederate monument in the 1920s. (Courtesy of Claudia Brinn Bunch.)

Margaret Ainsley is pleased with her birthday gift in 1951. (Courtesy of Margaret Ainsley Brewin.)

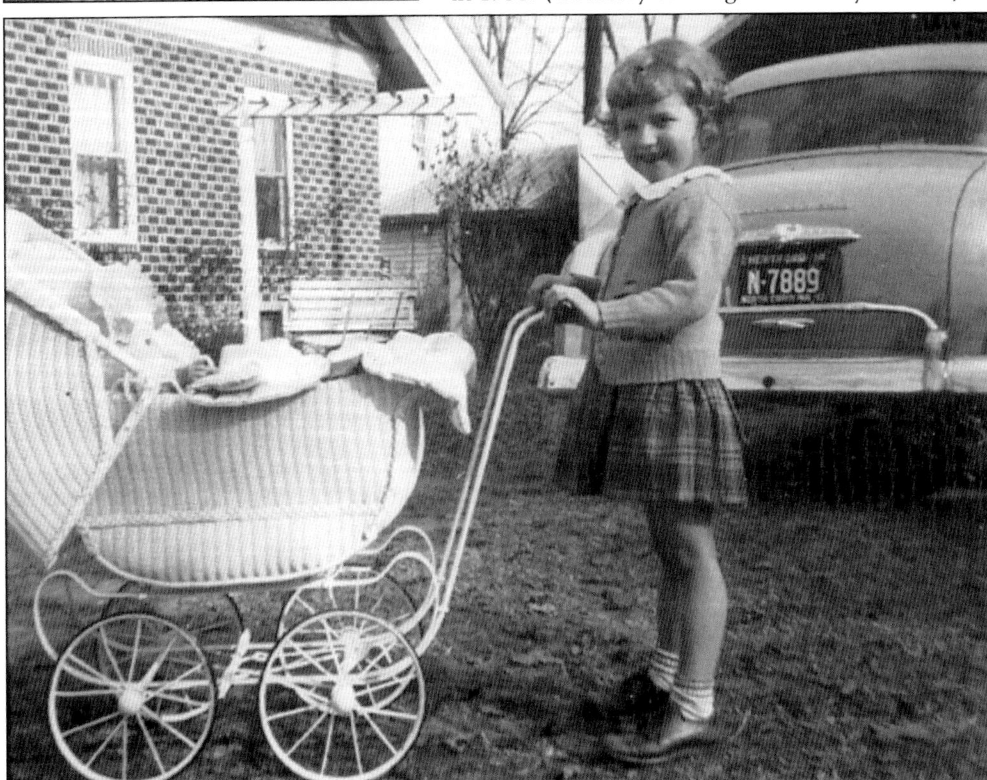

The girl with the beribboned bonnet may be Frances Newby in the 1920s. (Courtesy of Claudia Brinn Bunch.)

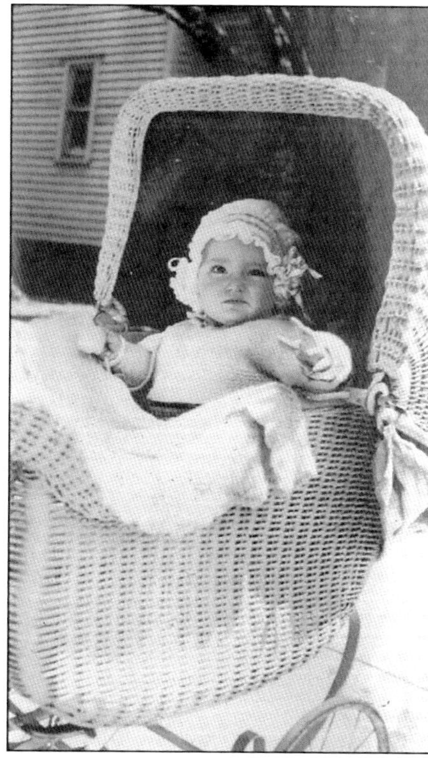

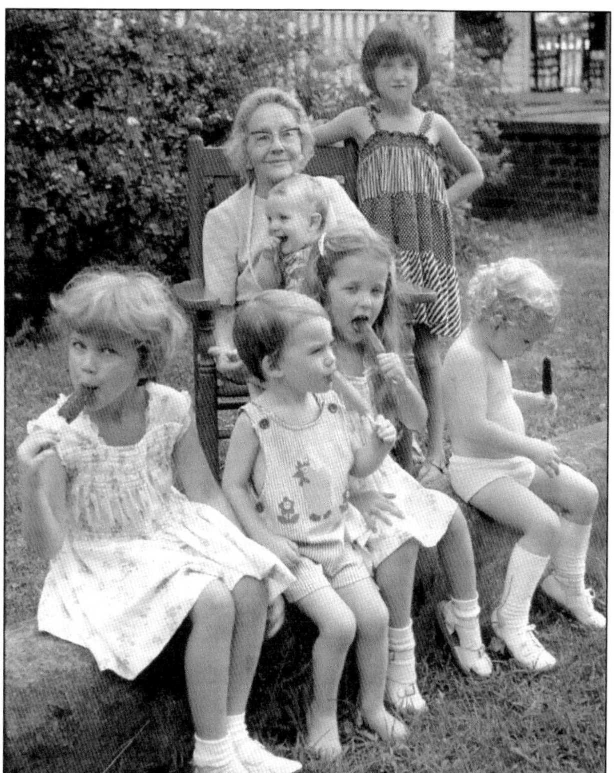

Pencie (Hunter) Gregory (1894–1980), in the armchair holding Wesley Beck, enjoys the summer of 1977 with her great-grandchildren. From left to right are (front row) Susan Ainsley, Michael Beck, Alice Brewin, and Mark Ainsley; (standing) Laura Brewin. (Courtesy of Margaret Ainsley Brewin.)

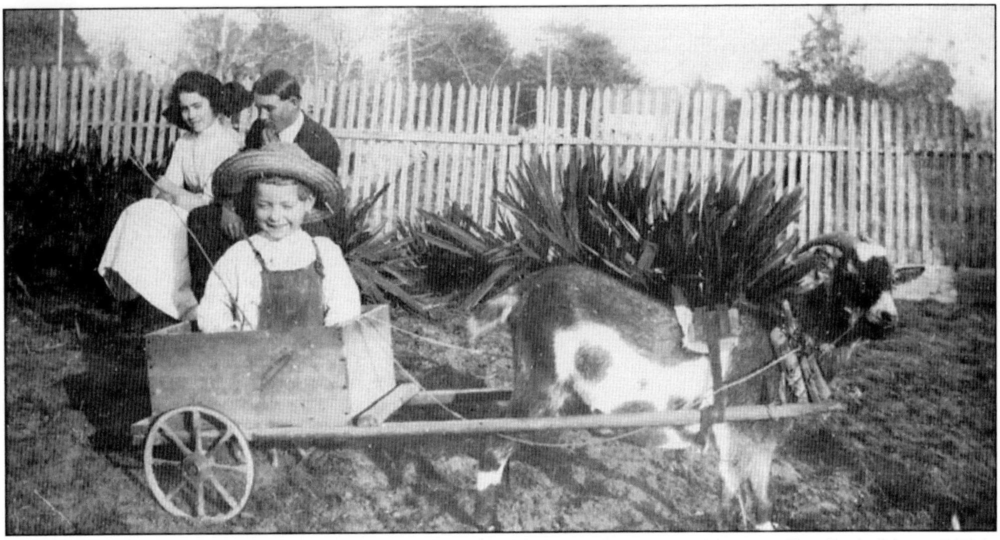

Henry Hunter is on patrol in his goat cart, chaperoning his sister Pencie (back, left) in 1912. (Courtesy of Margaret Ainsley Brewin.)

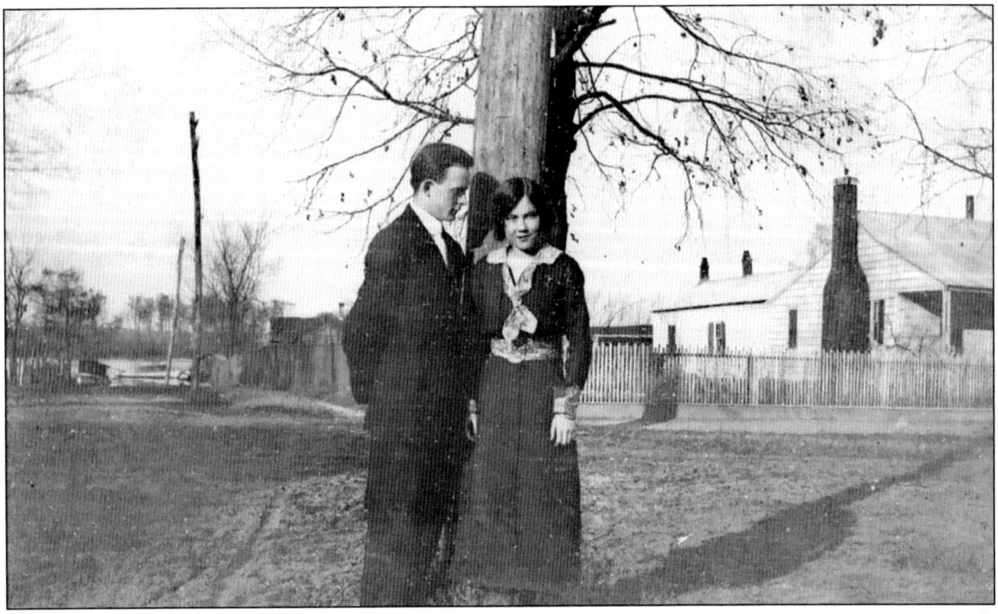

A courting couple was allowed to stroll about town, under watchful eyes of course. Mark Gregory and Pencie Hunter stand at a barely discernible intersection with Covent Garden Street dwindling away to the river (left), c. 1912. At right is the Rev. Josiah Elliott's house on Grubb Street. (Courtesy of Margaret Ainsley Brewin.)

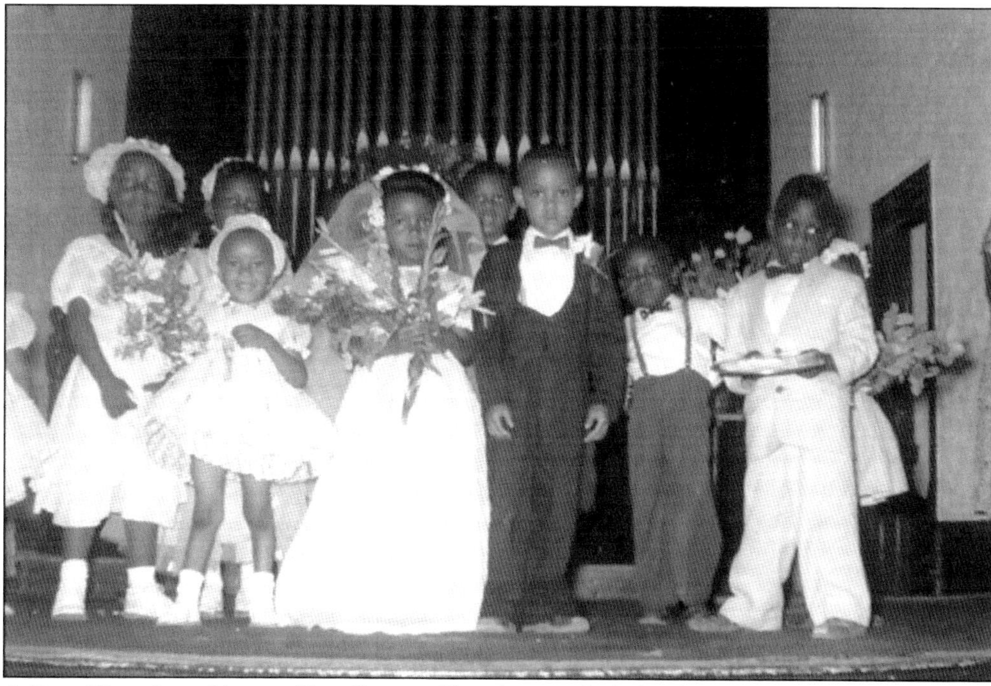

A Tom Thumb wedding at First Baptist Church in 1956 helped raise funds for a needy cause. Who can resist a smile and a contribution at the sight of children performing? (Courtesy of Helen Thompson Shaw.)

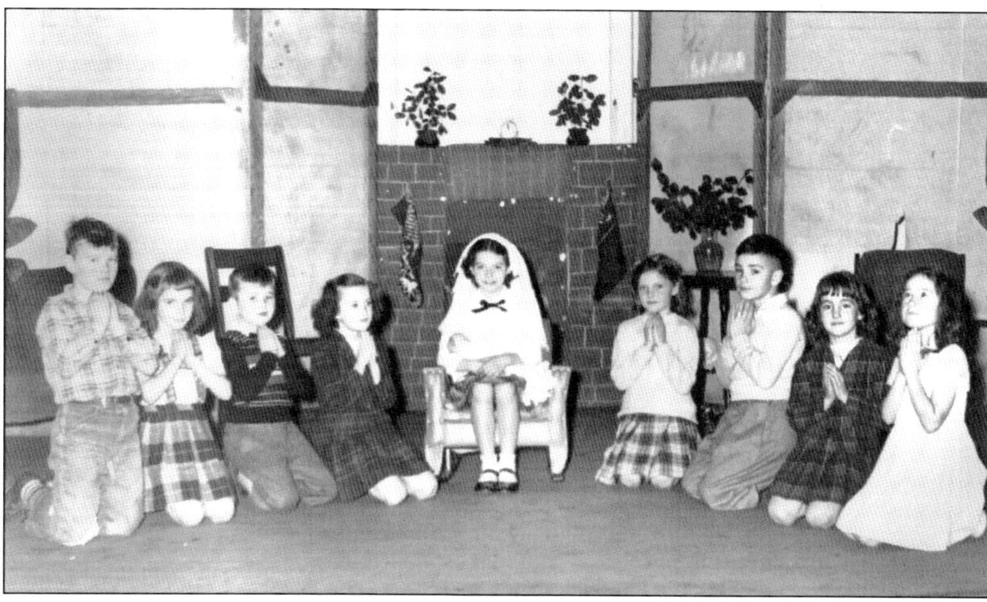

Second graders at Hertford Grammar School in the mid-1940s could perform a Christmas play and exhibit prayerful attitudes in the public school. From left to right are Tommy Matthews, Jane Keel, Sonny Matthews, Patsy Elliott, Becky Cox, Kay Nixon, Skip Matthews, Amanda Corprew, and unidentified. (Courtesy of Ruth Elliott Winslow.)

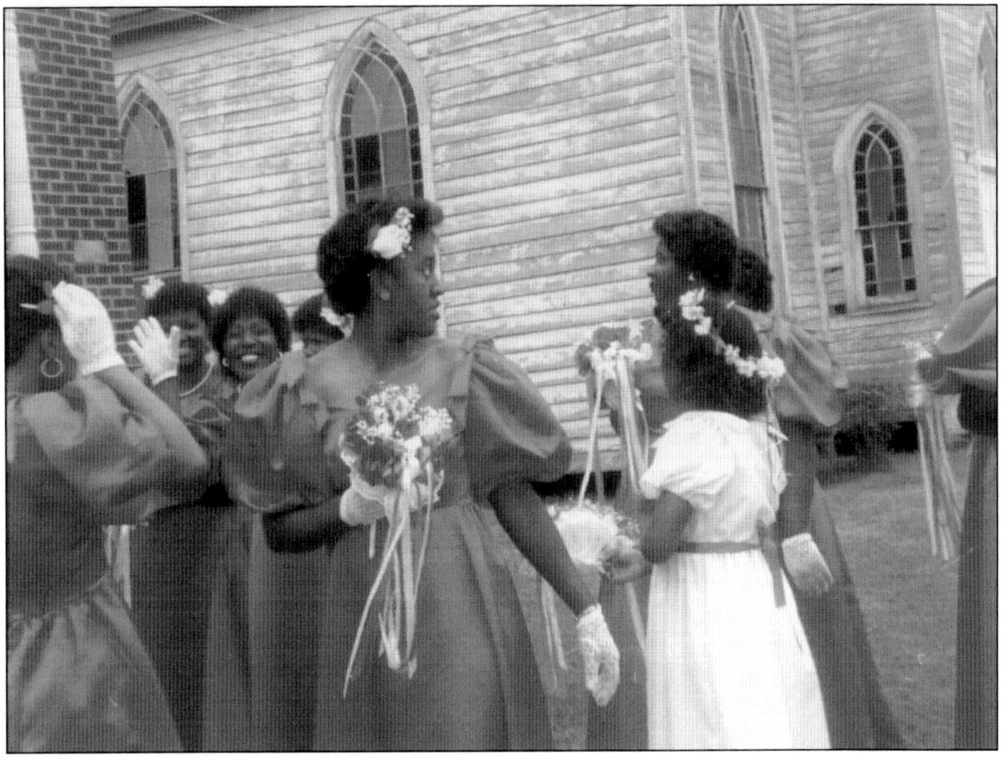

One of June Jordan's bridesmaids (center) turns a wistful glance toward the old Ellis Temple Baptist Church in Winfall, c. 1984. (Courtesy of Margaret Jordan.)

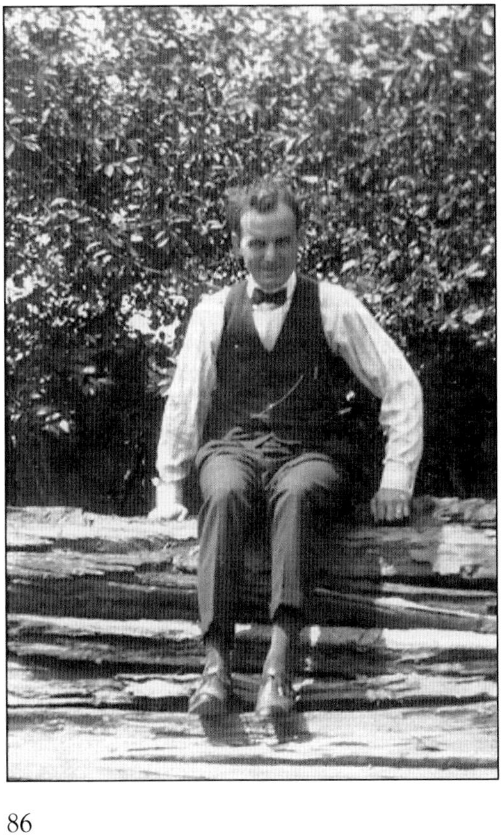

Even at play, an Edwardian gentleman retained his vest and necktie. Vivian Norfleet Darden (1892–1980) operated one of Hertford's leading clothing stores for nearly 65 years. He was also mayor, city manager, and fire chief for many years. (Courtesy of Florence Darden Christensen.)

The baggy look was fashionable for boys when Eugene Watson Chappell posed at the edge of the woods, *c*. 1920. He would go on to Wake Forest College before joining the sizable number of local men who took jobs at Newport News Shipbuilding and Dry Dock Company. (Courtesy of Peggy Lane.)

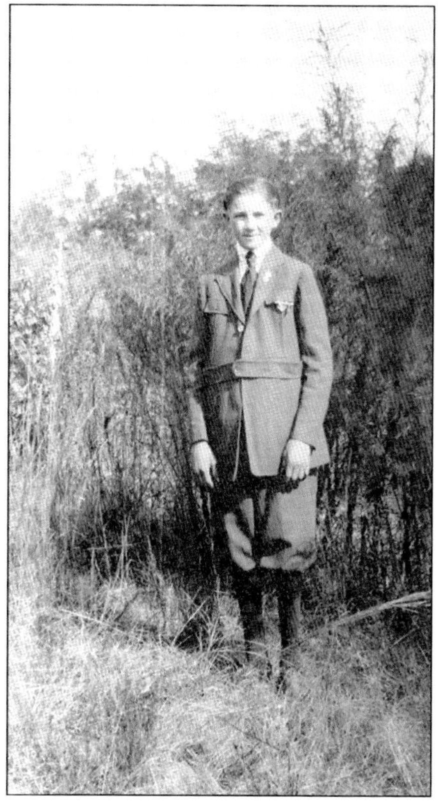

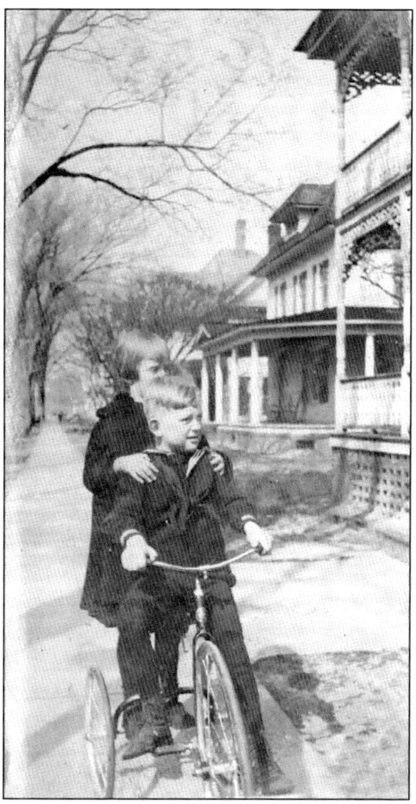

Claude Brinn (front) gives his cousin Sarah Brinn a ride past their adjacent Front Street homes in the early 1920s. (Courtesy of Claudia Brinn Bunch.)

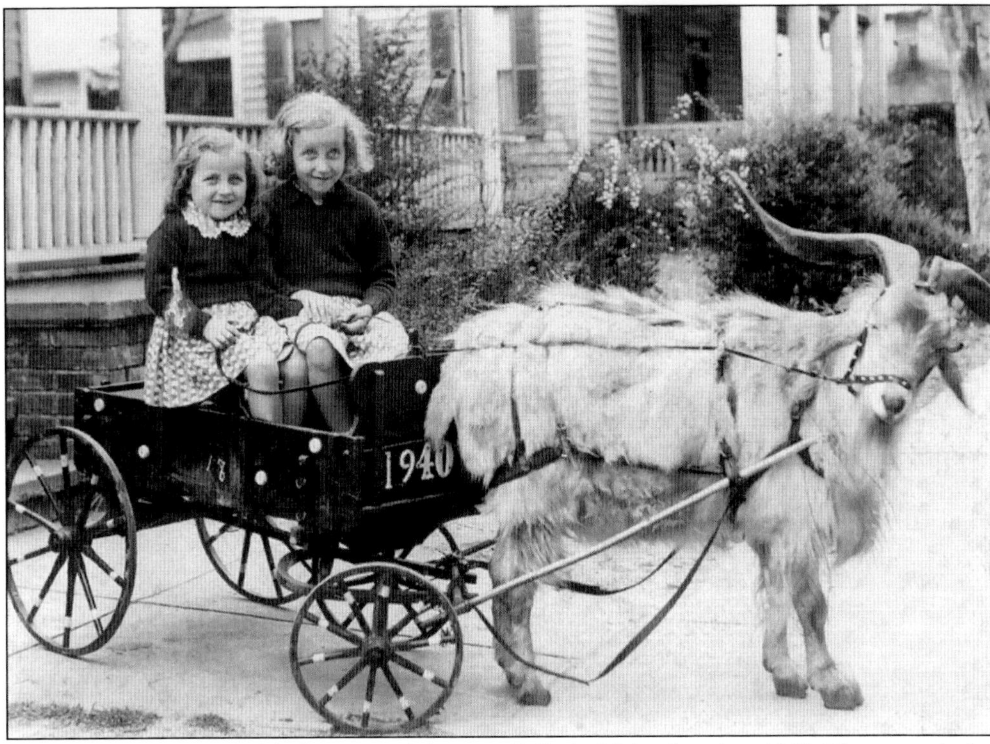

Shirley Skinner (left) holds the reins while sister Billie holds her hand, c. 1940. The goat tilts his head quizzically, perhaps wondering how a camera would taste. (Courtesy of Sybil Skinner.)

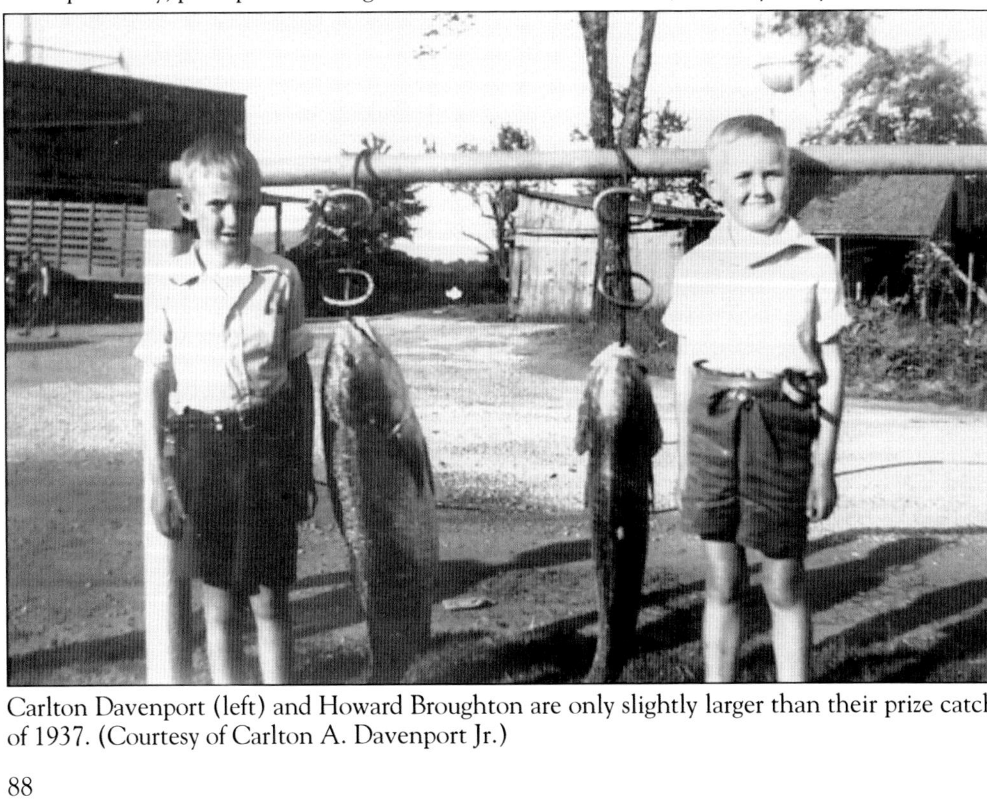

Carlton Davenport (left) and Howard Broughton are only slightly larger than their prize catch of 1937. (Courtesy of Carlton A. Davenport Jr.)

The dog needs a sniff to verify identities since the young ladies put on manly attire, *c.* 1900, in the New Hope vicinity. (Courtesy of Kay Matthews Whedbee.)

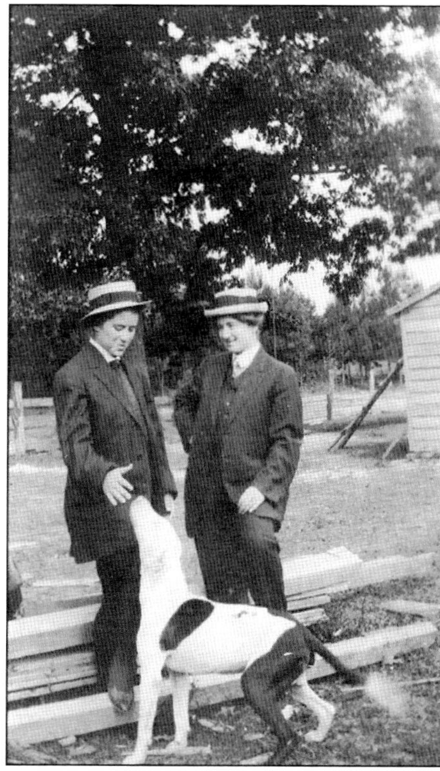

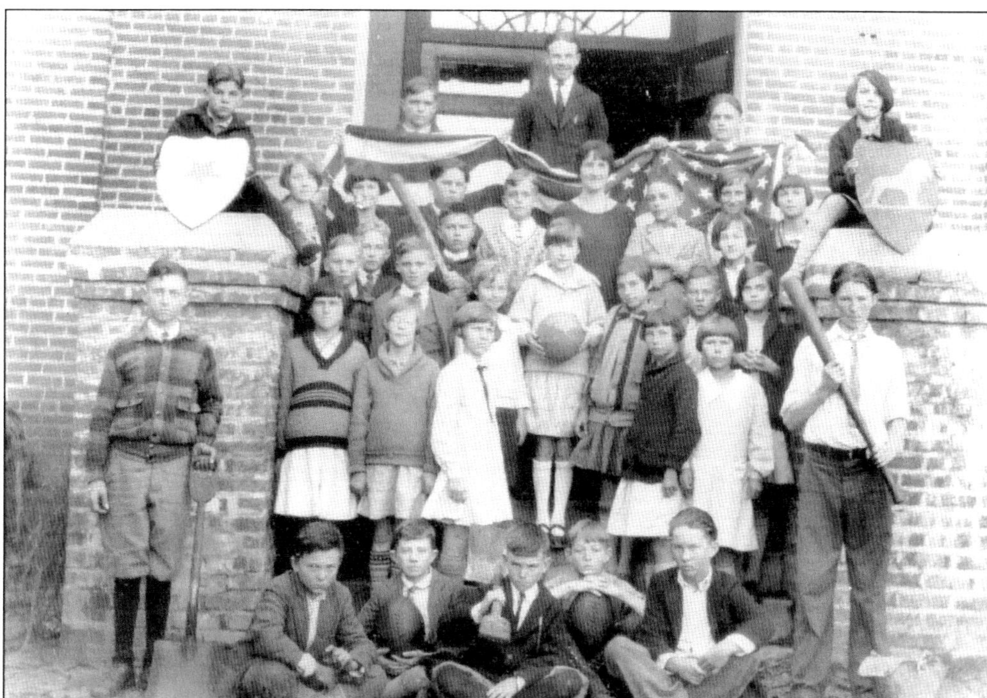

It is expected that children will be seen with balls and bats, but shovels and shields? Was this Hertford Graded School group preparing for Arbor Day? (Courtesy of John V. Matthews.)

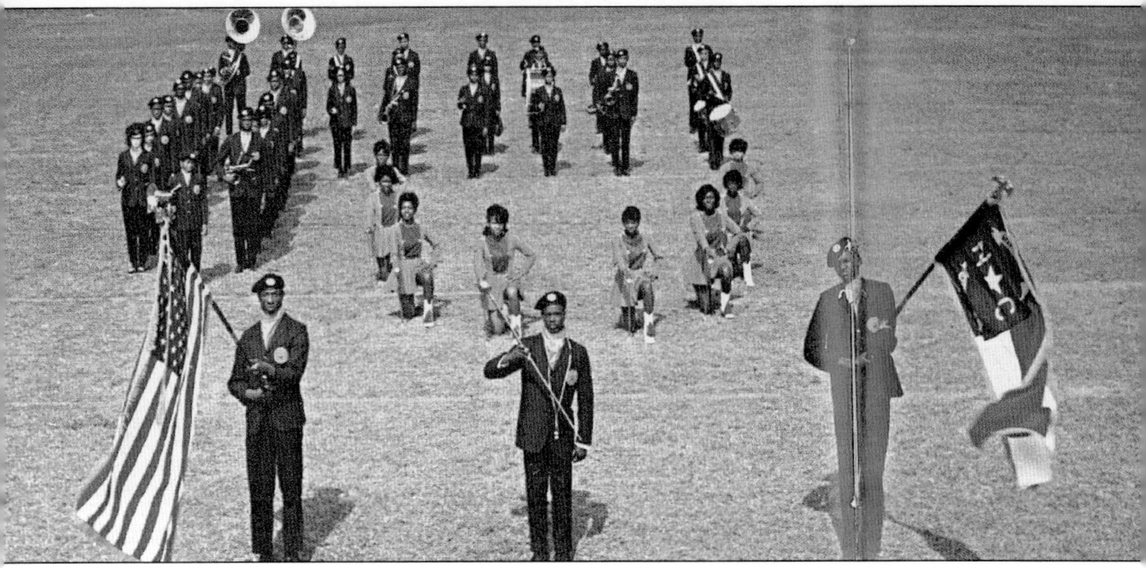

The 1968 Perquimans County Union School Marching Band poses in formation. Drum major Stanley Everett is flanked by U.S. flag bearer Larry Jordan and North Carolina flag bearer Willie Parson. Union School would cease to exist in 1970 as integration was implemented in the county. The building now is home to Perquimans County Middle School. (Courtesy of Evelyn Stubbins.)

Five

At Worship

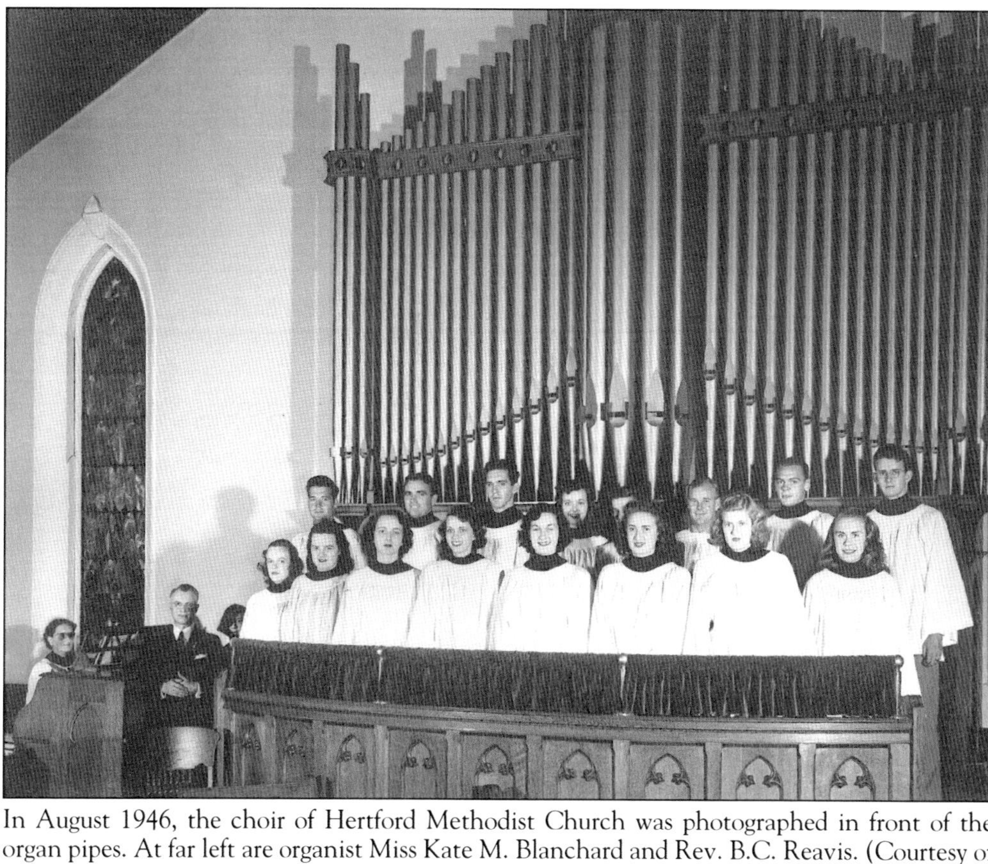

In August 1946, the choir of Hertford Methodist Church was photographed in front of the organ pipes. At far left are organist Miss Kate M. Blanchard and Rev. B.C. Reavis. (Courtesy of Charles T. Skinner Jr.)

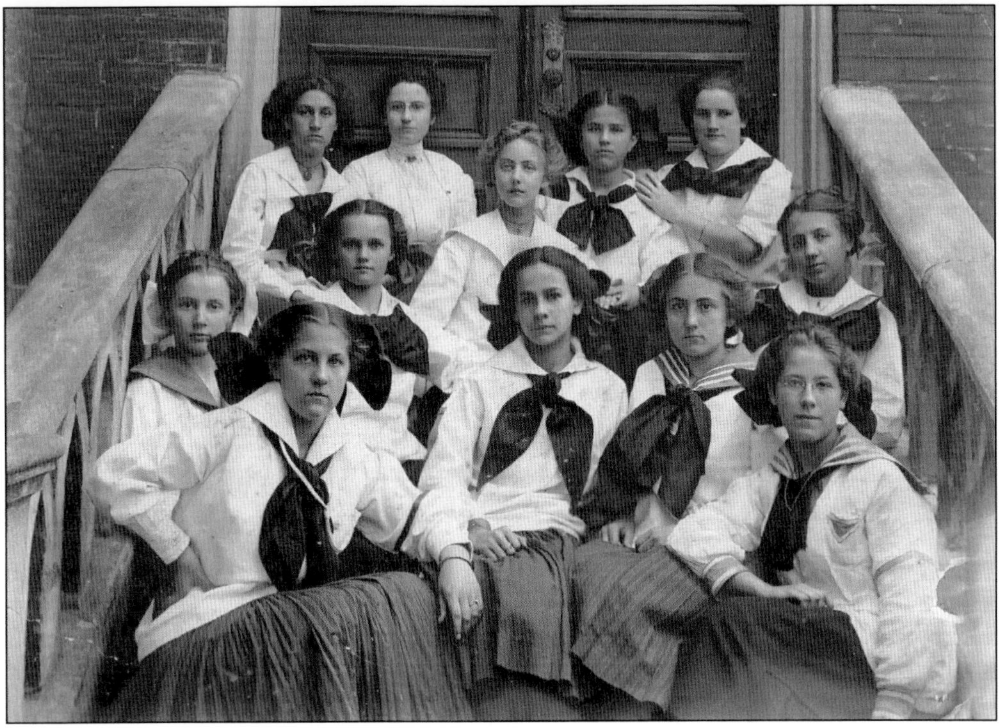

Middy blouses with bold bows grace the young ladies' Sunday school class at Hertford Methodist Church in 1914. Pictured on the church steps are, from left to right, (front row) Susie Morgan, Jessie McMullan, Evelyn White, and Mary Morris; (middle row) Julia Barber, Annie White, Katherine Newby, and Ida Ballance; (back row) Myrtle Chappell, teacher Mrs. R.T. White, Belle Walters, and Nellie Elliott. (Courtesy of Charles T. Skinner Jr.)

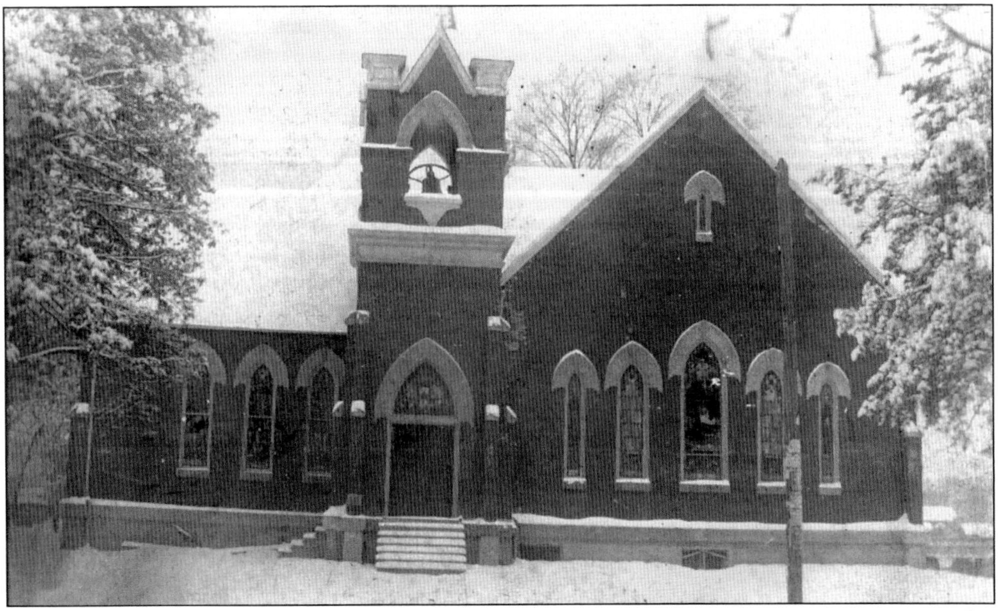

Hertford Methodist Church was built in 1901 for a congregation that began in the 1820s. This winter scene was probably photographed in 1902. (Courtesy of Charles T. Skinner Jr.)

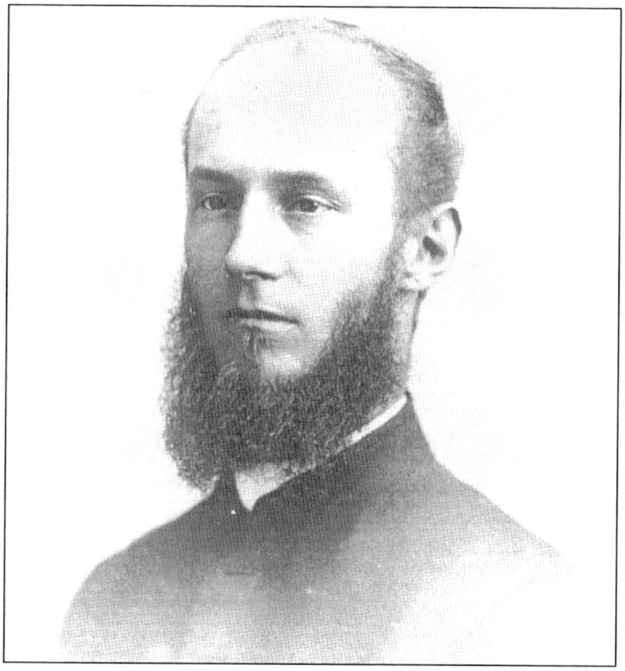

Seen here c. 1890 is Rev. Benjamin Skinner Lassiter, who accepted a call to serve as rector of Holy Trinity Episcopal Church, which his grandfather Benjamin S. Skinner had founded. He served the church in Hertford from 1901 to 1912. (Courtesy of Holy Trinity Episcopal Church.)

The Holy Trinity Episcopal Church, built in 1849, was featured on a c. 1905 postcard. Since then, the house to the left of the church has been demolished and replaced by the church's Parish House, while the vacant lot to the right has acquired a house of its own. (Courtesy of Holy Trinity Episcopal Church.)

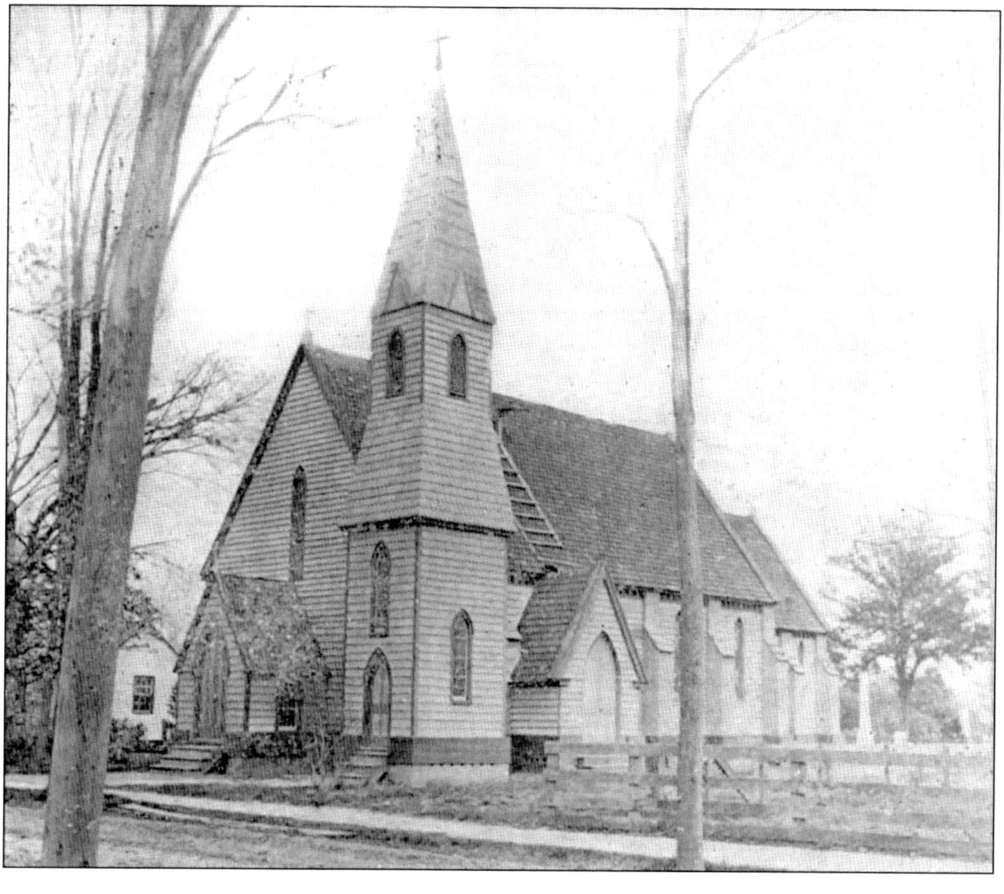

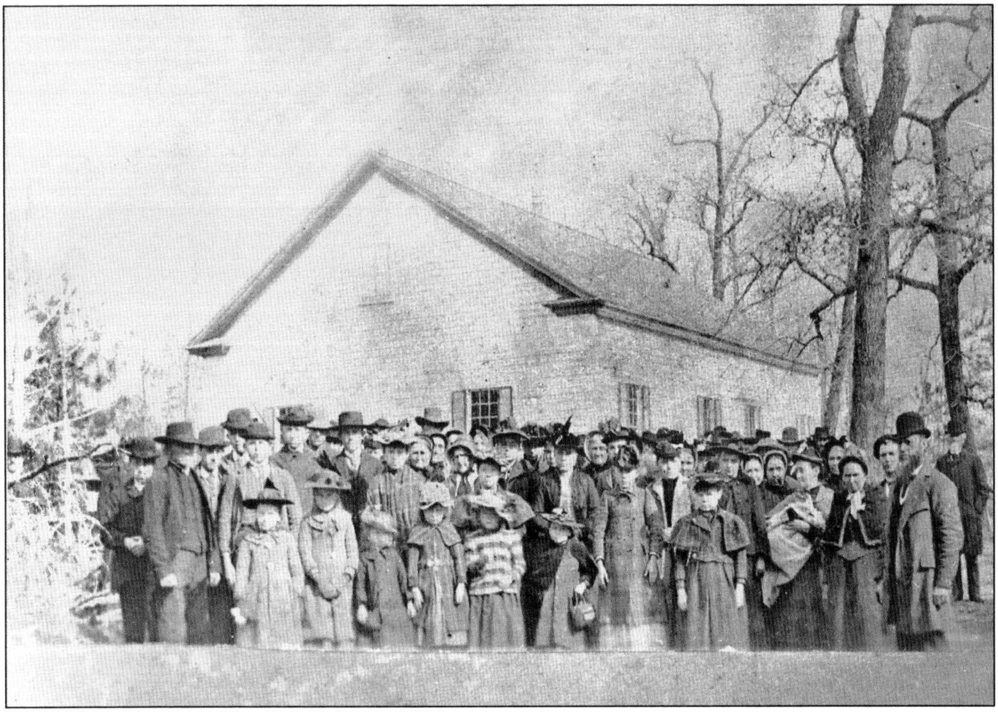

Probably taken in 1893, this photograph shows the congregation at Piney Woods Friends Meeting House near Belvidere. Friends, or Quakers, were once known for the wearing of hats and, indeed, there hardly seems to be a hatless person in the entire group. (Courtesy of Ruth Elliott Winslow.)

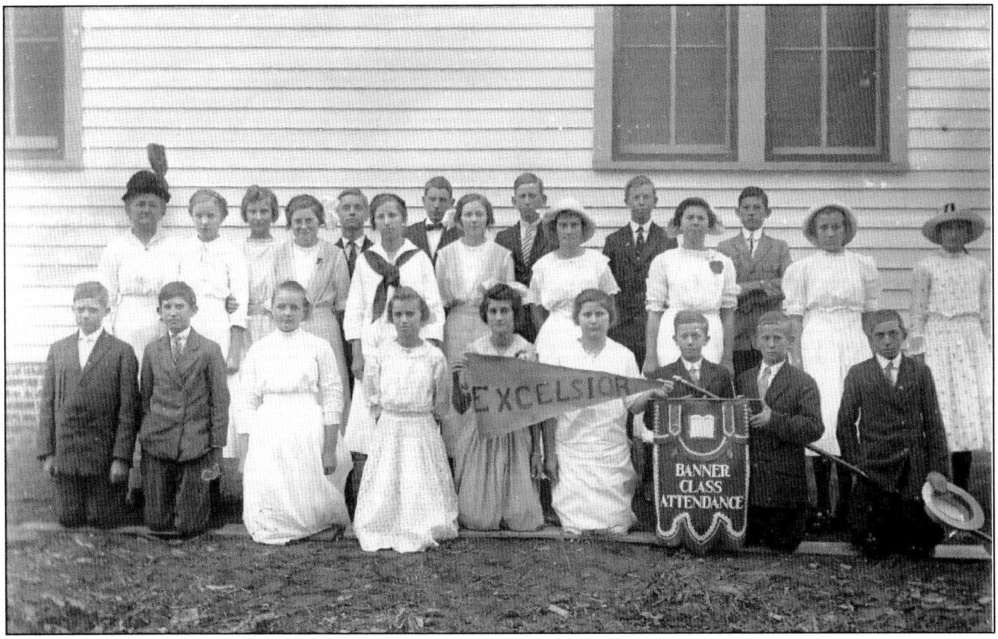

The 1915 "Excelsior" Sunday school class at Up River Friends Meeting appears to be the teenage group. (Courtesy of Lynwood C. Winslow III.)

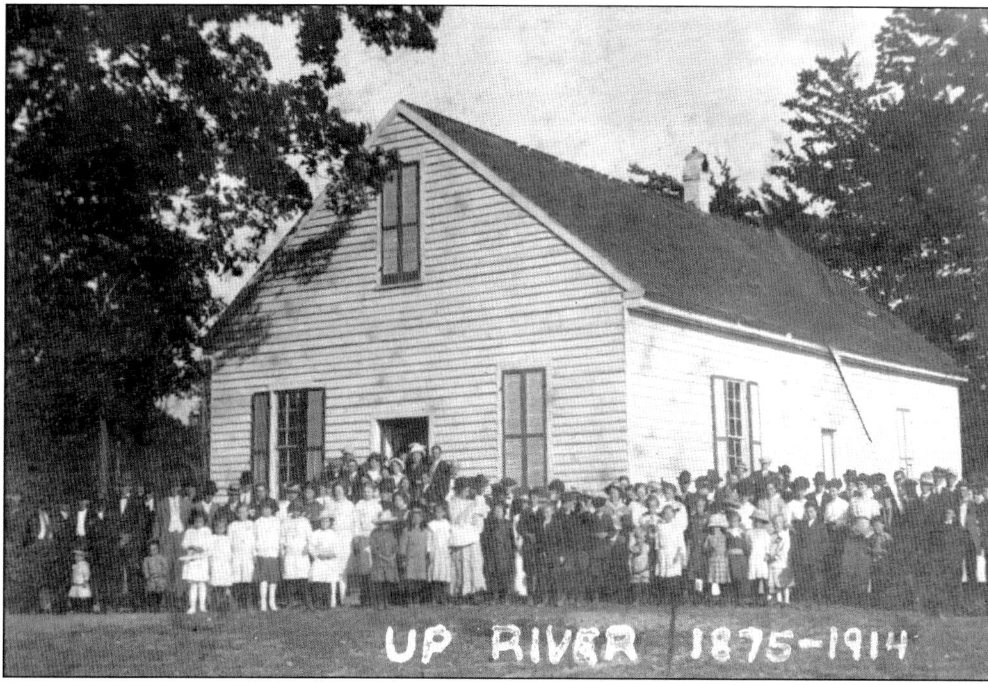

Friends at Up River Meeting built their first meetinghouse in 1875. This c. 1914 photograph shows the clean and simple lines of a utilitarian structure, with entrances on the front and side. The congregation was outgrowing the building, and a new meetinghouse would soon replace this one. (Courtesy of Lynwood C. Winslow III.)

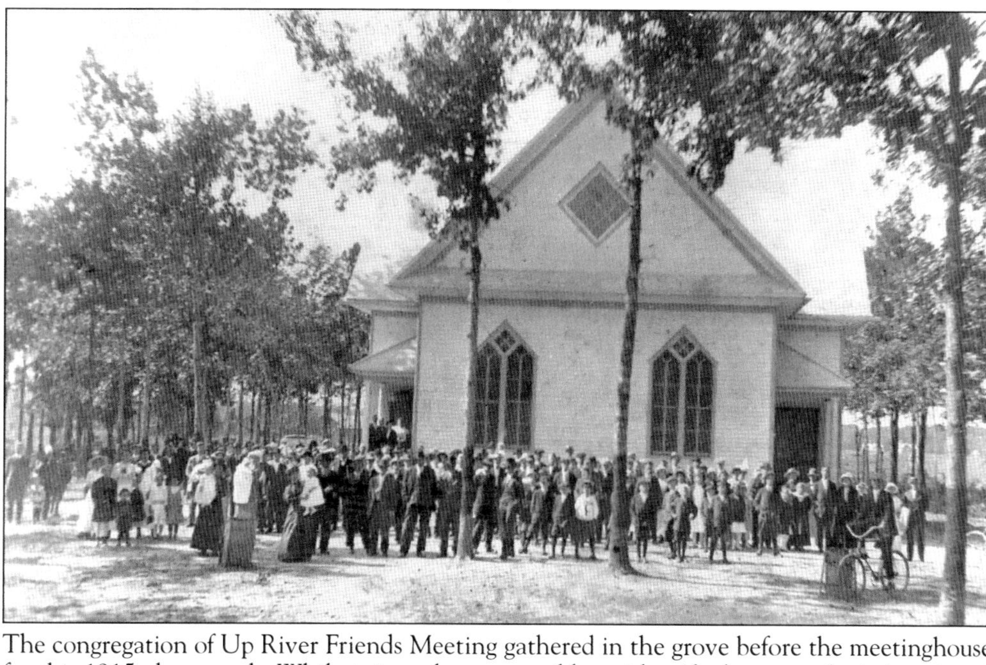

The congregation of Up River Friends Meeting gathered in the grove before the meetinghouse for this 1915 photograph. While it is no longer possible to identify these people, it is a virtual certainty that nearly all of them are related to the White and Winslow families. (Courtesy of Lynwood C. Winslow III.)

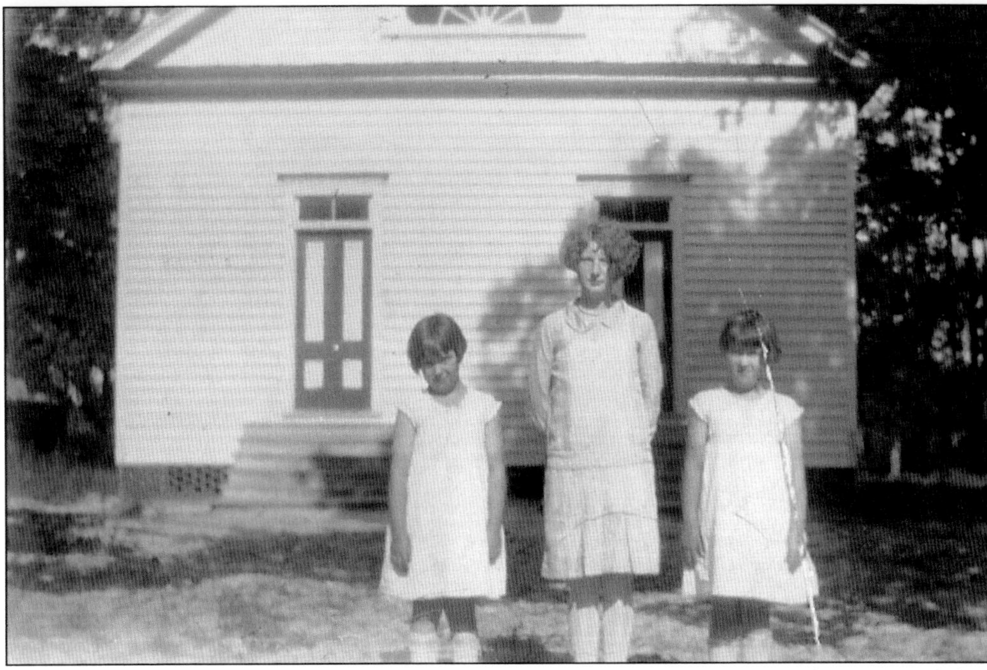

Chappell Hill Baptist Church forms a background for the Chappell sisters, shown from left to right to be Beulah, Piccola, and Eula, *c.* 1927. It was once common for Perquimans churches to have two entrances, one for males and one for females, and for men and women to sit in separate sections inside. (Courtesy of Peggy Lane.)

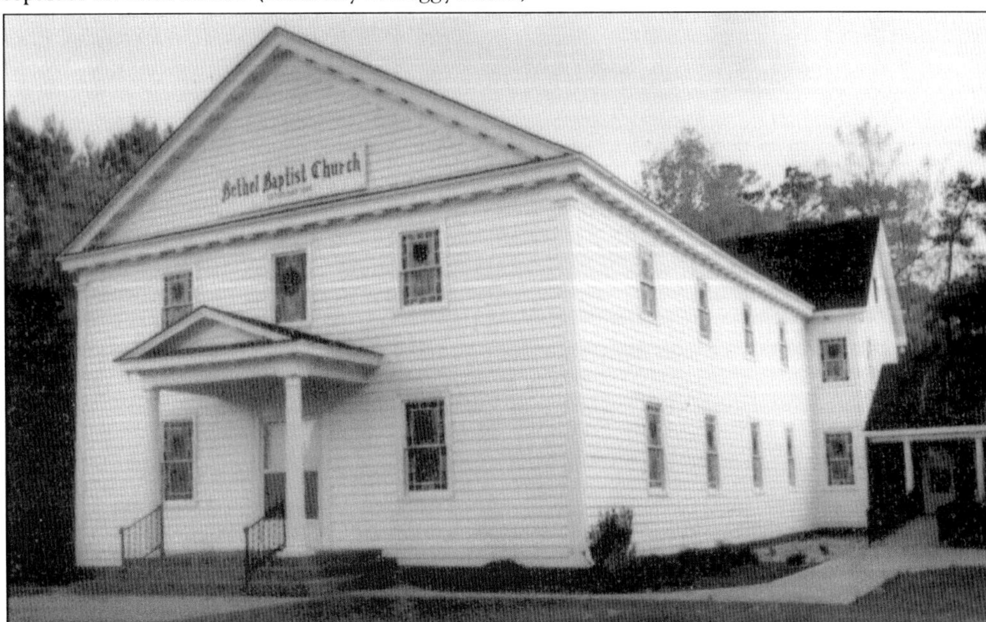

Bethel Baptist Church was organized in 1806 and is the oldest Baptist congregation in the county. The building was erected in 1837, but it has been substantially enlarged and remodeled in recent years. Since this photograph was taken, the exterior has been bricked over. (Courtesy of Joyce Hobbs.)

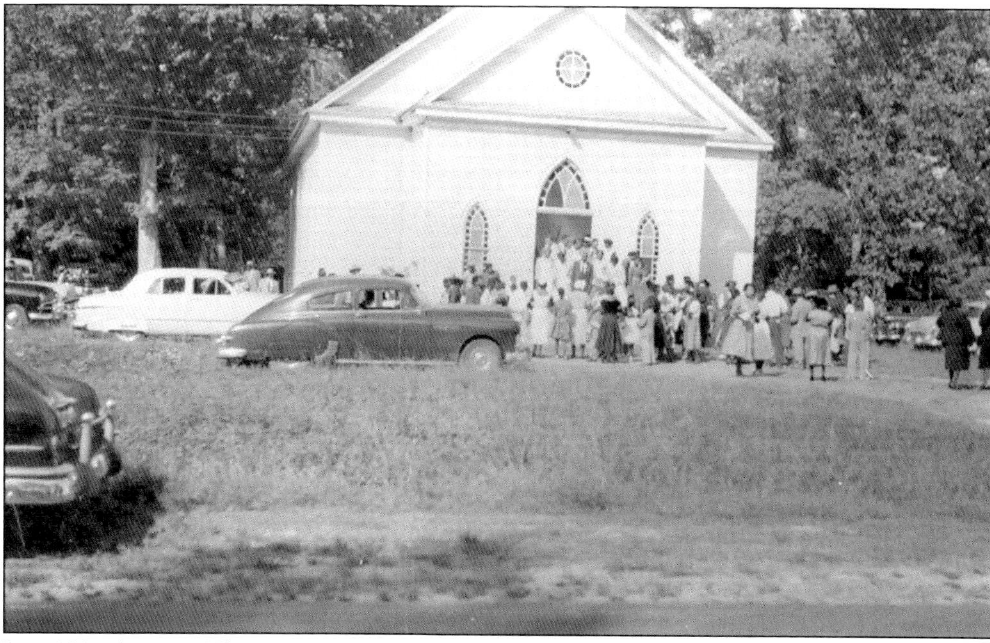

In 1888, deacons Thomas Nixon, Augustus White, Bacchus Hoskins, and Alfred Elliott purchased the lot near Winfall on which Melton's Grove Baptist Church would soon be built. In this 1950s photograph, the congregation is shown leaving the church. (Courtesy of Bertha Dixon.)

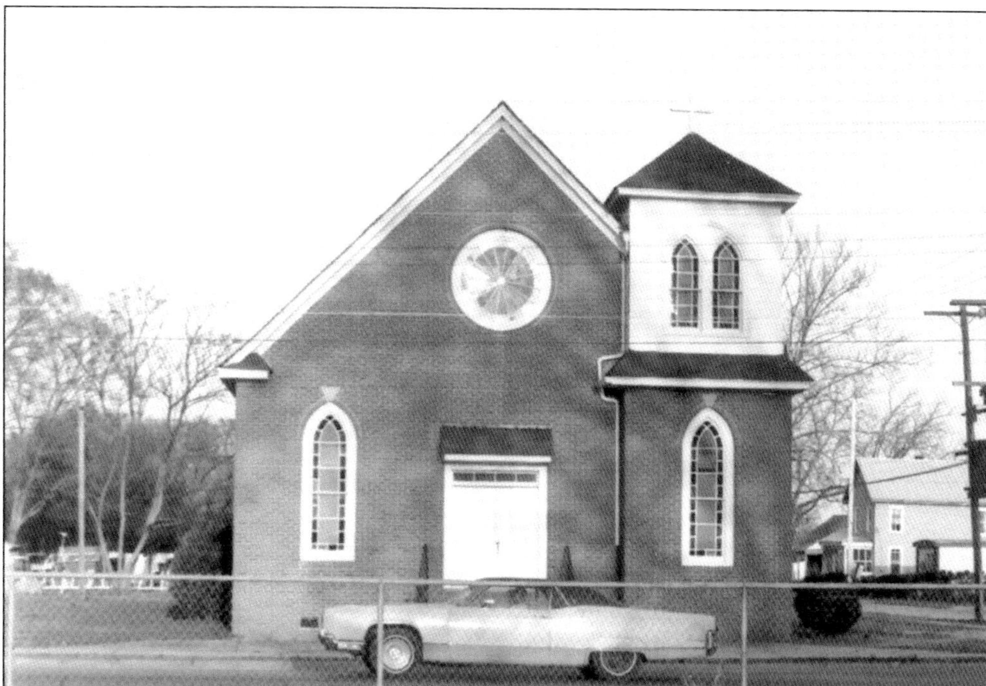

First Baptist Church was organized in 1866 by freedmen and the congregation has worshiped on this site on Hyde Park Street since 1871. The oldest part of the present building dates from c. 1897. (Courtesy of Town of Hertford.)

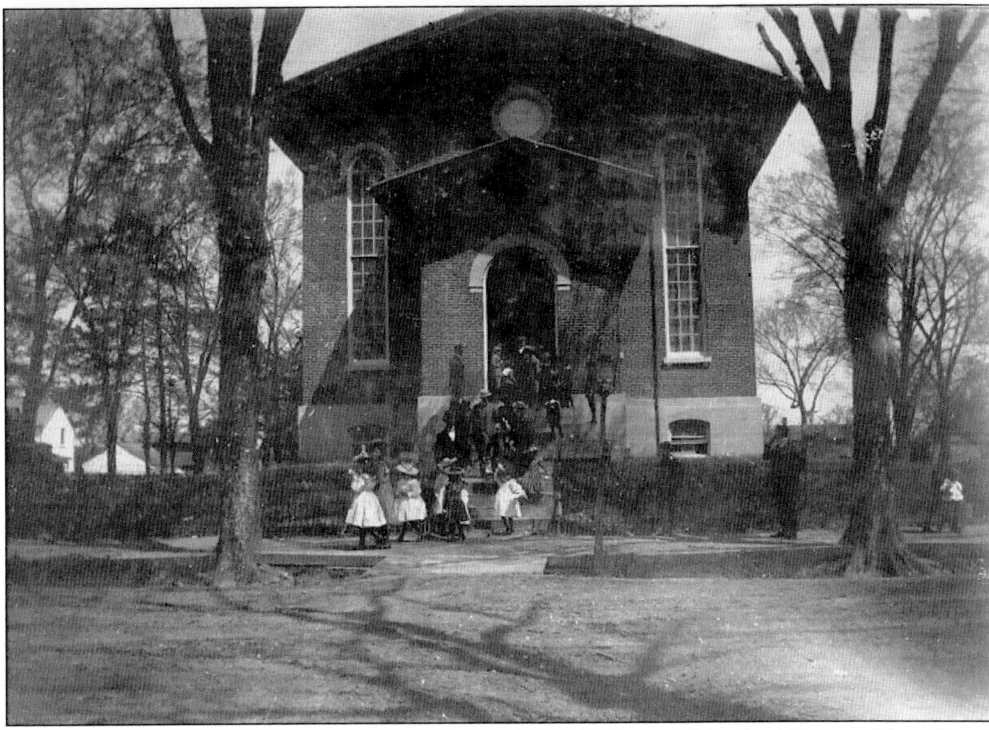

In this early view of Hertford Baptist Church, built in 1854, there are numerous trees that add a pleasant appearance to the town. Less attractive is the little bridge (center) crossing the ditch lying between sidewalk and street. (Courtesy of Hertford Baptist Church.)

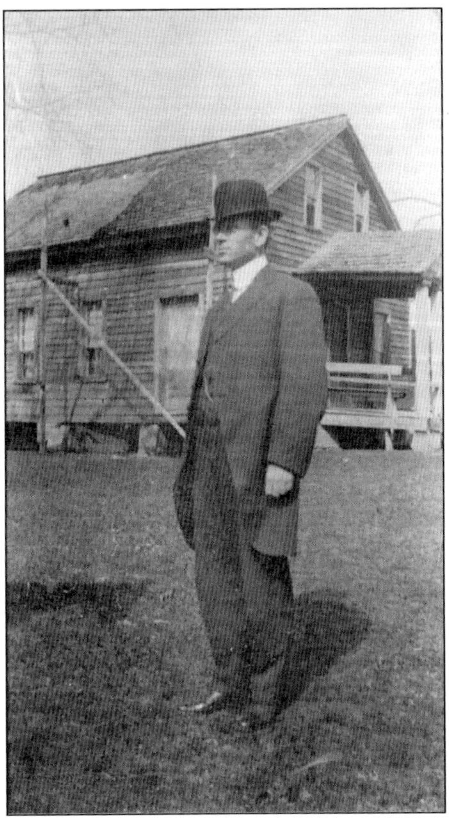

The Rev. Alexander A. Butler was a Baptist minister who served Hertford Baptist Church from 1908 to 1914. He was still living in Hertford in 1930. The house may be the Thomas D. Perry House in the Bay Branch vicinity. (Courtesy of Thelma Chappell Riddick.)

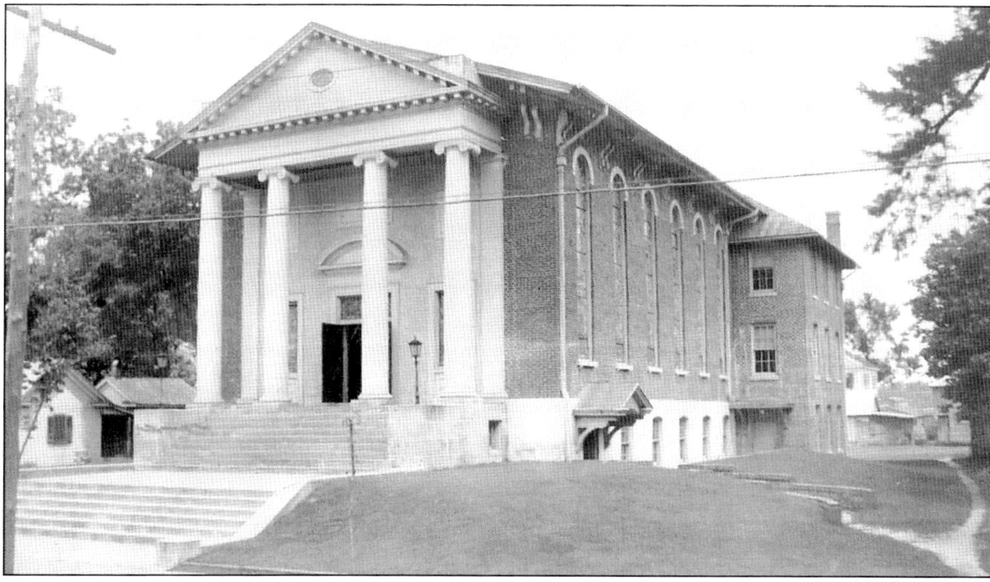

An intermediate stage in the expansion of the Hertford Baptist Church is depicted here. An imposing portico has enhanced the front of the building, while congregational needs have been addressed by the addition of an educational annex at the rear, but the crowning steeple is yet to come. (Courtesy of Hertford Baptist Church.)

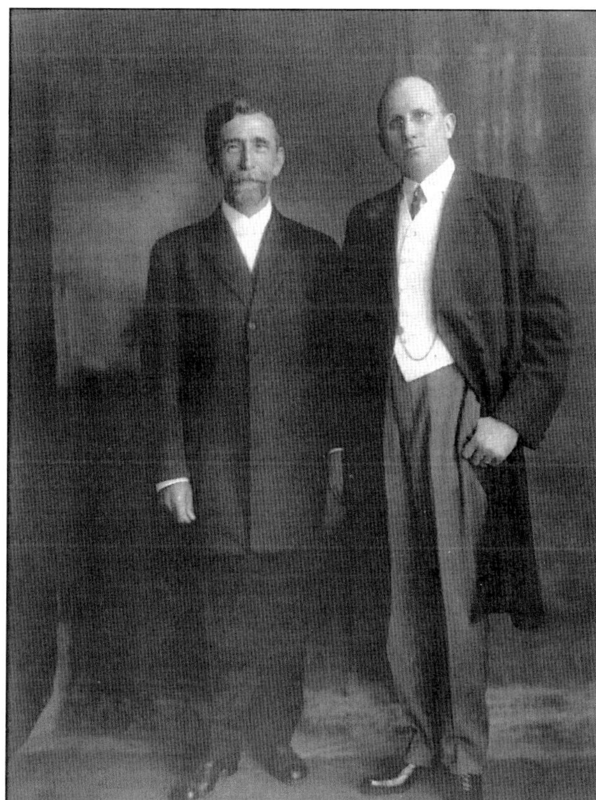

Two pastors of Hertford Baptist Church joined for a photograph, c. 1920. Josiah Elliott (left) was pastor from 1893 to 1897, while Beecher L. Rhodes served from 1919 to 1923. Elliott was the epitome of the local man called to a Perquimans pulpit, while Rhodes was typical of the outsiders called to serve county churches. (Courtesy of Charles T. Skinner Jr.)

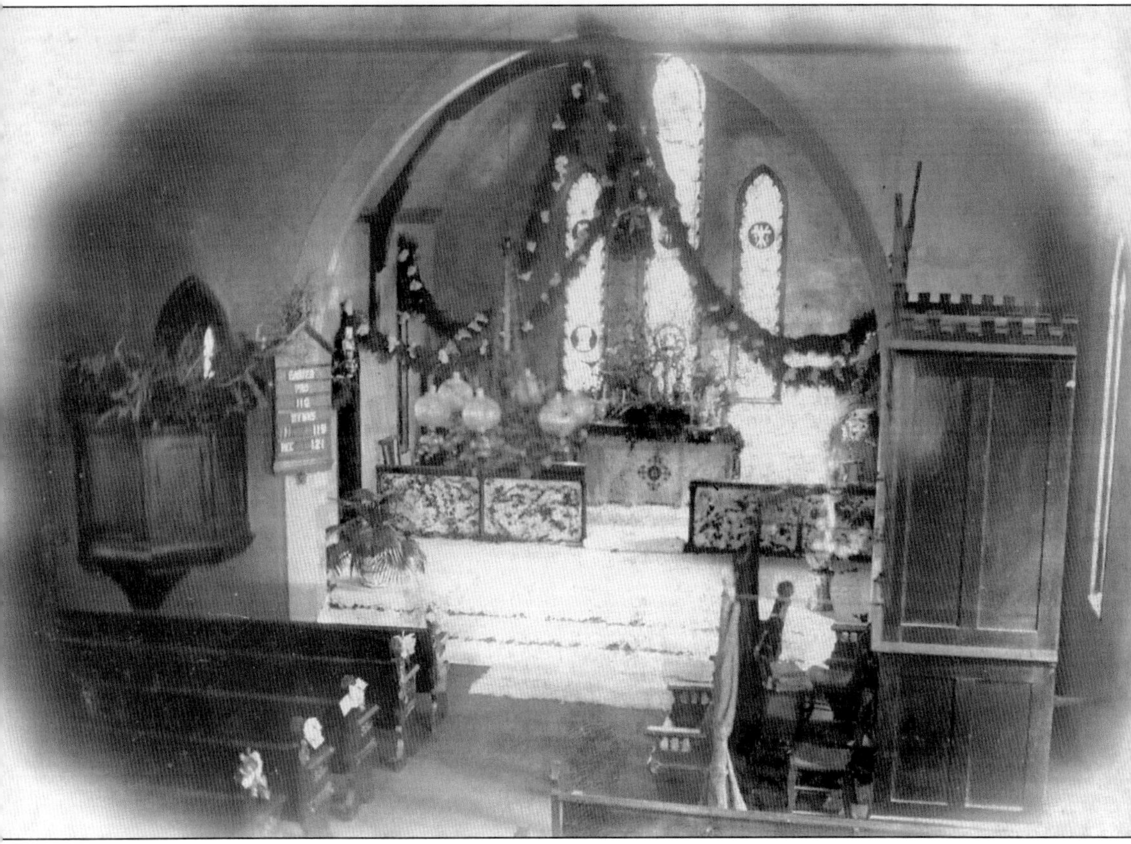

Easter garlands festoon Holy Trinity Episcopal Church, *c.* 1905. The *c.* 1854 Jardine organ (right) is still in regular use. (Courtesy of Museum of the Albemarle.)

Six

IN TOWN

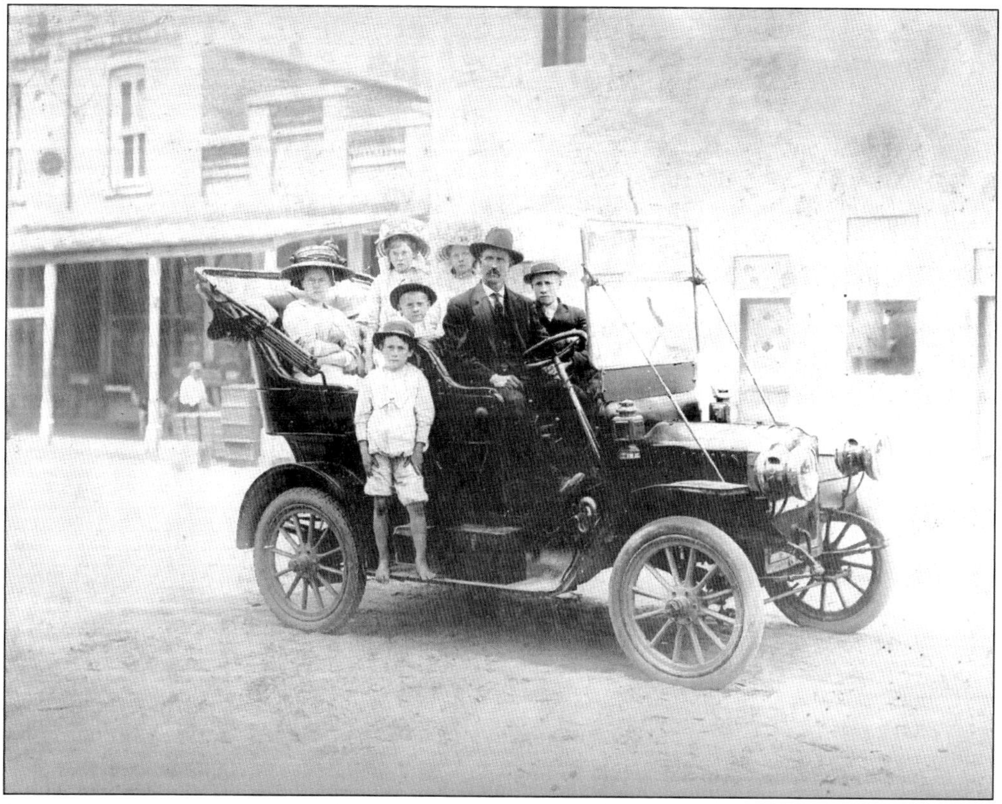

A new car is exciting, especially when it is one of the first in your neighborhood. Fernando C. White (at wheel) and family of Whiteston motored to Hertford and stopped in the middle of Market Street for a photograph in 1912. In the background are the Mills Eure Building, Benbury's Barber Shop, and Smith's Drug Store. (Courtesy of Lynwood C. Winslow III.)

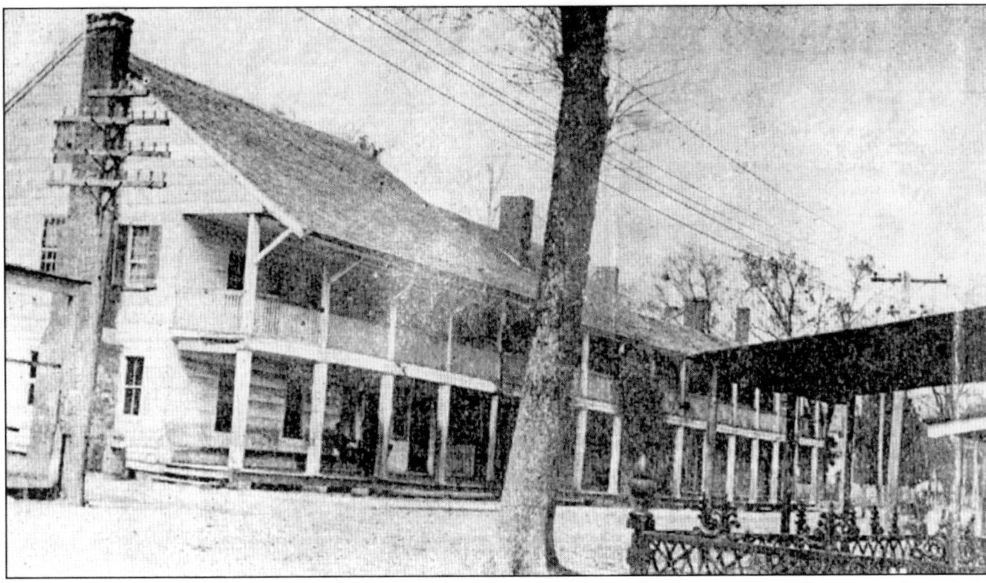

One of Hertford's most notable buildings was the Eagle Hotel. It began modestly in the 1760s and grew under various names and managements to become the principal hotel/boardinghouse in town. It stretched along the west side of Church Street south of Grubb until progress demolished it, *c.* 1915. (Courtesy of Dorothy Oakey Read.)

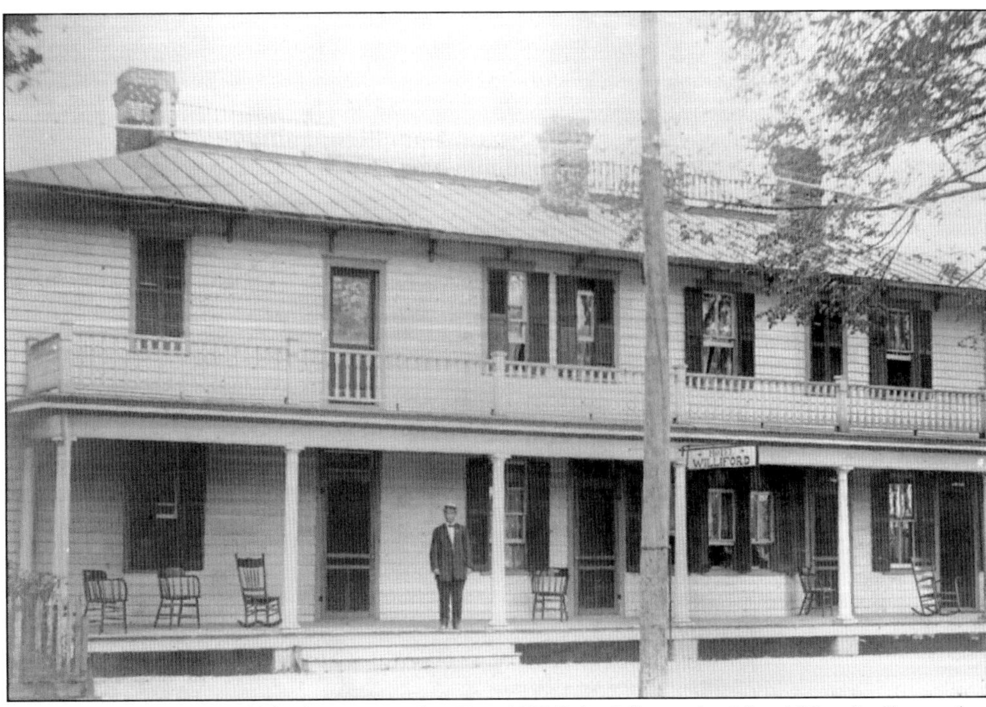

Built by Charles V. Williford in 1911, the Hotel Williford (later the Hotel Hertford) stood on Market Street just east of Hertford Baptist Church. It was patronized by commercial travelers and visitors who could not stay with relatives. (Courtesy of Charles T. Skinner Jr.)

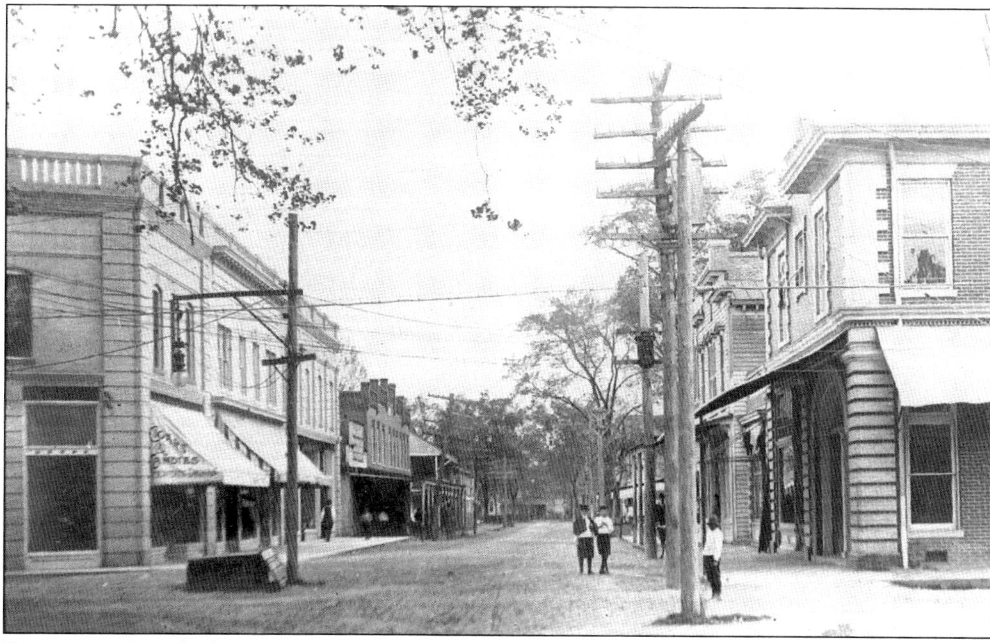

Downtown Hertford was sprouting utility poles in this *c.* 1912 view up Church Street from the Market Street intersection. Many of the visible buildings no longer exist, including the Eagle Hotel (near center in distance), Charles Morgan's store (frame building right of poles), and the old Hertford Bank (far right). (Courtesy of Charles T. Skinner Jr.)

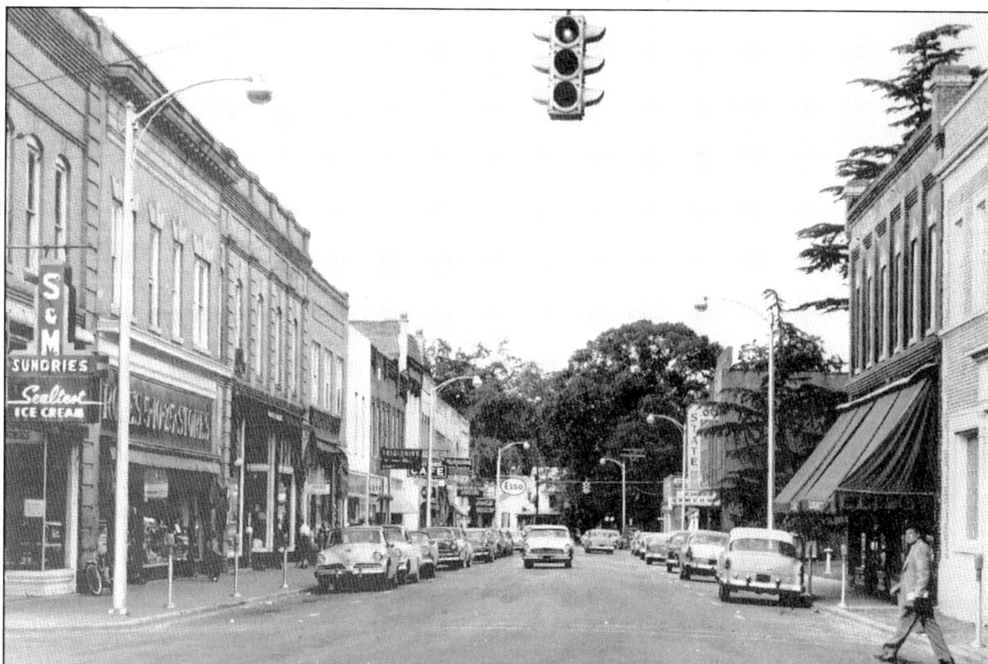

The buildings shown in this *c.* 1964 view of Hertford (looking north up Church Street from Market Street) still stand, but many of the signs advertise businesses no longer in operation. (From *Kilcocanen*, 1964.)

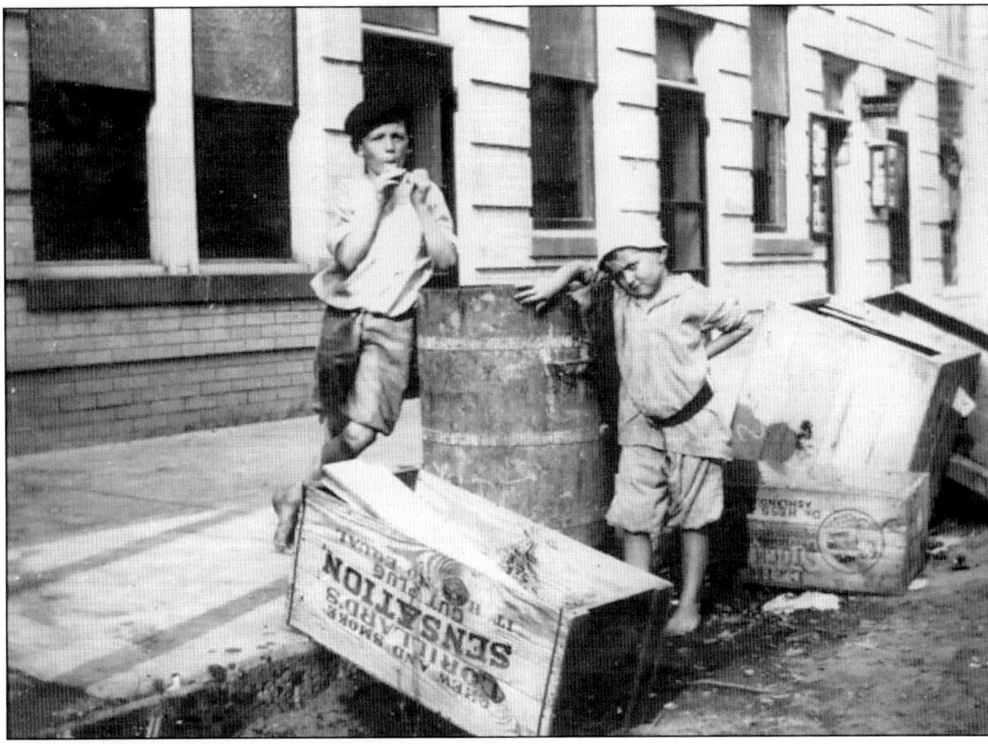

We hope "our gang" has not been partaking of the contents of the cut plug box in the foreground. In the background is the Market Street side of the drugstore Dr. Robert W. Smith built in 1911, which now houses Woodard's Pharmacy. (Courtesy of Charles T. Skinner Jr.)

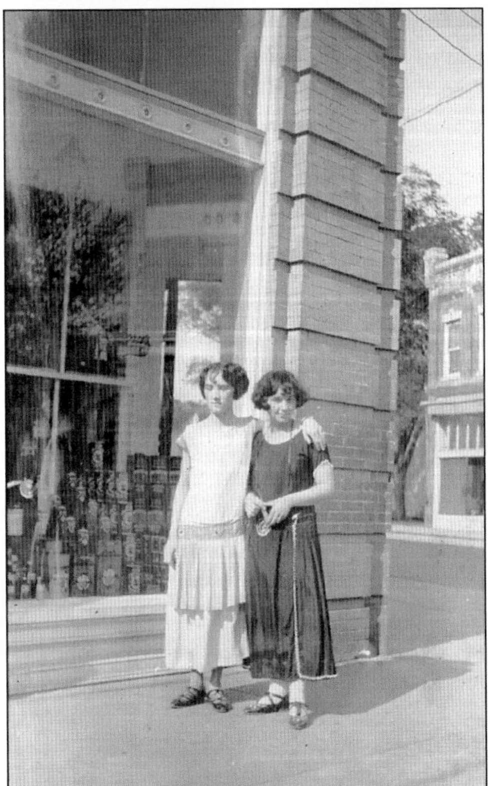

Two stylish young ladies promenade down Market Street past Dr. Smith's drugstore (left), c. 1923. Blanchard's general store appears across Church Street at right. (Courtesy of Claudia Brinn Bunch.)

William Shannonhouse leans against the well near the corner of Market and Church Streets before 1913. The rustic Shannonhouse general store at the left would soon be demolished to make way for a brick building. The well would disappear when the streets were paved. (Courtesy of Charles T. Skinner Jr.)

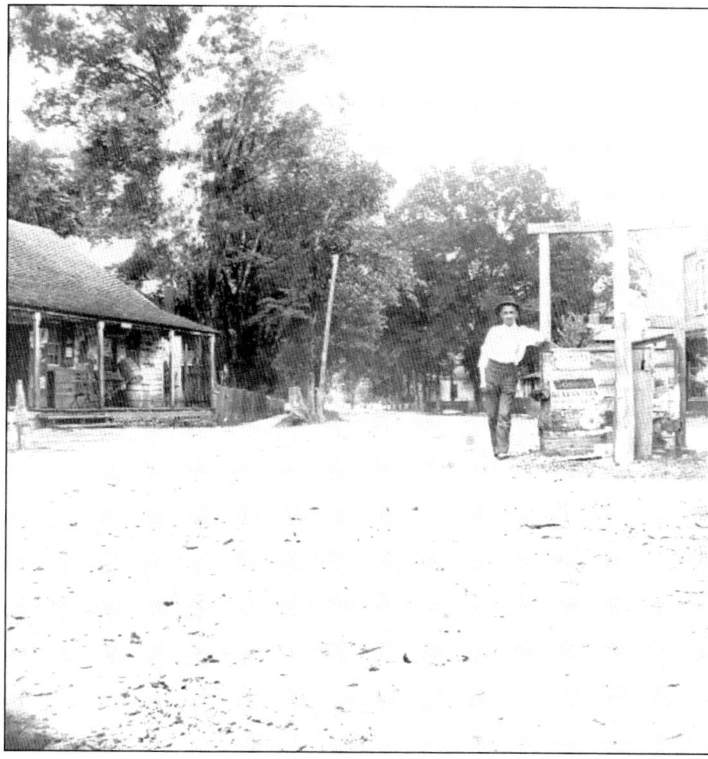

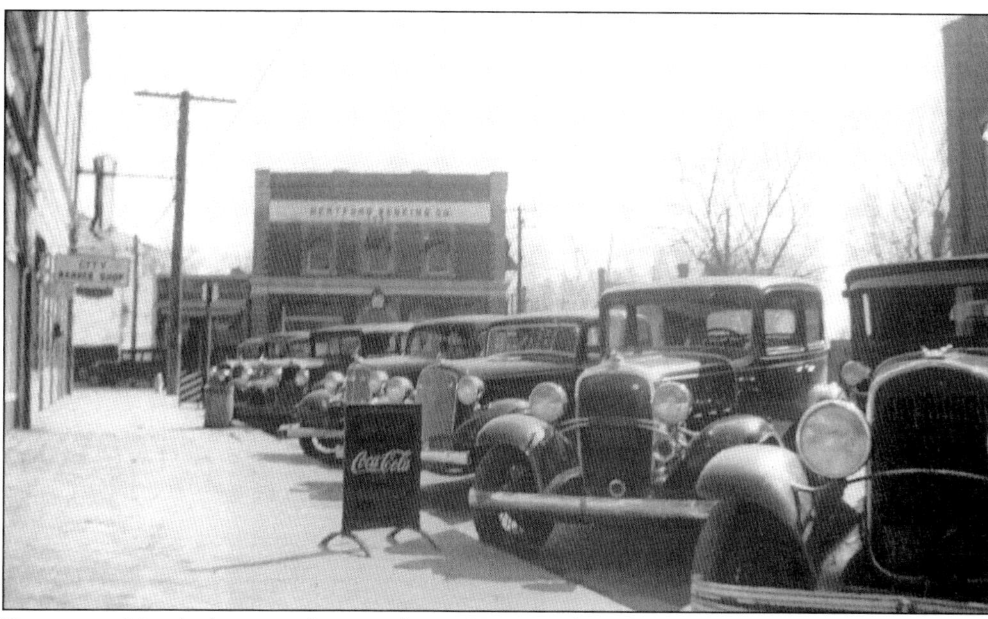

Downtown Hertford appears busy in this 1937 view of Market Street looking towards Church Street. Of the visible commercial buildings, only those to the left of the utility pole still exist. City Barber Shop and Hertford Banking Company have modern counterparts next to the old sites. (Courtesy of Charles T. Skinner Jr.)

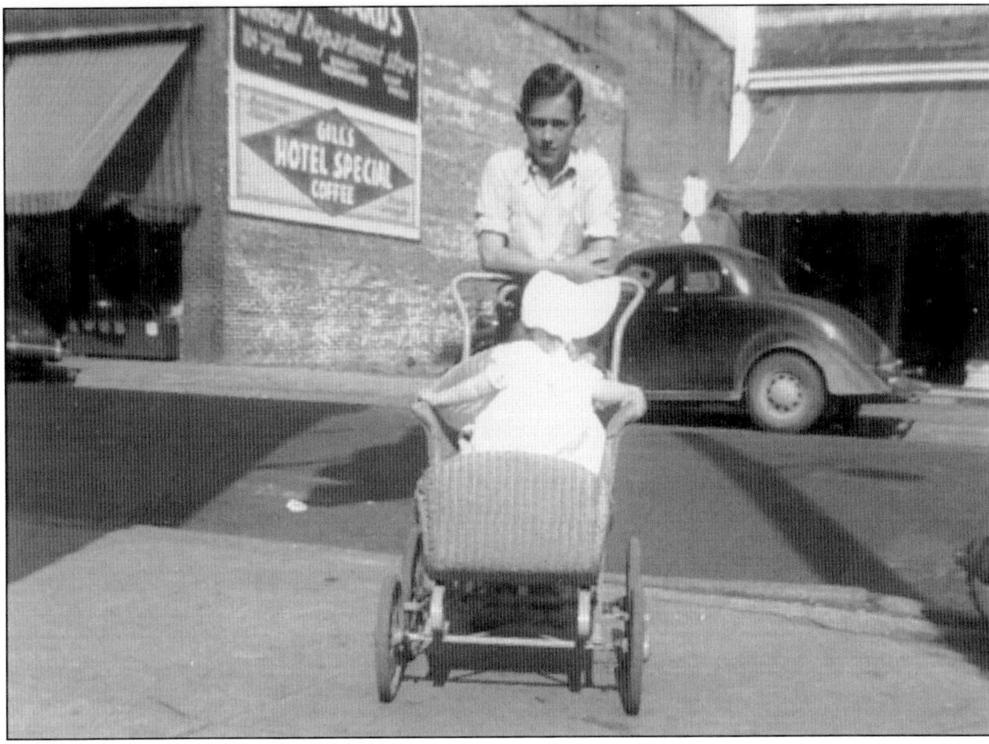

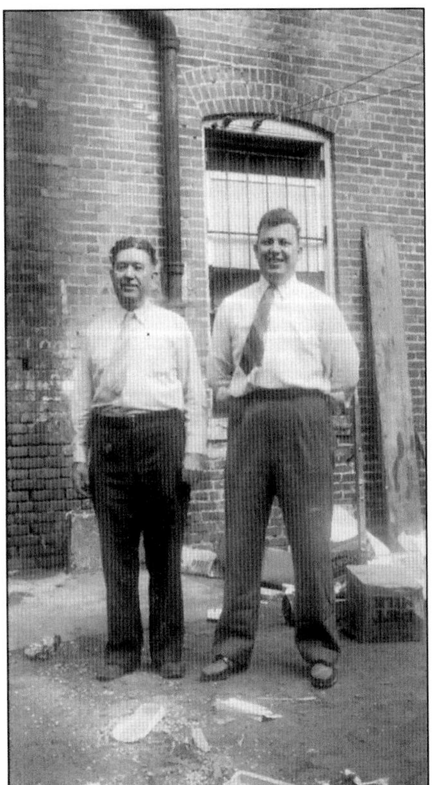

Since Billy White is watching the camera, baby Kay Matthews has to look out for traffic on Church Street, c. 1940. In the background (left) is Blanchard's store, housing a firm then over a century old; the building is now the Courthouse Annex. (Courtesy of Kay Matthews Whedbee.)

Robbins Blanchard (left) and G.A. "Frog" White were longtime employees of J.C. Blanchard & Company. This 1942 photograph shows the back of Blanchard's store, with sewage pipes and electrical wires visible in the background. (Courtesy of Carolyn Lane.)

The ground behind Darden Department Store has been mostly paved over since Vivian N. Darden posed with his daughter Florence, *c.* 1924. The wooden building at the left was soon to be replaced by a two-story brick store. (Courtesy of Florence Darden Christensen.)

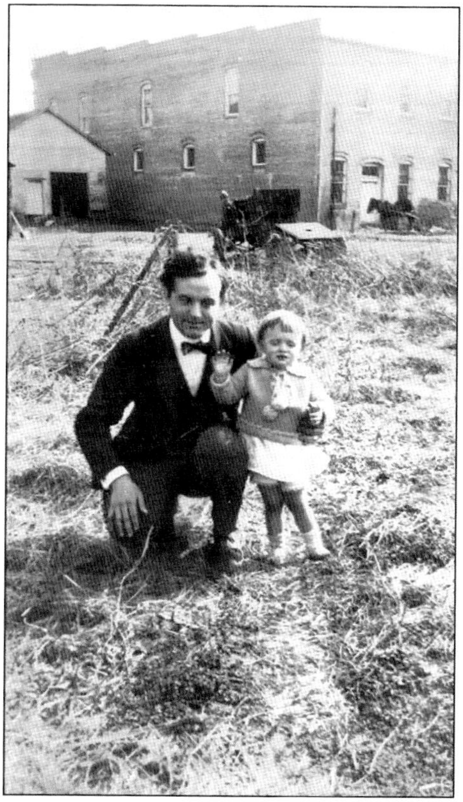

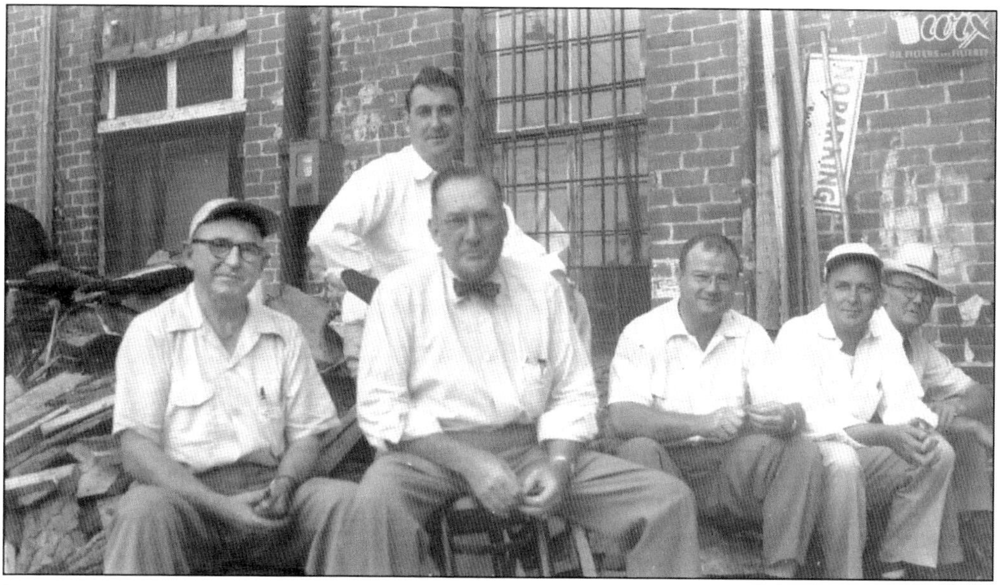

Despite a no-parking sign in the background, several gentlemen are relaxing behind Hertford Café in 1952. They are, from left to right, (front) auto parts dealer Ralph Murray, general practitioner Carlton Davenport, dentist Allan Bonner, Mr. Jackson, and mail carrier Charles Sumner; (back) Charles Murray. (Courtesy of Carlton A. Davenport Jr.)

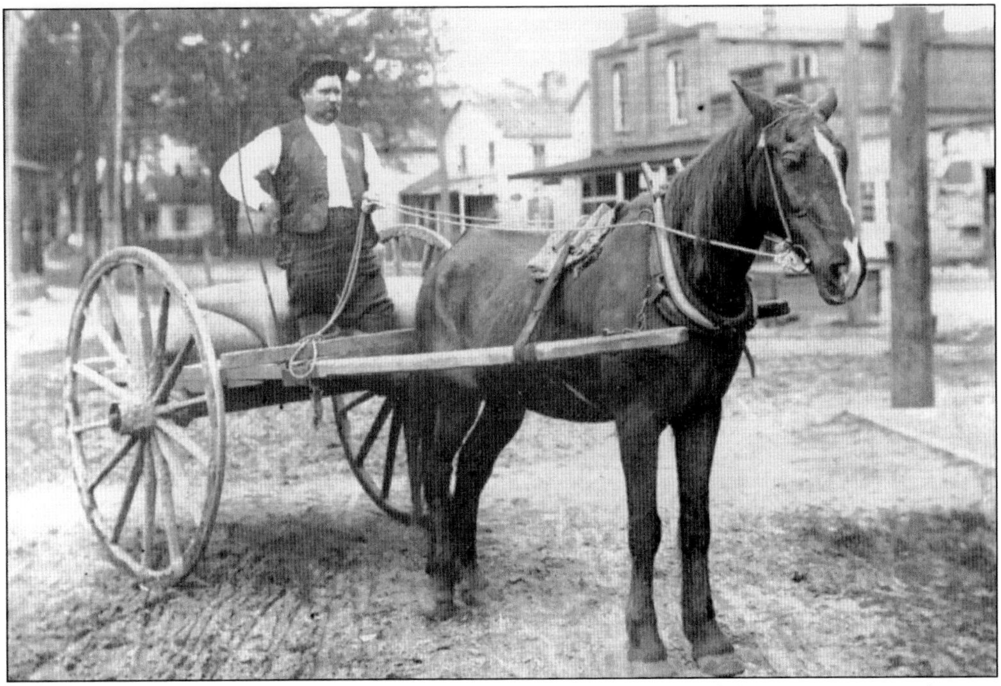

John R. "No Legs" Jackson (1862–1918) did not let a physical disability prevent a productive life. A drayman, he transported all manner of freight. He was keeper of the Hertford bridge and a grocer for a time. In this c. 1909 photograph, he poses his rig at the corner of Market and Church Streets. Behind the horse's head is a public well. (Courtesy of Charles T. Skinner Jr.)

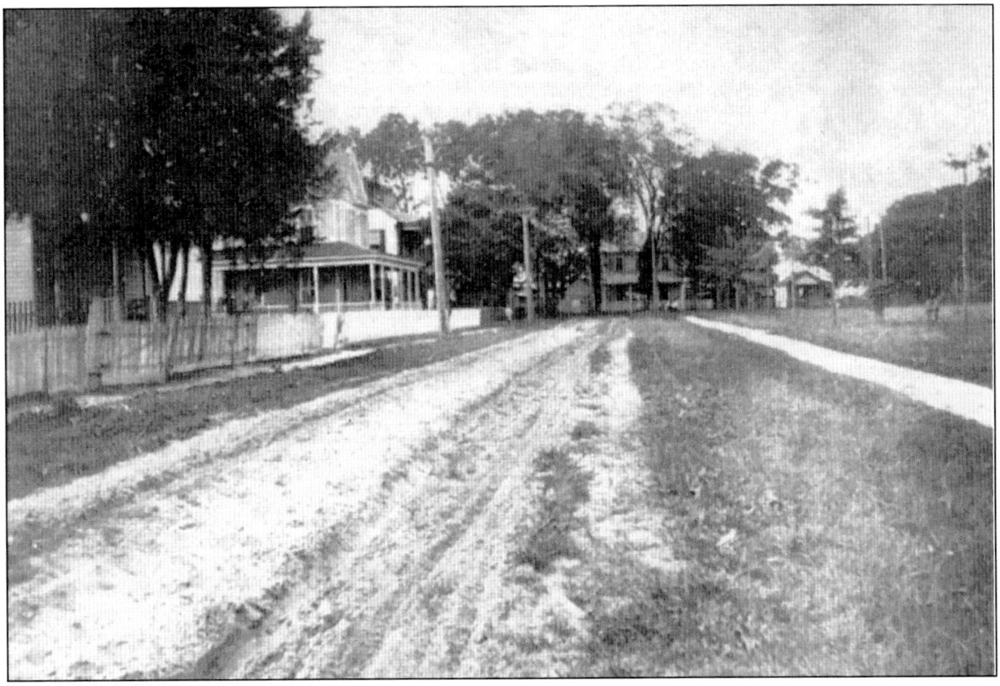

West Academy Street, looking north toward Grubb Street, has a rustic air in this c. 1920 view. Most of the buildings shown no longer exist. (Courtesy of Charles T. Skinner Jr.)

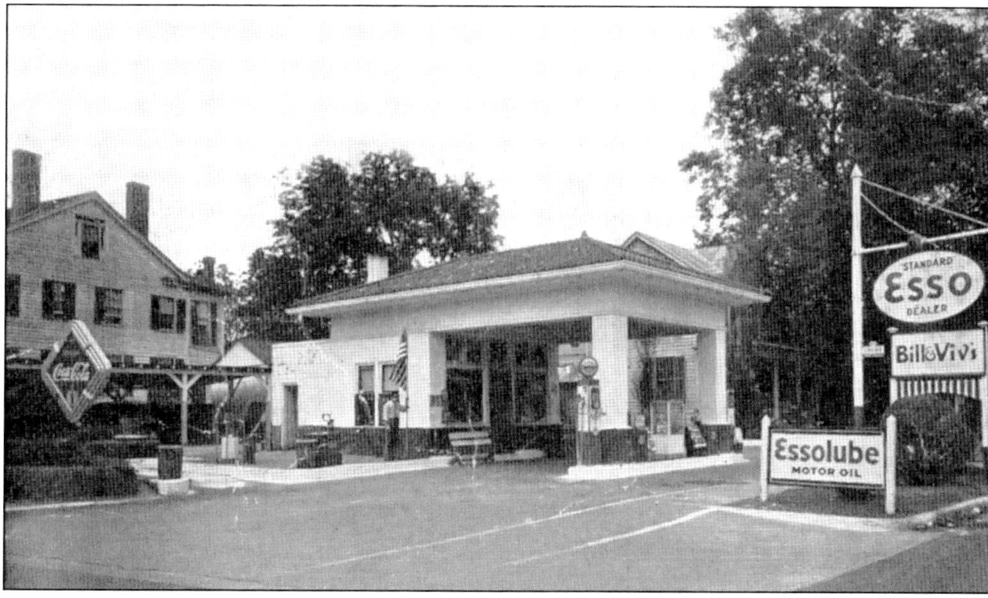

When automobiles became prevalent, filling stations sprang up on many Hertford corners. Bill and Viv's, seen here c. 1940, was on the northwest corner of Church and Grubb Streets. Bill Divers and Vivian Matthews were proprietors of this Esso dealership. At left is the old Wilson Reed house, which formerly stood on this same corner; it was moved several feet down the street, no doubt in the name of "progress." (Courtesy of Kay Matthews Whedbee.)

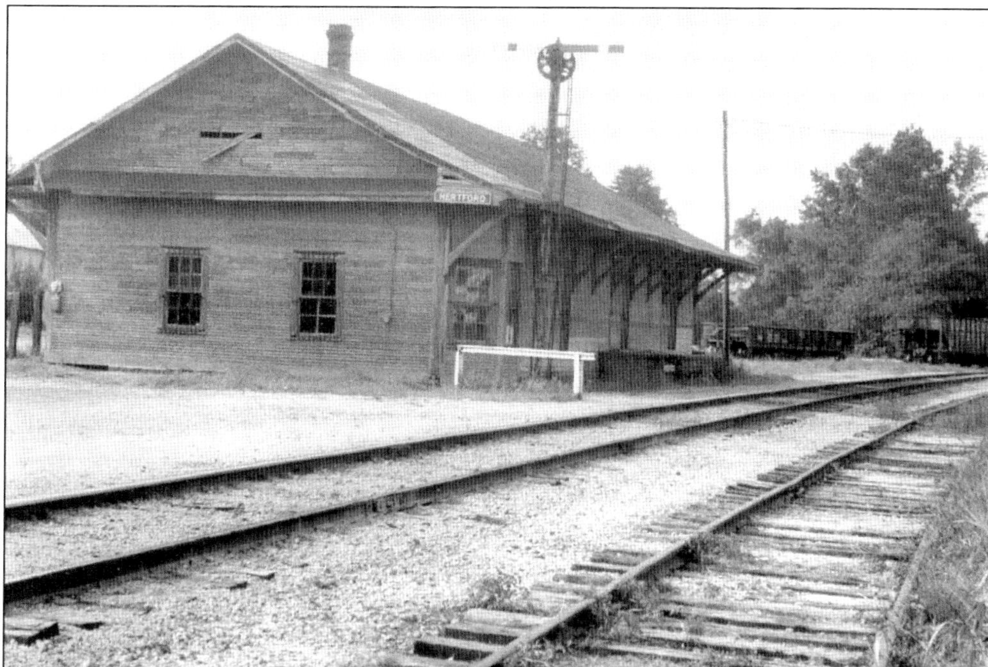

The Hertford railroad station is shown in decline. In its heyday, from the 1880s until the 1940s, the Norfolk & Southern Railroad brought freight and passengers to town. The availability of such convenient transportation encouraged several growth spurts in the local economy. (Courtesy of Frank Roberts.)

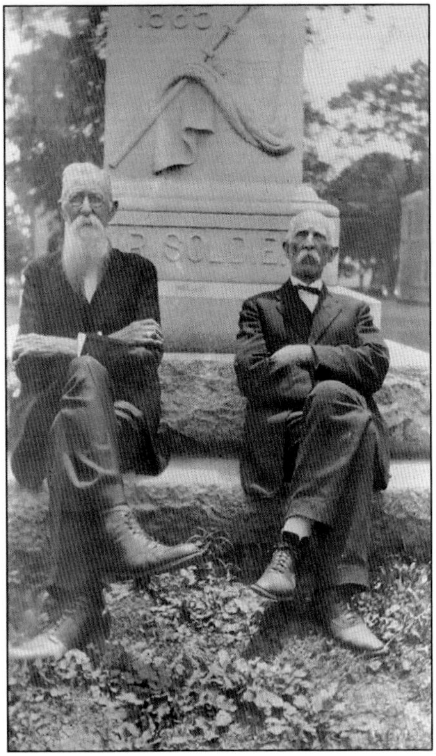

Perquimans sent hundreds of men to the Confederate Army. Few of them were still living when the photographer found two unidentified veterans at the Confederate monument in the 1920s. (Courtesy of Claudia Brinn Bunch.)

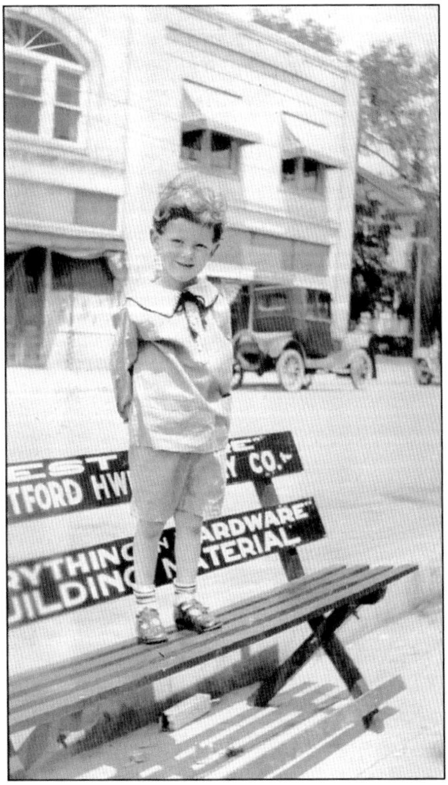

An unidentified little tyke stands on a Hertford Hardware bench in the 1920s, with Church Street behind him. The Grubb Street intersection appears at right. (Courtesy of Claudia Brinn Bunch.)

The Confederate monument on the Courthouse Green is decorated with flag, flowers, and cannon. The McCallum house in the background would be shorn of its porches, c. 1920. (Courtesy of Margaret Ainsley Brewin.)

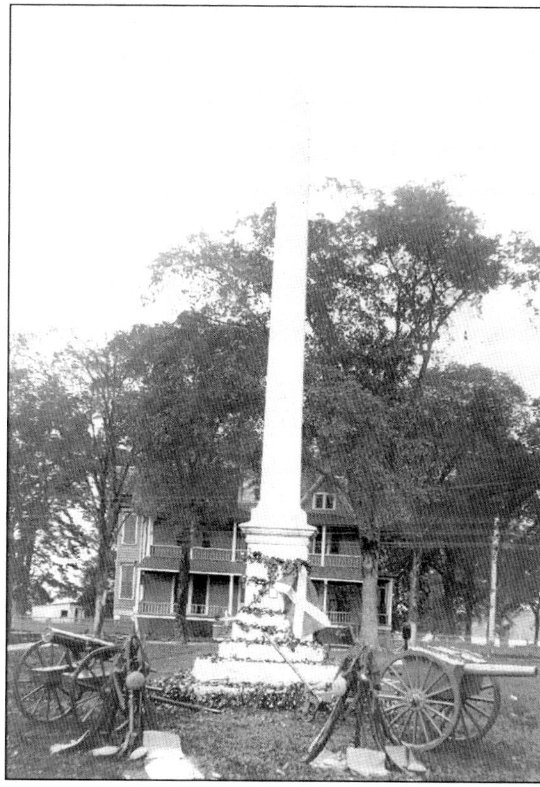

Perquimans County Courthouse has served the county since 1825. In this mid-20th–century photograph, the Federal-style structure has yet to undergo several major alterations and enlargements. The building still houses some of the oldest public records in North Carolina. (Courtesy of Florence Darden Christensen.)

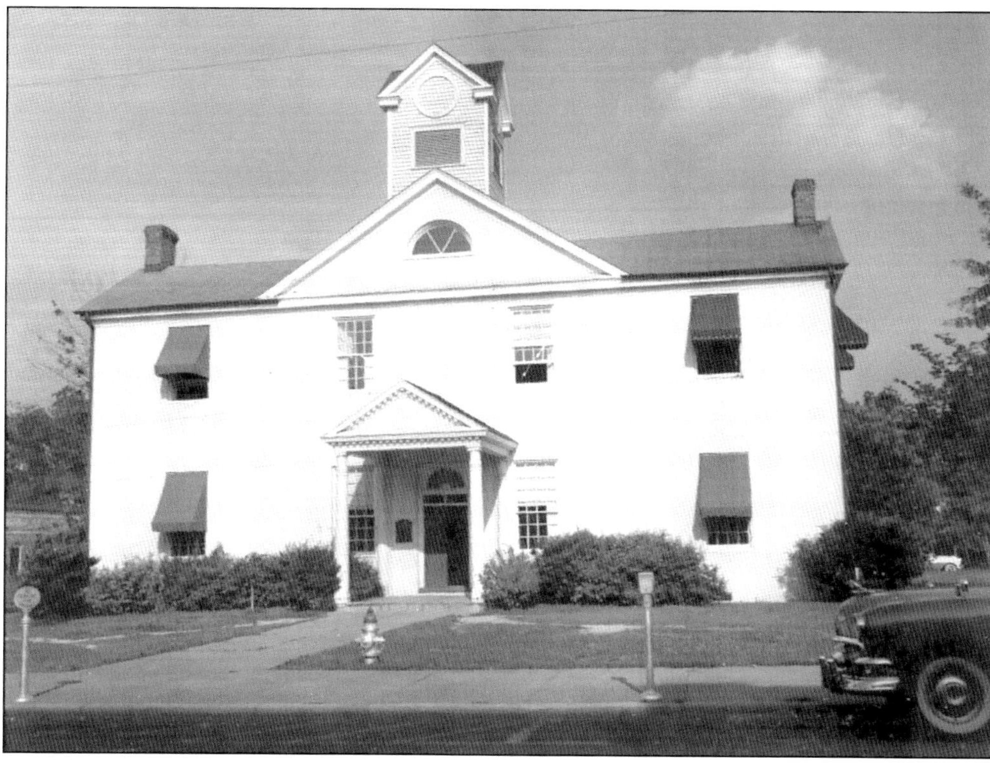

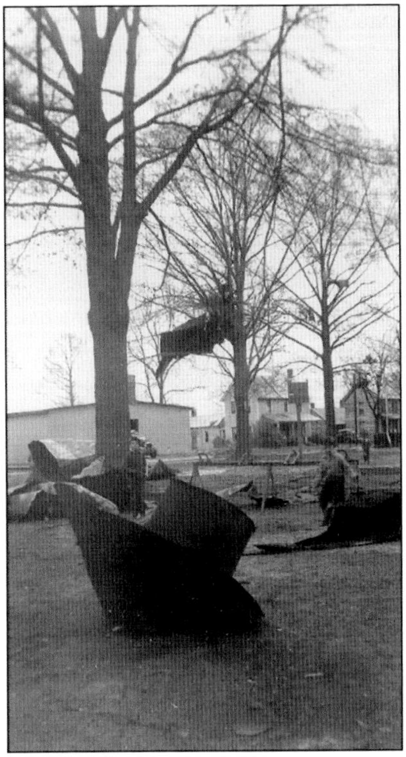

Sections of the Hertford Grammar School roof litter the playground after a tornado in 1944 or 1945. Tornadoes and hurricanes are not uncommon in Perquimans. (Courtesy of Ruth Elliott Winslow.)

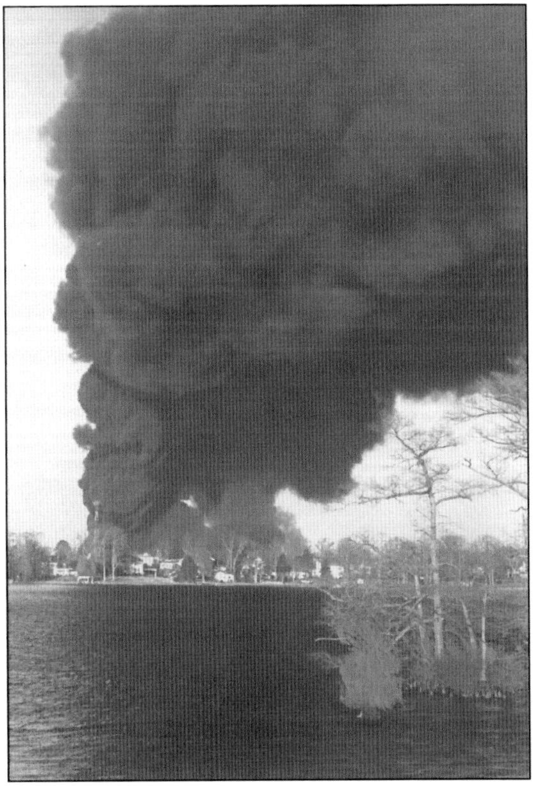

Looking west from the Perquimans River Bridge, the plume of smoke emanating from the oil fire of January 10, 1978, seems larger than the town of Hertford. U.S. Coast Guard personnel assisted in containing the fuel, which threatened to spread the fire across the river. (Courtesy of Charles T. Skinner Jr.)

Seven

ON THE WATER

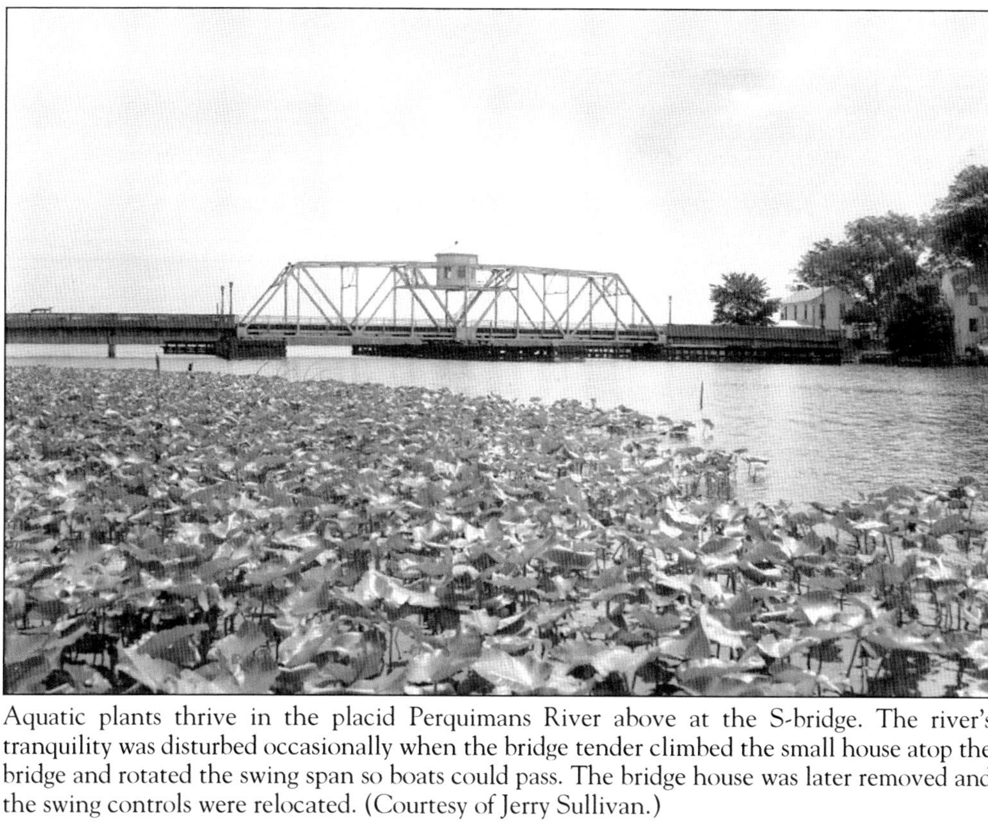

Aquatic plants thrive in the placid Perquimans River above at the S-bridge. The river's tranquility was disturbed occasionally when the bridge tender climbed the small house atop the bridge and rotated the swing span so boats could pass. The bridge house was later removed and the swing controls were relocated. (Courtesy of Jerry Sullivan.)

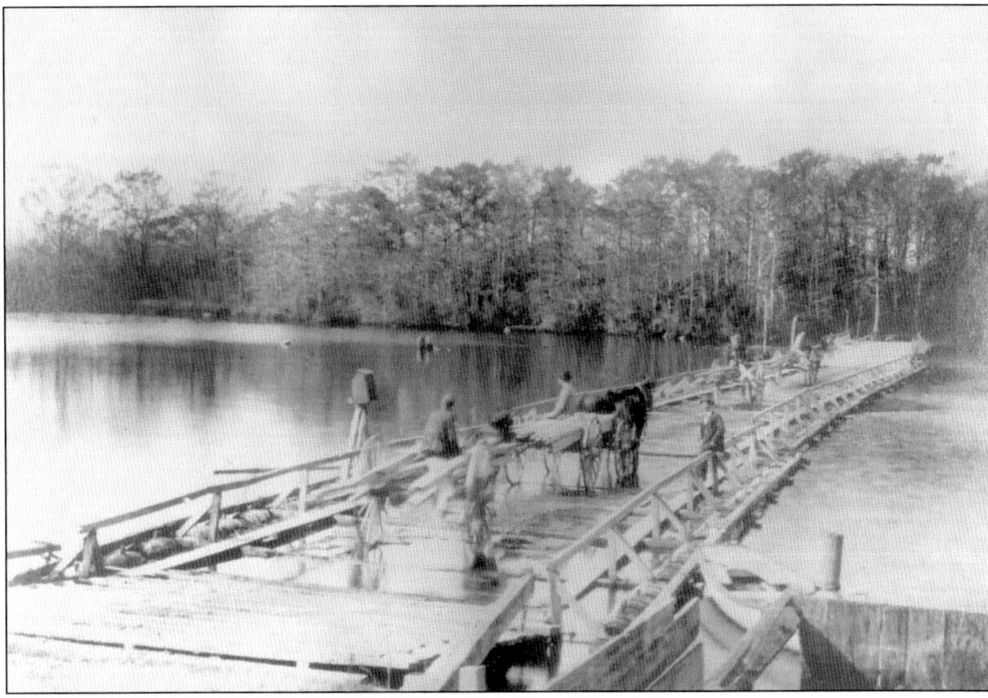

The float bridge across Perquimans River at Hertford was photographed, *c.* 1895. Serving the public for about a century, the bridge rested on the water, buoyed up by empty barrels down the sides. Boats could not pass unless a hinged draw in the center was opened. (Courtesy of Prue Newby Reed.)

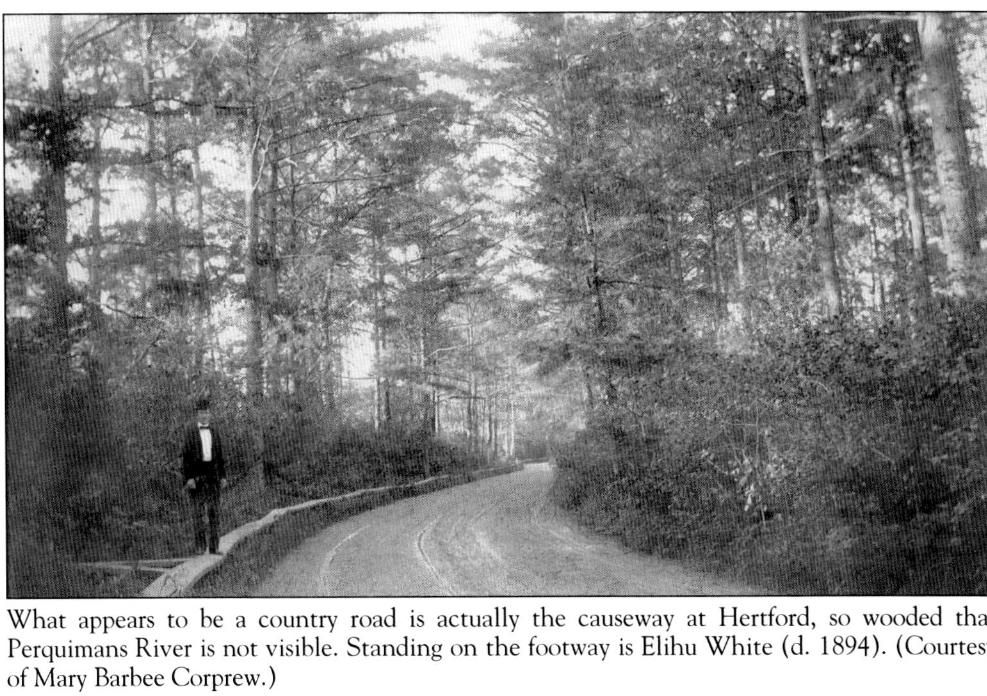

What appears to be a country road is actually the causeway at Hertford, so wooded that Perquimans River is not visible. Standing on the footway is Elihu White (d. 1894). (Courtesy of Mary Barbee Corprew.)

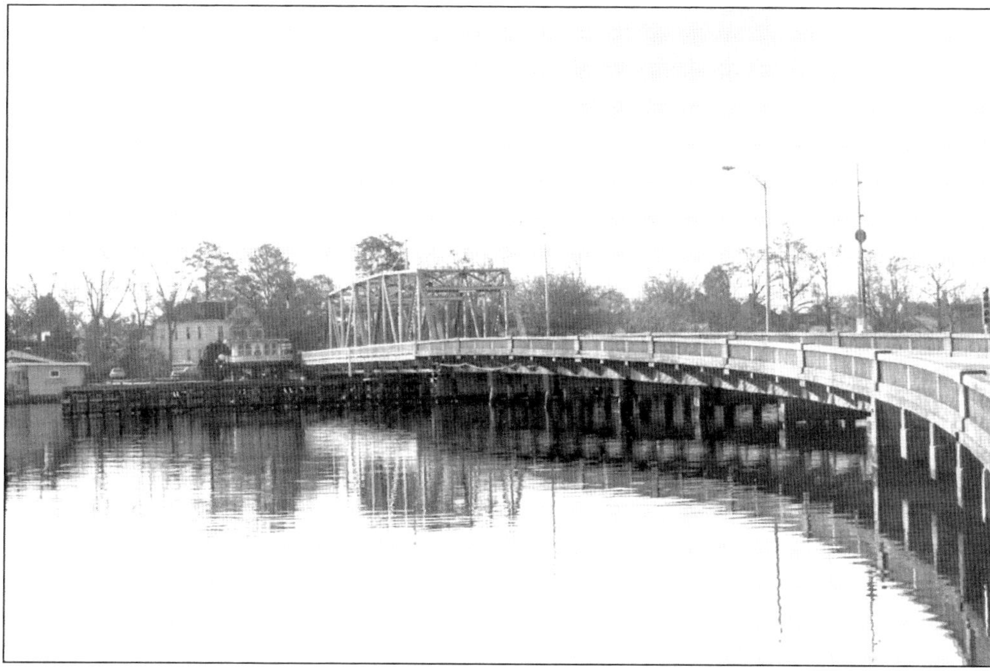

This view clearly emphasizes the curvature of Hertford's S-bridge. The unusual shape of the bridge gives a claim to fame as the only known S-shaped bridge. (Courtesy of Charles T. Skinner Jr.)

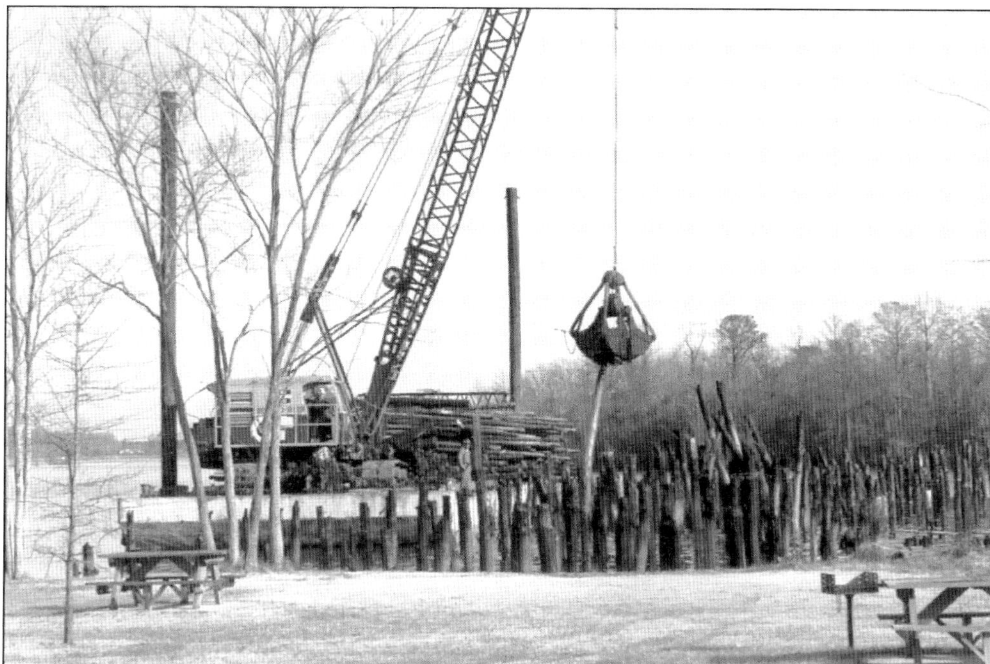

Generations of wharves, piers, docks, bulkheads, and industrial buildings littered the Hertford waterfront with pilings. Here, the shore of Missing Mill Park is being cleared. (Courtesy of Town of Hertford.)

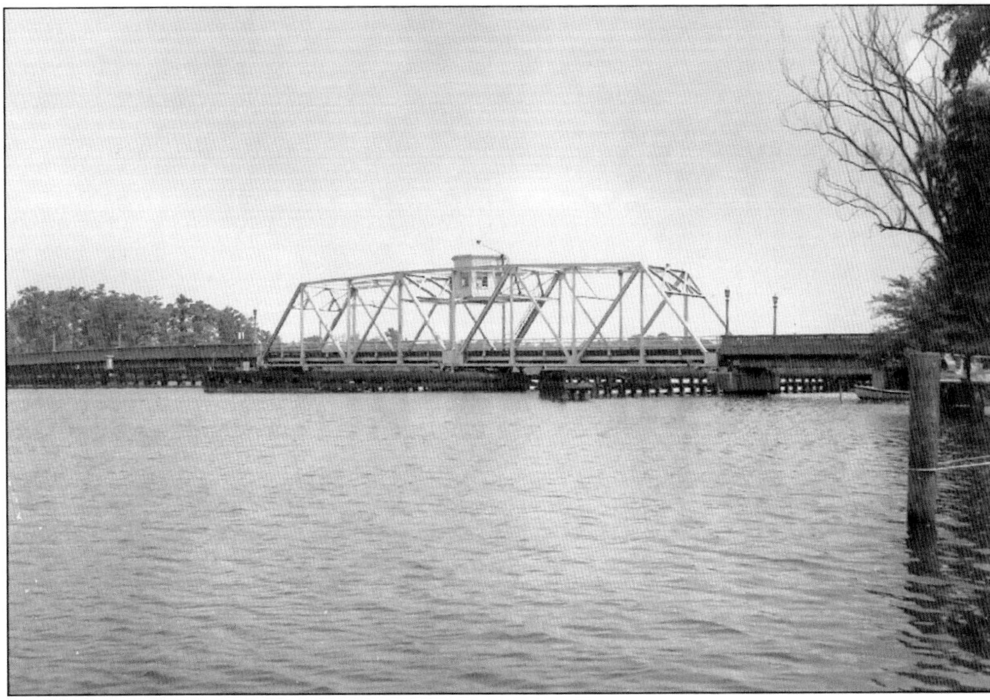

The steel Warren-truss center section of Hertford's S-bridge can pivot to open a passage for boats. The bridge was constructed in 1928. (Courtesy of Florence Darden Christensen.)

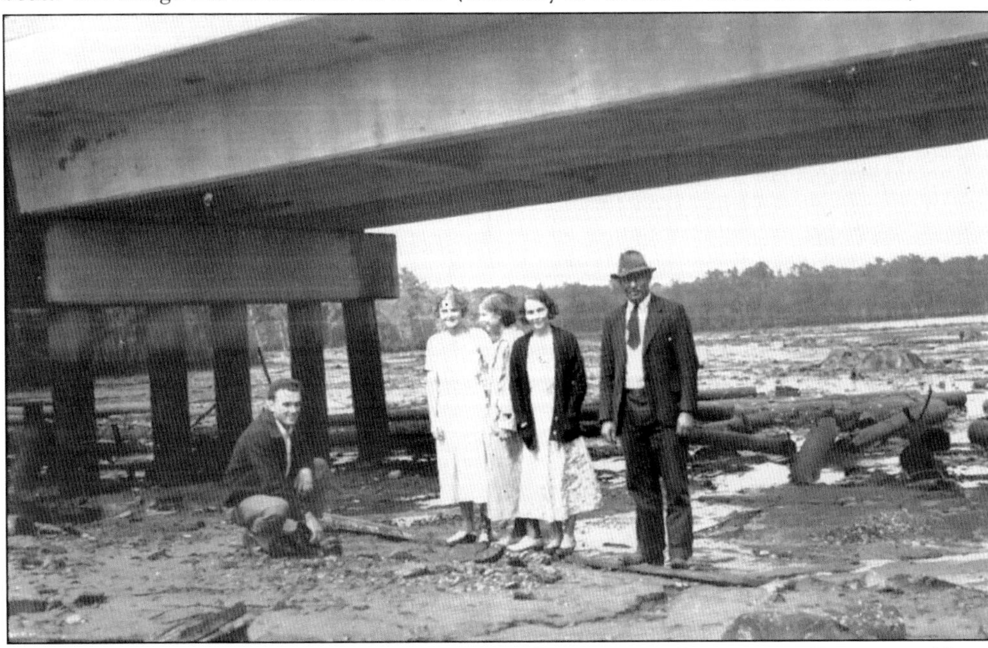

In an extraordinary freak occurrence in 1935, the water in Perquimans River was blown out into Albemarle Sound, exposing the river bottom for some time until the wind changed. From left to right are Willie Ainsley, Eugenia Gregory, Doris Gregory, Pencie Gregory, and Robert White, who were able to stand under the S-bridge at Hertford. (Courtesy of Ruth Elliott Winslow.)

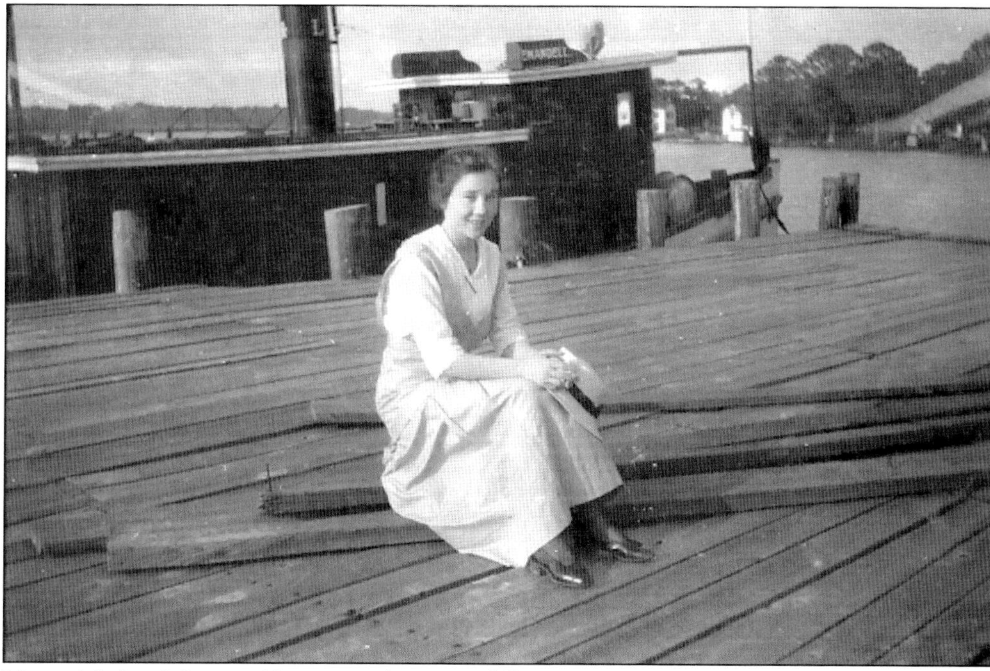

Moored behind Pencie Hunter is the *Emandell*, a tugboat belonging to Major and Loomis Lumber Company, in 1915. (Courtesy of Margaret Ainsley Brewin.)

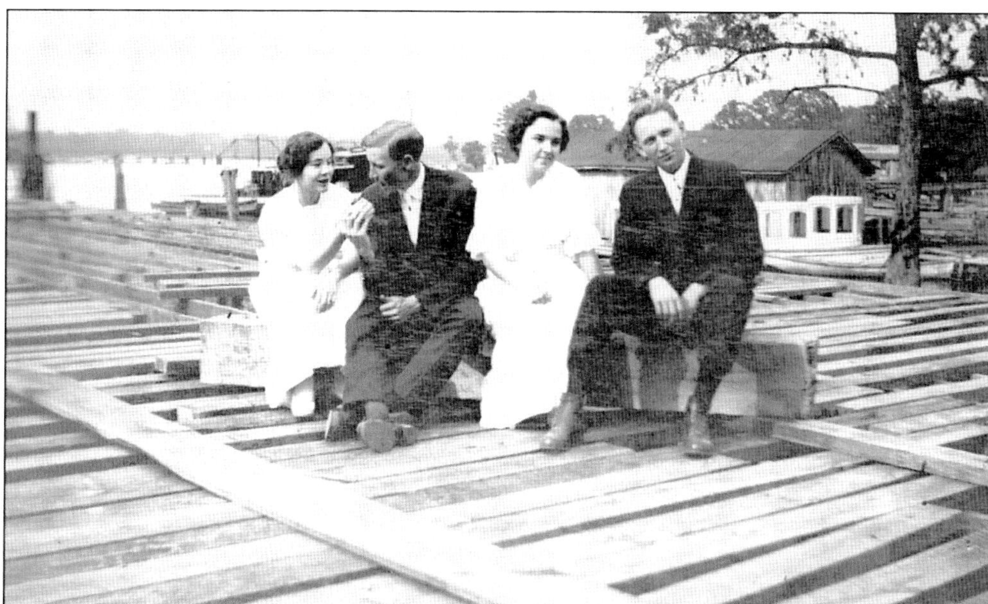

The Hertford waterfront near Grubb Street was formerly crowded with commercial and industrial buildings and wharves. Pencie Hunter (left) and friends chat on a convenient beam, c. 1914. (Courtesy of Margaret Ainsley Brewin.)

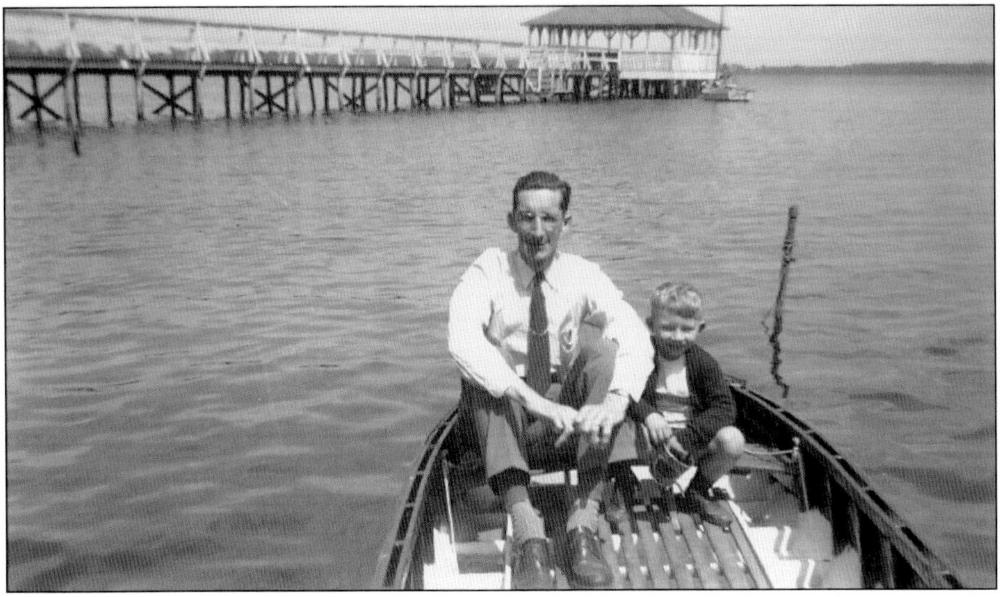

Surrounding the Hertford Town Pier, the expansive Perquimans River awaits drugstore-owner Henry Clay Sullivan and son Jerry, c. 1949. (Courtesy of Jerry Sullivan.)

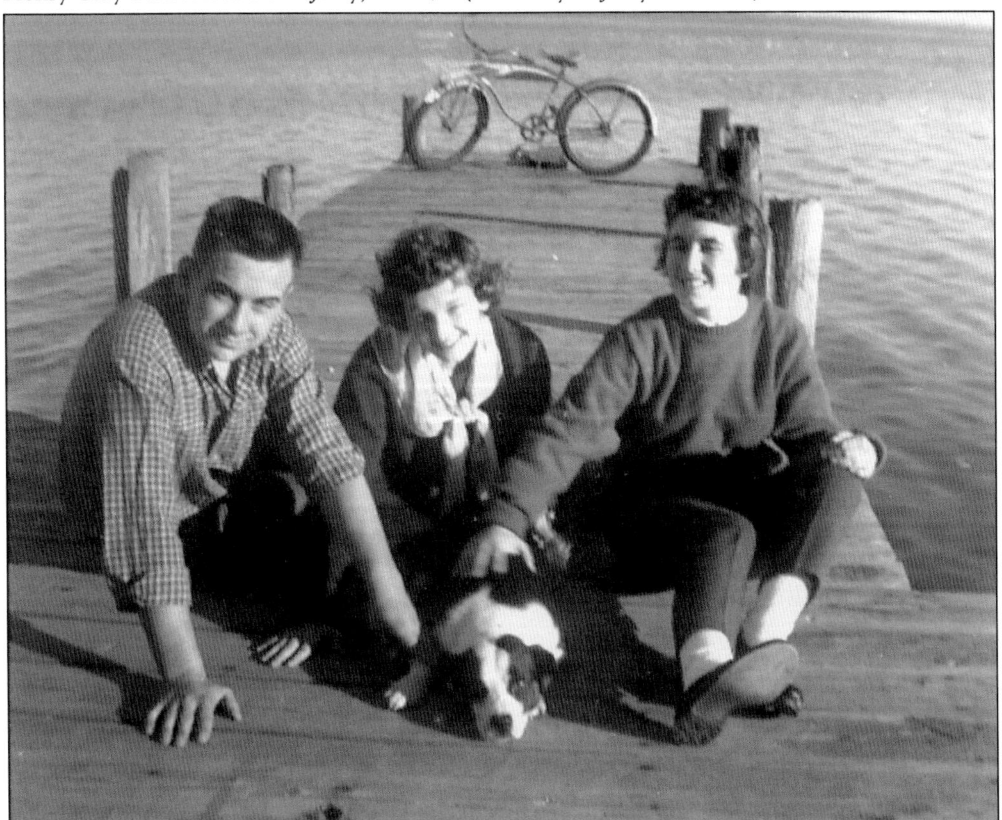

Cousins, from left to right, Edward Matthews, Ruthie Johnson, and Kay Matthews pet a canine friend at the end of the town pier, 1959. (Courtesy of Kay Matthews Whedbee.)

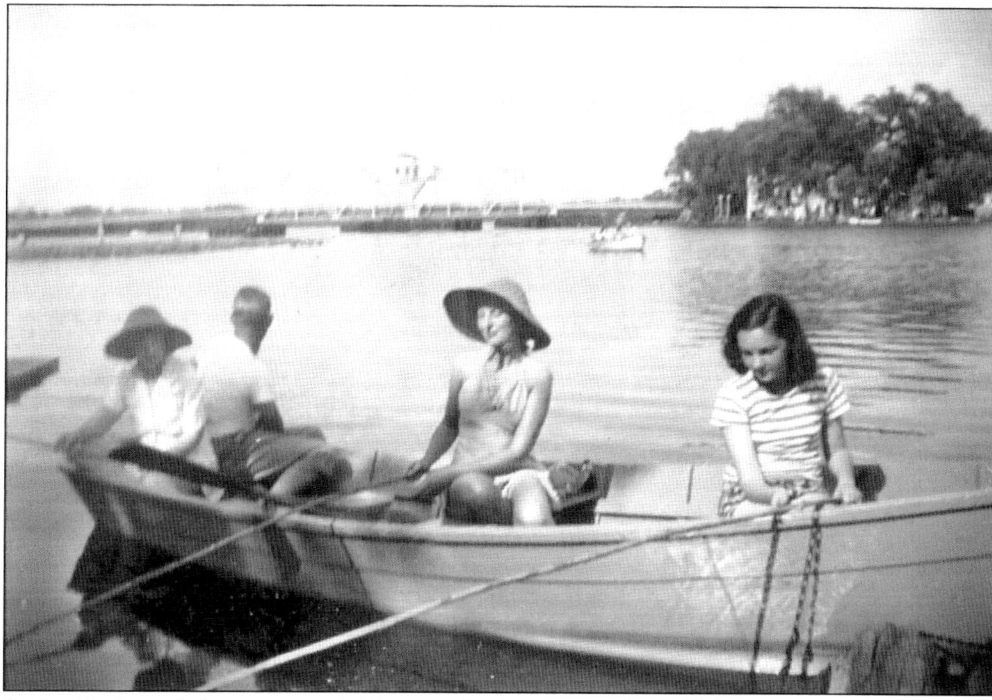

Ruth (Nachman) Stephenson (left) treats the family to a day of fishing on the river, *c.* 1945, with the S-bridge in the background. (Courtesy of Mary K. Vidaurri.)

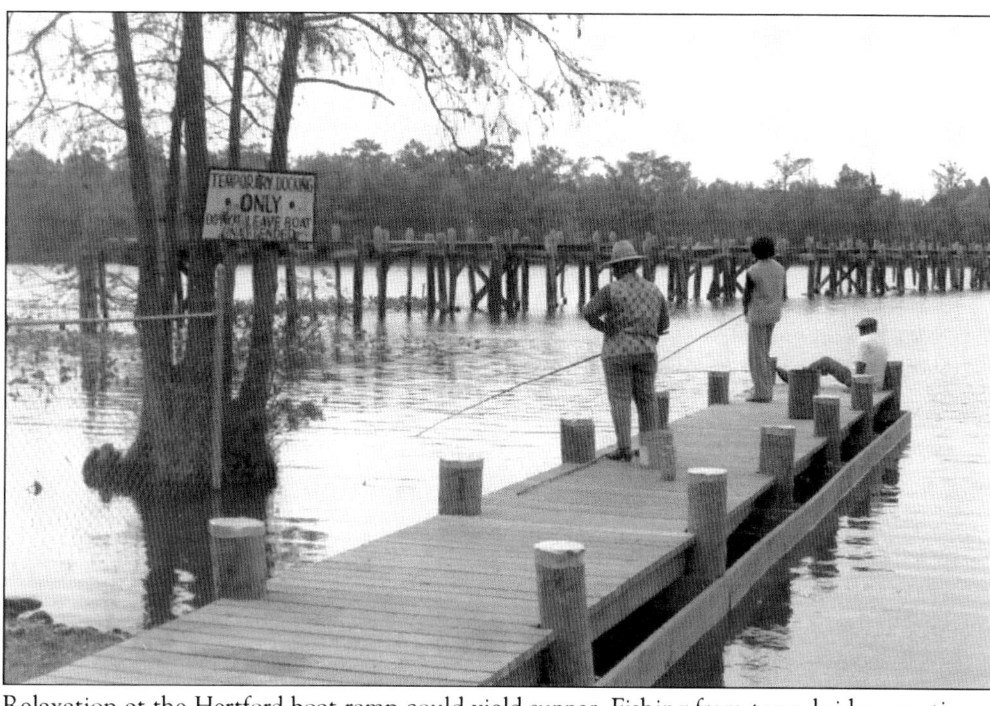

Relaxation at the Hertford boat ramp could yield supper. Fishing from town bridges continues to be a popular pastime today. (Courtesy of Town of Hertford.)

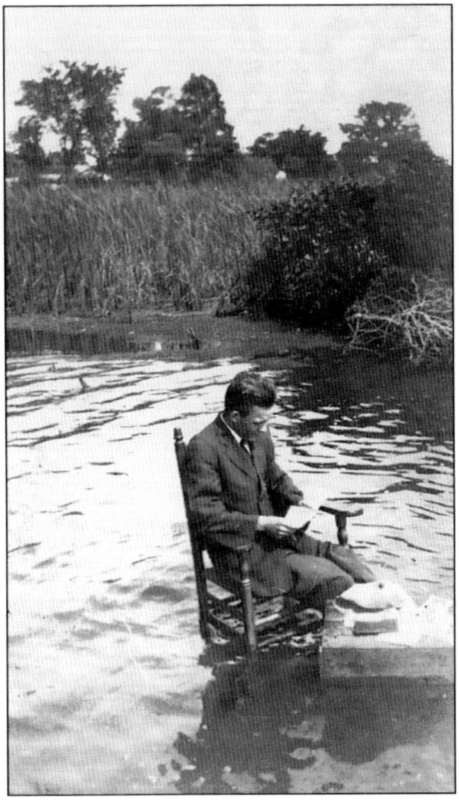

Mark Gregory submitted to wet feet in a risky seat for this 1913 gag photograph. (Courtesy of Margaret Ainsley Brewin.)

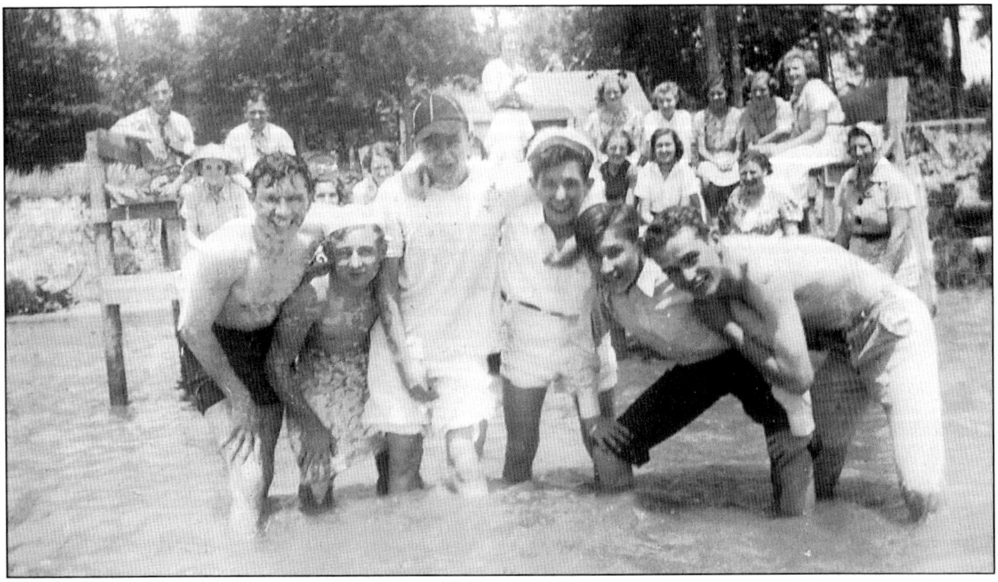

At this dressy Perquimans County High School picnic, some of the group wound up in the water anyway. (Courtesy of Florence Darden Christensen.)

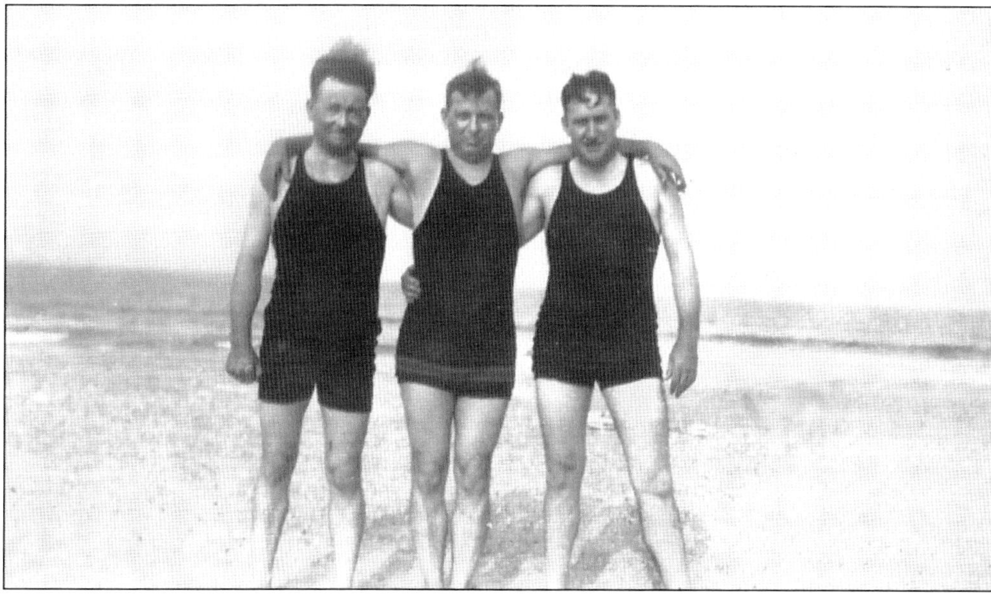

A favorite getaway for Perquimans folk has long been Nags Head. Enjoying the beach in 1929 were, from left to right, store clerk Herbert Whitley, trucker Thomas Sumner, and family doctor Carlton Davenport. (Courtesy of Carlton A. Davenport Jr.)

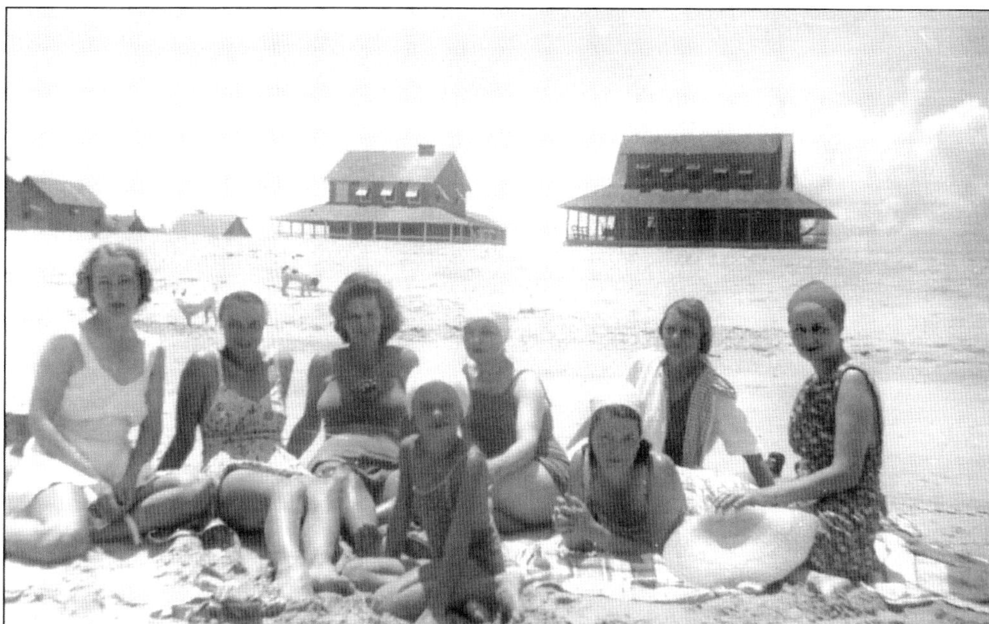

Since Francis Nixon of Perquimans began acquiring Outer Banks property about 1830, many local families have made regular vacation pilgrimages to the Nags Head area each summer. Many of them for years have owned cottages like those in the background. This group of Hertford ladies sunned on the beach in 1940. (Courtesy of Carlton A. Davenport Jr.)

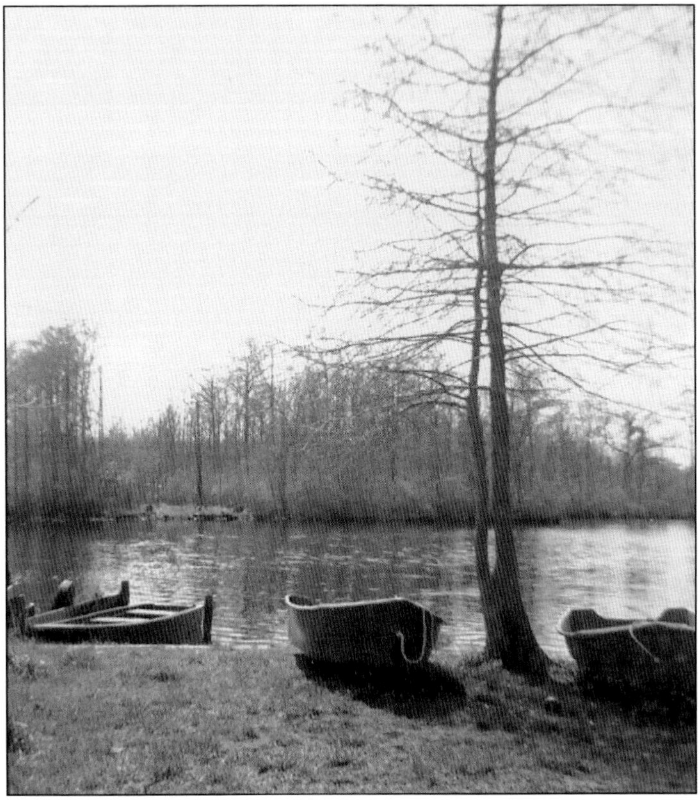

This tranquil spot in the narrows of Perquimans River west of Winfall was a ferry crossing in the early 18th century. The ferry was replaced in the 1760s by a floating bridge that survived until Union forces destroyed it in 1863. Close by Nixon's (later Blanchard's) Bridge were a store and other commercial buildings. (Courtesy of Raymond A. Winslow Jr.)

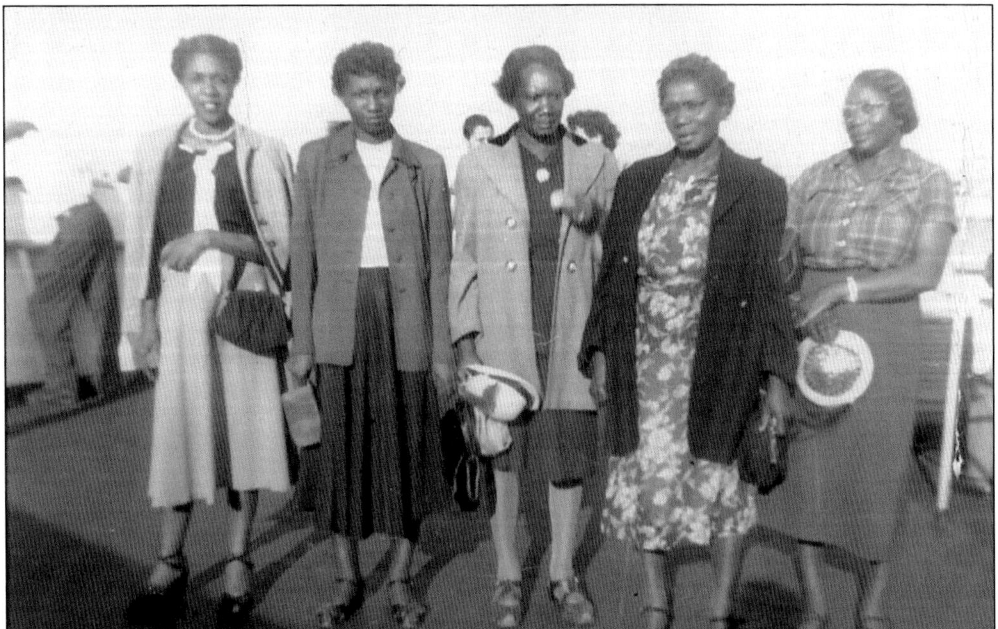

The five ladies in the foreground enjoy an outing aboard a barge near Winfall in the 1950s. They are, from left to right, Elizabeth Billups, Eula Hill, Hattie Billups, Georgette Billups, and Pearl Billups Rumbler. (Courtesy of Brenda Dillard.)

Mark Gregory admires Pencie Hunter's hat as they lean against the railing of a pier off Grubb Street in May 1913. (Courtesy of Margaret Ainsley Brewin.)

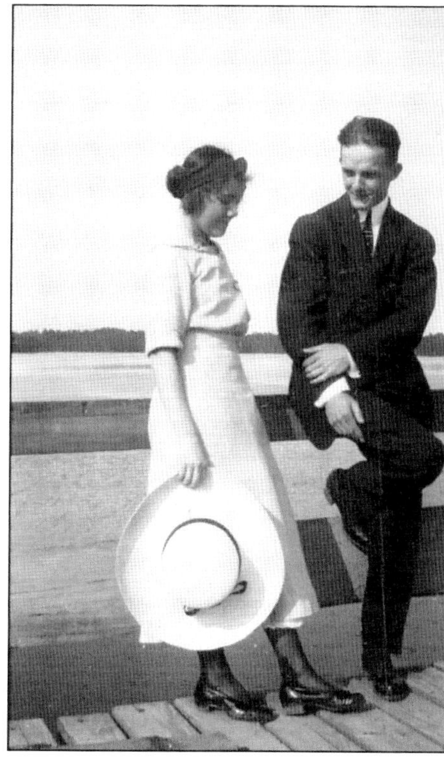

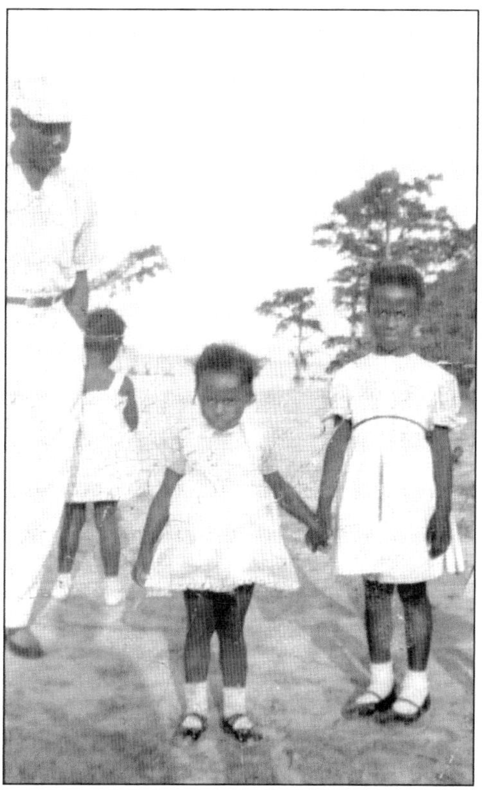

In their Sunday best, the Stepney sisters share an outing at Lowe's Beach on the Perquimans River in 1955 with their father, Lee Stepney (left). The children, from left to right, are Carolyn, Wonder, and Gloria Stepney. (Courtesy of Wonder Lewis.)

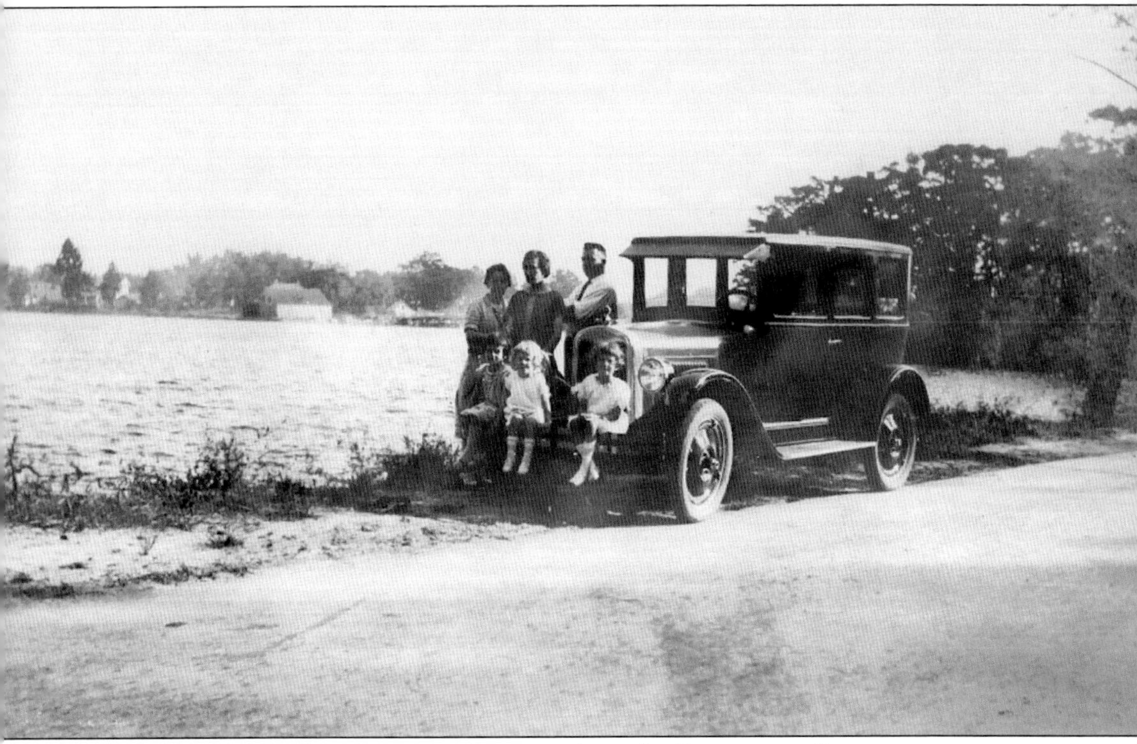

Behind some Sunday afternoon pleasure riders, the Perquimans River causeway curves to meet the bridge at the entrance to Hertford, *c*. 1925. Dominating Phelps Point and the town waterfront is the old McMullan oyster warehouse. (Courtesy of Margaret Ainsley Brewin.)

In the 1940s, the Historic American Buildings Survey identified the Newbold-White House as contributing to America's architectural heritage, leading to local interest in historic preservation. The house had been enlarged and modified, but the c. 1730 structure was still sound. (Courtesy of Library of Congress, Prints & Photographs Division, HABS, HABS, NC, 72-HERF.V, 5-2.)

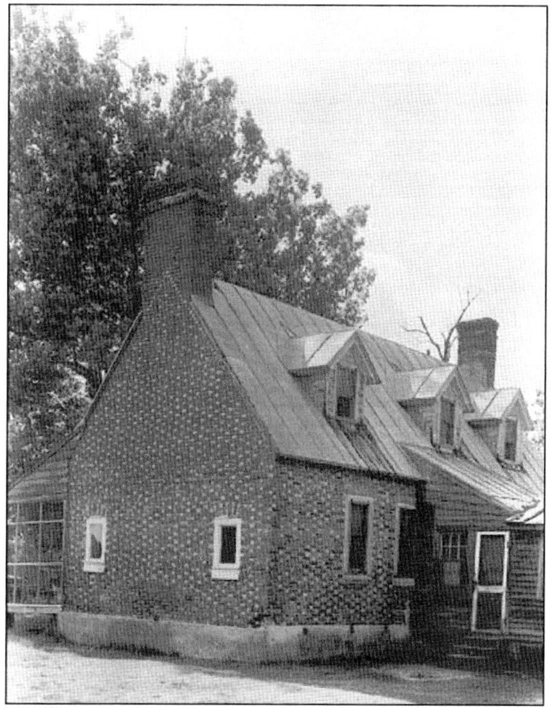

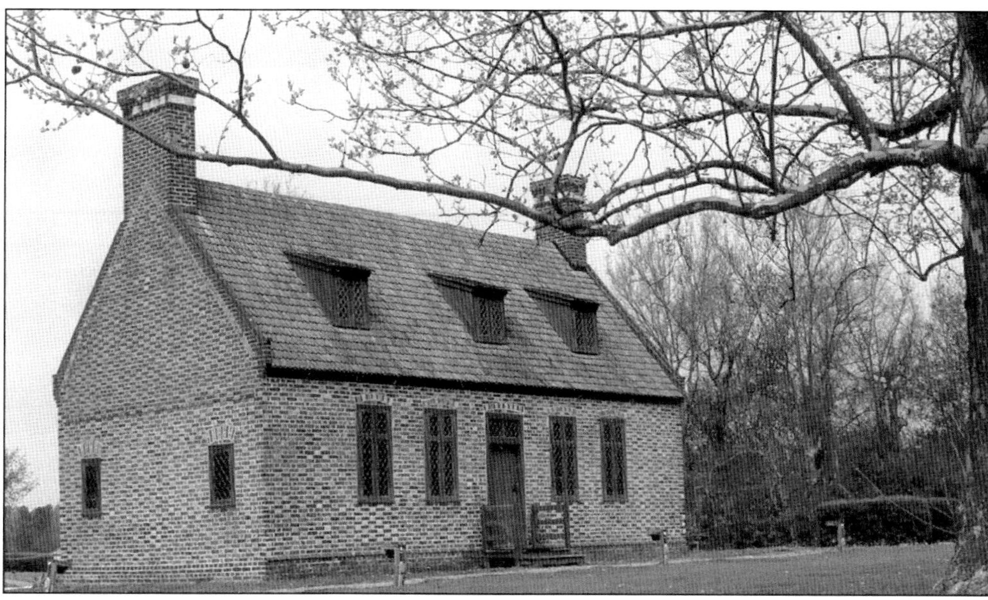

In 2003, the county's history is prized as a great public asset. Open to the public for over 20 years, the Newbold-White House tells the story of a colonial Quaker family and is widely recognized as one of North Carolina's most notable historic preservation accomplishments. Local preservation efforts have led to documenting other areas of the county, resulting in historic districts established in the Perquimans communities of Hertford, Old Neck, Winfall, Belvidere, and Bethel. (Courtesy of Perquimans County Restoration Association.)

INDEX